Transnational Civil Society and the World Bank

Interest Groups, Advocacy and Democracy Series

Series Editor
Darren Halpin, Australian National University, Australia

The study of interest groups and their role in political life has undergone somewhat of a renaissance in recent years. Long standing scholarly themes such as interest groups influence, mobilization, formation, and 'bias', are being addressed using new and novel data sets and methods. There are also new and exciting themes, such as the role of ICTs in enabling collective action and the growth of global advocacy networks, are being added. Contemporary debates about the role of commercial lobbyists and professionalized interest representation are also highly salient. Together, they draw an ever larger and broader constituency to the study of interest groups and advocacy. This series seeks to capture both new generation studies addressing long standing themes in new ways *and* innovate scholarship posing new and challenging questions that emerge in a rapidly changing world.

The series encourages contributions from political science (but also abutting disciplines such as economics, law, history, international relations and sociology) that speak to these themes. It welcomes work undertaken at the sub-national, national and supra-national political systems, and particularly encourages comparative or longitudinal studies. The series is open to diverse methodologies and theoretical approaches. The book series will sit alongside and complement the new Journal of the same name.

Titles include:

Darren Halpin and Grant Jordan (*editors*)
THE SCALE OF INTEREST ORGANIZATION IN DEMOCRATIC POLITICS
Data and Research Methods

Chris Pallas
TRANSNATIONAL CIVIL SOCIETY AND THE WORLD BANK
Investigating Civil Society's Potential to Democratize Global Governance

Daniel Stockemer
THE MICRO AND MESO LEVELS OF ACTIVISM
A Comparative Case Study of Attac France and Germany

Interest Groups, Advocacy and Democracy Series
Series Standing Order ISBN 978-113702871-6 (hardback) and 978-113702839-6 (paperback)

You can receive future titles in this series as they are published by placing a standing order. Please contact your bookseller or, in case of difficulty, write to us at the address below with your name and address, the title of the series and the ISBNs quoted above.

Customer Services Department, Macmillan Distribution Ltd, Houndmills, Basingstoke, Hampshire RG21 6XS, England

---

Transnational Civil Society and the World Bank

Investigating Civil Society's Potential to Democratize Global Governance

Christopher L. Pallas
Assistant Professor of Conflict Management, Kennesaw State University

First published 2013 by
PALGRAVE MACMILLAN

Palgrave Macmillan in the UK is an imprint of Macmillan Publishers Limited, registered in England, company number 785998, of Houndmills, Basingstoke, Hampshire RG21 6XS.

Palgrave Macmillan in the US is a division of St Martin's Press LLC, 175 Fifth Avenue, New York, NY 10010.

Palgrave Macmillan is the global academic imprint of the above companies and has companies and representatives throughout the world.

Palgrave® and Macmillan® are registered trademarks in the United States, the United Kingdom, Europe and other countries

ISBN: 978-1-137-27760-2

This book is printed on paper suitable for recycling and made from fully managed and sustained forest sources. Logging, pulping and manufacturing processes are expected to conform to the environmental regulations of the country of origin.

A catalogue record for this book is available from the British Library.

A catalog record for this book is available from the Library of Congress.

Contents

List of Tables

Acknowledgements

I am deeply grateful to the many civil society leaders and World Bank staff who generously gave of their time in answering my questions and sharing their reflections on events past and present. I expect that the conclusions of this book will disappoint some of them, who may have hoped for a more sympathetic depiction of their organizations' activities. I can only stress that the purpose of this book is to assess transnational civil society's impact on the democratization of global governance, not the merits of any particular organization or activity. That civil society activism has achieved numerous positive outcomes, in human rights, environmental protection, development policy, and economic justice, is beyond question. The challenge, as this book reveals, is that the current functioning of transnational civil society gives power to a small elite. This book seeks to understand this challenge and to develop strategies by which the current, elite system can give way to a more democratic one.

In addition to the participants in the research, I wish to thank the Center for Democracy and Civil Society at Georgetown University for hosting me during my research in Washington; Jude Howell, David Lewis, Jan Aart Scholte, and Ngaire Woods for their input on the preliminary project; Jonas Tallberg for the encouragement to publish in book form; Abraham Pallas, Pamela Pallas, and Genevieve Scirica for their support in my academic endeavors; and Sarah Pallas for her input, patience, prayers, and encouragement.

List of Acronyms

ADF	Asian Development Fund
ASCE	American Society of Civil Engineers
BDI	Federation of German Industries
BIC	Bank Information Center
CIEL	Center for International Environmental Law
CSO(s)	Civil Society Organizations
CWS	Church World Service
Development GAP	Development Group for Alternative Policies
DFI	Development Finance International
EBRD	European Bank for Reconstruction and Development
EDF	Environmental Defense Fund
EPI	Environmental Policy Institute
FAVDO	Forum of African Voluntary Development Organizations
FoE	Friends of the Earth (US)
GCS Team	Global Civil Society Team
GEF	Global Environmental Facility
IBRD	International Bank for Reconstruction and Development
IDA	International Development Association
ILO	International Labor Organization
IMF	International Monetary Fund
INGO(s)	International Non-Governmental Organizations
INHURED	Institute for Human Rights, Environment, and Development
IO	Intergovernmental Organization
IRN	International Rivers Network
MDB	Multilateral Development Bank
NAM	National Association of Manufacturers
NBA	Narmada Bachao Andolan
NGO(s)	Non-Governmental Organizations
NGOWG	NGO Working Group on the World Bank
NRDC	Natural Resources Defense Council
NWF	National Wildlife Federation

OECD	Organization for Economic Cooperation and Development
OECD-DAC	OECD Development Assistance Committee
OED	Operations and Evaluations Department
OPCS	Operations Policy and Country Services
PAD	Project Appraisal Document
PID	Project Information Document
PTI(s)	Poverty-Targeted Interventions
SAL	Structural Adjustment Lending or Loan
TAN	Transnational Advocacy Network
TCS	Transnational Civil Society
TCSO	Transnational Civil Society Organization
UCS	Use of Country Systems (for Procurement)
UN	United Nations
UNICEF	United Nations Children's Fund
USAID	United States Agency for International Development
WDM	World Development Movement
WTO	World Trade Organization
WWF	World Wildlife Fund

1
Waiting on Democracy

At their best, global governance institutions reflect a certain form of optimism. Many of the most prominent institutions, including the United Nations, World Bank, and International Monetary Fund, were created at the close of World War II to preserve peace and enhance global economic prosperity. International institutions and regimes founded in subsequent decades help regulate everything from the trade in endangered species to transnational aviation, and facilitate global responses to epidemics, climate change, and criminal activity. Taken together, global governance institutions can seem to reflect a world trying to work together toward some common good.

Yet academics and practitioners alike recognize that global governance institutions suffer from a democratic deficit. Global governance institutions often reflect the balance of power among the states most involved in their founding. In the UN, the permanent members of the Security Council exercise veto power over military interventions. In the World Bank and IMF, voting rights on the governing boards are assigned based primarily on the capital each state contributes to the institution, privileging wealthy states over poorer ones. The trade rules enforced by the WTO favor free trade in the manufactured goods produced by industrialized states while allowing restrictions on trade in the agricultural goods produced by developing countries.

In the midst of such inequality, many activists and observers have looked to transnational civil society as a means of remediation. Activist leaders appealing for changes in global policies claim to speak on behalf of marginalized stakeholders, and academics describe transnational civil society as the basis of a new, more democratic international order. Yet, as this book explains, such claims must be evaluated critically – not because transnational civil society is still nascent and has yet to reach full maturity, as some have argued, but rather because civil society is already becoming an established player in international policy processes and a clear gap has begun to emerge between normative expectations and empirical reality.

Purpose of the book

This book examines the potential for TCS to democratize global governance by assessing TCS impacts on policymaking at the World Bank. This book asks: do data about the World Bank support the idea that TCS can democratize global governance? To answer this question, the book focuses primarily on whether transnational civil society is democratizing Bank policymaking already. There are several reasons for this retrospective approach. First, the best and most definitive evidence of transnational civil society's capacities is demonstration of concrete achievement. This is particularly important in the realm of global governance, where the hypothesized capacities of international actors and regimes have frequently failed to live up to expectations. Just because the architecture of a global governance institution is structured in a particular way does not mean it will produce the outputs that one might logically expect from such a structure.[1]

Second, it has been twenty years since civil society's capacity to impact global governance was first discussed by scholars like Lipschutz and Shaw, who started to frame the issue in 1992. In the intervening decades, civil society has demonstrated that it is indeed capable of changing the international system. If its capacity to democratize global governance is real, then one would expect to find concrete evidence of democratizing impacts. Indeed, a substantial portion of the literature on civil society and the democratization of global governance argues that civil society is democratizing on the basis of the impacts that civil society has already achieved. Therefore, testing whether civil society is democratizing global governance on the basis of civil society's concrete impacts is not only logical; it also allows this book to investigate directly many of the claims made in the literature.

This book, however, is more than just an investigation of previous claims. As noted, transnational civil society has real power and has used its influence to telling effect over the past several decades. If TCS is not making global governance more representative, transparent, accountable, or otherwise democratic, then one must ask: what is the net effect of TCS on the functioning of global governance?

This chapter provides the background and framework for this research. The first half of the chapter elaborates on the points made above by describing the democratic deficit in global governance, defining transnational civil society, and outlining the claims made about transnational civil society's impacts. The second half of the chapter explains the design of the research and enumerates the specific questions it seeks to address. The chapter concludes with an overview of the book's argument.

The democratic deficit in global governance

In the past half-century, the forces of globalization have increased the importance of global governance at an ever-accelerating pace, connecting people through new technologies and increasing economic interdependence. At the same time, the world has encountered new problems, such as ozone depletion, climate change, and transnational pandemics, that require a coordinated global response. These evolutions have increased the power and importance of global governance institutions.

As the power and importance of international institutions has increased, so too have concerns about how who controls their power and how it is used. In the 1980s, the growing environmental movement drew public scrutiny to the work of the World Bank. Concerns about the impact of structural adjustment focused attention on both the World Bank and the IMF in the late 1980s and early 1990s. The IMF's handling of the Southeast Asian financial crisis led to accusations that its policies favored rich-world business interests over developing country citizens. Protests against the WTO in Seattle in 1999 created greater awareness of the problems posed by globalization and the arguments of its detractors. Alternative 'people's forums' have sprung up around meetings of global power brokers, like the World Economic Forum in Davos, and popular protests are now a regular feature of the meetings of the G8. The net impact of such critical activism has been to challenge the legitimacy of existing power arrangements. The activists participating in these challenges do not, in general, seem to argue that global cooperation is unnecessary; indeed, the protests themselves often represent a form of international cooperation. Rather, they argue that global cooperation must take place in a way that affords equal value and voice to all of the world's citizens.

As already noted, a significant part of the problem involves institutional architecture that privileges a minority of states over most others.

However, the problems in global governance go beyond self-interested manipulation of global governance mechanisms by state leaders. Institutions often develop considerable autonomy through their exercise of bureaucratic functions and their role as norm-setters (Barnett and Finnemore 1999) and national governments have often allowed global governance institutions 'considerable unchecked prerogative' in their activities (Scholte 2004, p. 212). The result is that international institutions can become autonomous players with limited accountability to any outsider. One of the best examples of this is the IMF, which has been accused of pushing a neo-liberal agenda based on the economic ideology of its core staff (Stiglitz 1999; cf. Scholte 2012, pp. 195–196).

The combination of unequal state power and technocratic autonomy has resulted in what academics have described as a democratic deficit in global governance (Scholte 2011; Woods 2007). Zürn (2004, p. 262) writes:

> There is broad agreement that currently the functioning of international institutions such as the WTO or the UN does not meet democratic standards. Acknowledged democratic deficits include the lack of identifiable decision-makers who are directly accountable for wrong decisions made at the international level, as well as the inscrutability of international decision-making processes and thus the advantage the executive decision-makers have over others in terms of information. Furthermore, particularly the prime actors in international politics, such as multinational businesses and superpowers, are at best accountable only to a fraction of the people affected by their activities.

In short, the vast majority of people impacted by global governance have generally been without any effective voice or vote in the decisions affecting them. Yet if the problems in global governance are rooted in the political and bureaucratic structure of global governance institutions, then it seems possible that global governance could be made more democratic, even in a world marked by persistent imbalances in economic and political power between states.

Transnational civil society defined

Transnational civil society (TCS) is often suggested as a key part of this solution. TCS is a category of non-state actors ranging from advocacy groups like Amnesty International and the World Wildlife Fund to faith groups like the Catholic Church and even some social movements, like Occupy Wall Street and its global spin-offs. Yet while the actors within TCS are readily recognized – we know transnational civil society when we see it – arriving at a precise definition can be challenging. Therefore, before discussing its possible role as a solution to the problems of global governance, it is necessary to discuss and define the term itself.

Definitional debates over the meaning of TCS occur for several reasons: because of a minority of writings that conflate contemporary definitions of civil society with a much older, Hobbesian usage that depicts civil society simply as the citizens of the state; because of normative arguments over whether 'uncivil' civil society organizations should be excluded from study; and because transnational civil society often looks quite different from civil society in the domestic setting where, as Robert Putnam (2000) has pointed out, civil society includes groups like bowling leagues and bridge clubs that have no explicit policy agendas. In addition, a variety of labels besides TCS have been used to denote non-state actors working in the transnational realm. Some research refers to 'transnational advocacy networks' and others to 'global civil society'. A number of authors pragmatically focus on the most visible actors, writing about 'non-governmental organizations' (NGOs) or 'international non-governmental organizations' (INGOs). These definitional ambiguities and variations in nomenclature can inhibit scholarly dialogue and obstruct empirical research.

This book uses the term transnational civil society and defines it as referring to all associations of individuals meeting two criteria. These associations (a) are not primarily a part of a government or a governance organization, nor of a profit-making enterprise and (b) are engaged in activity that takes place beyond the borders of the state in which they are headquartered, is intended to impact events outside their state, or is linked to non-governmental, non-commercial actors outside their state. Individual groups meeting these criteria are referred to as transnational civil society organizations (TCSOs).

It is important that the reader not think of TCSOs as equivalent to 'international non-governmental organizations' or 'INGOs'. The popular use of the INGO term obscures more than it reveals. The term is generally used to describe a class of NGOs characterized by their resources rather than their transnational activities, and thus applied almost exclusively to well-resourced actors from the US and Europe. Calling these actors international NGOs, rather than American or European, can obscure fundamental characteristics of these organizations (including funding base, staff culture, and language) that may influence their behavior. The use of the term INGO to refer to this limited group also obscures the presence of transnational organizations in other parts of the world. By creating a false dichotomy between 'international' and 'local' NGOs, the term depicts many developing country NGOs as perpetual objects of assistance and ignores the contributions they make (or seek to make) to global governance.

Admittedly, to define actors by the transnationality of their activities or associations creates opportunities for confusion, insofar as a purely local CSO may become a TCSO by dint of entering an international campaign. It is important to recall, however, that the purpose of this book is to understand the democratic credentials of transnational civil society. The definition of TCSO is designed to delimit the membership of TCS.

TCS is conceptualized as the collective body of TCSOs. This is not to say that TCS represents some sort of homogenous whole or to assume that TCSOs consistently arrive at consensus agendas. We can readily observe that not all TCSOs participate in all instances of international policy advocacy and, as this book will make abundantly clear, TCSOs frequently disagree with one another on policy priorities and advocacy strategies. However, insofar as we are evaluating the impacts of TCS on global governance, we must consider the aggregate impact of all TCSOs, whether they choose to participate in policymaking, abstain from involvement, or are otherwise excluded.

Defining TCS in this way has two virtues. First, the definition stated above best describes the empirical reality of non-state engagement with global governance institutions. Civil society typically refers to that realm of human association that is neither explicitly profit-making nor a formal part of state government. The vast majority of policy advocacy has been conducted by professional NGOs – organizations in which the majority of the staff are full-time employees of the organization (as opposed to volunteers), such as Amnesty International, Greenpeace, and Christian Aid. Yet faith-based organizations have also played a crucial role in areas like development policy and human rights. Protestant and Catholic churches, for instance, helped support the Jubilee debt relief movement, while Muslim organizations frequently sponsor development projects in Africa. Global justice movements, based around grassroots resistance to things like globalization or environmental degradation and often manifested in street protests during major world policy summits and in groups like Occupy Wall Street, have occasionally influenced international policy. The term 'non-governmental organization', in its most common usage, does not readily encompass these latter two types of organizations (however much a literal definition of the term ought to encompass them). If we wish to talk about all of the organizations impacting global governance, the term 'transnational civil society' is clearer.

Transnational civil society also seems preferable to other common terms like transnational advocacy networks (TANs) or global civil society. Transnational activity is inherent in seeking to influence global governance and one of the virtues of the TAN perspective is that it readily encompasses local actors involved in international campaigns, rather than focusing only on powerful international NGOs. Empirically, however, not all participants in transnational advocacy or activity are part of networks or – if they are – conduct their advocacy through those networks. While the idea of TANs is certainly useful for discussing the particular advantages of concerted action or information-sharing across state boundaries (or, as researchers such as Clifford Bob have revealed, the perils of such coordination), to focus only on TANs would exclude organizations that have chosen to go it alone. Environmental Defense, for instance, is said to have influenced climate change negotiations largely by pursuing an agenda independent of the other CSOs involved. Amnesty International frequently coordinates only with its own local chapters. Indeed, as this book will discuss, atomized action on the part of civil society organizations operating internationally may be more the norm than the exception.

The term 'global civil society' is more normative that descriptive. The community of transnational civil society organizations is not truly globe-spanning. Organizations with the resources and wherewithal to operate transnationally tend to be concentrated in the wealthier, more industrialized countries of what is often called the global North. As will be discussed later in this book, their partners elsewhere, while also part of transnational civil society, are often chosen selectively to suit the purposes of their rich-world partners. Moreover, even civil society organizations in developing countries that operate transnationally of their own initiative tend to be led and staffed by economic and social elites from within those countries. If the globe encompasses all people of all states and all socio-economic strata, there is little that is global about transnational civil society.

The TCS and TCSO definitions used in this book aim to bring together the most important parts of these alternative terms and definitions. The exclusion of government and commercial involvement, for instance, is in keeping with the commonly understood definitions of NGOs and civil society. Specifying transnational linkages, rather than transnational activity, allows us to include, as the

TAN model does, local organizations that form a crucial part of transnational advocacy efforts yet rarely undertake activities beyond their home state. Thus the term transnational civil society and its associated definition were chosen because they facilitate inductive, empirical research on non-state actors and the democratization of global governance, while also connecting to previous scholarship in clear, recognizable ways.

TCS to the rescue

Why do observers hope that TCS will democratize global governance? To begin with, transnational civil society has had a noticeable impact on global governance over the past 25 years. Transnational civil society organizations are credited with, or claim credit for, prompting developing country debt forgiveness, driving new environmental regulations, ending human rights abuses, and persuading most of the world to ban the use of anti-personnel landmines. In achieving these changes, TCSOs have forced the hands of states and global governance institutions alike, establishing TCS as what Florini (2000) describes as the 'third force' – a new power in international policymaking. TCSOs have helped create new institutions and policy regimes, such as the Forest Stewardship Council and Fairtrade labeling, that directly influence international trade. TCSOs have also been granted a seat at the table in established global governance forums. TCSOs participate in the Convention on the International Trade in Endangered Species, they have won the right to independently monitor state adherence to climate change agreements, and are formally consulted by organizations like the World Bank. In short, TCS has power and is able to wield that power in what was previously thought of as a state-centric system.

At the same time, TCS presents itself as the voice of popular dissent. Whether it is Occupy Wall Street groups protesting on behalf of the 99 per cent or developing country civil society leaders speaking out at a 'people's forum' against the activities of the World Bank or G8, transnational civil society presents an obvious counterpoint to the technocrats and Northern government leaders at the heart of global governance. In addition to claiming to represent a more diverse group of interests, TCS organizations operate more publicly, with seemingly greater transparency, and are more accessible to the general public. When these characteristics are considered alongside the obvious impact of TCS, it is unsurprising that many commentators hope that TCS will democratize global governance.

A multiplicity of hopes

That being said, exactly how the activities of a popular, transparent, or accountable TCS will lead to democratically accountable global governance is unclear. In essence, there is a continuum of possibilities ranging from the reform of international institutions to their outright replacement.

In one view, civil society promotes both representation and accountability. TCS is depicted as enunciating the needs of stakeholder populations in existing policymaking fora and monitoring the activities of governance institutions (see Price 2003, p. 581; Colas 2002). First, TCS magnifies voices that would otherwise be silenced; as one author writes, TCS 'rescue[s] the causes of marginalized or excluded groups', bringing them to the attention of policymakers and opinion leaders (Grzybowski 2000, p. 442). Second, when policymakers respond to popular demands with new policies or initiatives, TCS can push for implementation or monitor compliance (Keck and Sikkink 1998, p. 3; Clark 2001; cf. Rich 1994). TCS can either do this in an ad hoc way, holding policymakers to their promises in particular policy areas, or they can advocate for structural reform, promoting efforts to make international institutions transparent or externally accountable (Udall 1998; Fox 2003; cf. Scholte 2004).

An overlapping view is that TCS works by creating or promoting new global norms. In this view, the core activity of TCS is not so much representing the needs of specific populations to a narrow group of policymakers, but rather rallying broad public opinion on behalf of issues or people groups, creating waves of pressure to which international institutions are constrained to respond. The creation of environmental and social safeguards at the World Bank, for example, is attributable to civil society efforts to promote a global norm of environmental conservation (Wade 1997; cf. Rich 1994). Risse and Clark argue that transnational civil society has helped define and protect human rights via an iterative process of norm formation and implementation (Risse 2000; Clark 2001). Norms influence not only the current conduct of states and institutions, but form a standard for future conduct and may become enshrined in new international law.

A third view is that TCS represents the start of a new global order. Many of the discussions of norm formation convey the clear belief that civil society ruptured the old system of state dominance (Price 2003; Turner 1998; see also Shaw 1992; Lipschutz 1992). Some authors argue that as states decrease in power, TCS will form the basis for a new system of governance. Such a system might be anarchical and stateless (Korten 1998); involve new, globe-spanning structures that complement the state (Held 2004, 2006; Archibugi 2004); or replace representative systems of democracy with more deliberative ones (Nanz and Steffek 2004).

These visions are not always entirely reconcilable. Some of their diversity results from differences in data or from the gap between empirical and theoretical or normative writing. However, the diversity of views also indicates that discussion of TCS's democratizing potential has been inhibited by disagreement over exactly how TCSOs influence global governance and how TCS-driven democratization should be envisioned and assessed.

Doubts and concerns

At the same time that TCS has been hailed as a potential democratizer of global governance, positive views of TCS influence have been challenged by a countervailing body of scholarship. A growing body of relatively recent research has raised questions about many of the attributes of TCSOs, such as transparency, accessibility, popular participation, and grassroots accountability, that underlie claims of its democratizing potential. In essence, when the standards of accountability, transparency, equality of access, and representivity that Zürn and others use to critique international institutions are applied to transnational civil society, TCS is found lacking.

The value of international campaigns as representatives of stakeholder interests is predicated on the assumption that the policy positions presented by activists and advocates in fact represent the desires of the stakeholders they claim to represent. As indicated earlier, such campaigns generally claim to represent marginalized stakeholders in the developing world. However, abundant evidence exists that relations between CSOs are prone to disequilibrium. Christian Aid, for instance, has ignored or marginalized the opinions of its own local partners in constructing its global campaign against structural adjustment (Nelson 2000). Large Northern NGOs have endorsed the World Bank's plans for education in Niger, despite strenuous local objections (Murphy 2005). Northern NGO voices seem to dominate TCS input in World Bank and IMF policymaking processes (Woods 2000, 2005). Research in development studies indicates that even when Northern

NGOs provide funding to less well-resourced Southern partners, the result may be a Northern-dominated principal-agent relationship, rather than Southern empowerment (see, for example, Simbi and Thom 2000). In short, power imbalances among CSOs may marginalize developing country voices even within TCS.

A growing number of sources indicate that TCSOs based in the global North are motived or constrained in their behavior by economic considerations. The behavior of NGOs engaged in aid delivery in the Democratic Republic of the Congo and in Bosnia, for instance, has been shown to be driven by a need for organizational survival, particularly continued funding for overhead and staff salaries (Cooley and Ron 2002). Such considerations can prompt NGOs to compete against one another and curry favor with the international institutions that supply their funding, behaving 'much like firms do in markets' (Cooley and Ron 2002, p. 7). The focus on funders and the pressure of competition leaves little room for grassroots input and may undermine optimal aid outcomes. This theme is echoed by Manji and O'Coill (2002), who argue that development NGOs may advance and serve the political and economic agendas of their Western donors in a fashion reminiscent of some colonial-era missionaries and voluntary organizations. The result is that the work of development NGOs 'contributes marginally to the relief of poverty, but significantly to undermining the struggle of African people to emancipate themselves from economic, social, and political oppression' (Manji and O'Coill 2002, p. 582). While such critiques have focused primarily on NGOs involved in service delivery, they have direct relevance for TCSOs seeking to influence global governance. Manji and O'Coill point out that some of the major NGOs involved in international advocacy, groups like Oxfam and Christian Aid, still implement government-funded aid contracts as 'their "bread-and-butter"' activity (2002, p. 582). Clifford Bob's (2005) *The Marketing of Rebellion* also indicates that NGOs focusing on advocacy are constrained by their economic environment in much the same way as those NGOs focusing on service delivery.

Tensions between hopeful and critical views of TCS also highlight questions regarding the mechanisms of civil society impact. Insofar as many of the critiques of international institutions focus on their opaque or inaccessible power structures, understanding how civil society itself exerts power is important. Nonetheless, as Price writes, it is 'no small puzzle' how civil society has achieved its impacts (2003, p. 582). Although the traditional constructivist view of global civil society has focused on civil society's ability to create norms, some

authors note that civil society influence (including its capacity to propagate and enforce norms) is also often tied to the state (Keck and
Sikkink 1998; Risse 2000). Connections between the state and civil
society, in turn, 'may well undercut any claims of the autonomous
power of civil society' (Price 2003, p. 582).

What is striking in much of the critical writing is its detailed empirical evidence. Some of the academics who favorably discuss transnational civil society base their conclusions on detailed case studies (Keck
and Sikkink 1998; Risse 2000; Clark 2001), but others write in a more
purely theoretical vein (Held 2004; Lipschutz 1992; Matthews 1997;
Nanz and Steffek 2004). Detailed pro-TCS case studies often appear in
academic-edited volumes, but are frequently written by civil society
leaders previously involved in the campaigns they describe (see
Edwards and Gaventa 2001; Florini 2000; Fox and Brown 1998b;
Walker and Thompson 2008). Thus some of the best empirical data in
support of transnational civil society are also possibly the least objective. Moreover, many of the plaudits given to TCS come from political
scientists who neglect the extensive empirical data in development
studies, much of it produced by anthropologists, on the complex and
ambiguous impacts of TCSOs (see Tvedt 2002).

There is a reasonable concern that transnational civil society may
not be able to stand up to the very critiques its proponents have
leveled at international institutions. Transnational civil society as a
whole has been shown to impact international policymaking.
However, there is a substantial body of critical literature that challenges the benefits of civil society influence for those populations currently lacking power in international policymaking and that questions
the independence of transnational civil society organizations. While
not all authors critiquing TCSOs specifically address the question of
democracy, the points on which they touch directly challenge the pre-
vailing conception of TCS as a democratizing force. Indeed, taken as a
whole, their work seems to indicate that TCS may not only fail to
remedy the problems of global governance; it may actually make the
existing democratic deficit worse.

Approach to the research

This book examines the make-up of transnational civil society campaigns advocating for change in Bank policy, the mechanisms of TCS
influence, and the outcomes of TCS engagement on stakeholder representation in transnational policymaking using a series of detailed case

studies. The data generated present new insights into the impacts of TCS policymaking at the World Bank and add generally to the historical understanding of Bank engagement with TCS. The Bank is an extremely influential global governance institution with direct influence in those nations to which it lends money and strong ties to the donor nations that help fund it. Developing new data on the World Bank is itself significant simply because of the institution's reach and impact, and it is hoped that the findings will be useful for policymakers and activists alike in understanding the Bank and its interlocutors.

Examining TCS engagement with the World Bank fits well with the research approach described above. The Bank's level of intervention makes it easy to identify many of its stakeholders (including the farmers, fishermen, school children, and others affected by its lending) and its stakeholders may be precisely delimited as the populations of the 186 countries that make up the International Bank for Reconstruction and Development (IBRD), the Bank's core unit. This stakeholder base is extremely large. At the same time, the World Bank has been heavily targeted for reform by TCSOs and, compared with other global governance organizations of similar power and influence, the Bank has been relatively amenable to engagement with civil society (cf. Ebrahim and Herz 2011). Assuming that TCSOs demonstrate an equal will for engaging other international institutions and that the stakeholders of other institutions can be invoked as grounds for reform, the Bank has the potential to act as a leading indicator of TCS's potential impact on global governance. Thus this book's findings in the context of the World Bank constitute an important confirmation of certain elements of existing theories, as well as a starting point for new theory-building.

Research for this book focused on three case studies: the 10th replenishment of funding for the World Bank's International Development Association, the Bank's cancellation of funding for the Arun III dam in Nepal, and the Bank's decision to allow borrowing countries to use their own national systems to management procurement for Bank projects. Research was conducted over twelve months, primarily in Washington, DC and involved extensive archival research using TCSO, government, and Bank documents. This was supplemented by over two dozen intensive interviews, primarily with senior government, Bank, and civil society leaders with firsthand knowledge of key events, and by participant observation of Bank policymaking workshops. Data analysis was conducted over an additional twelve months at the Centre for Civil Society at the London School of Economics.

Case selection

The IDA-10 was a landmark case featuring an unprecedented number of TCSOs from extremely diverse backgrounds engaging with the Bank and culminating in far-reaching changes to the Bank's internal structures and its engagement with TCS. Because of its seminal role in Bank history and the ways in which it illustrates TCS behavior, much of this book is dedicated to analysis of the IDA-10. The International Development Association (IDA) was established by the Bank's donors in 1960 to provide loans to clients on concessional terms, i.e. with long repayment periods and little or no interest. The IDA can also provide outright grants. It is the World Bank's primary tool in addressing poverty in the world's least developed countries. Because IDA lending, unlike normal Bank lending, is not readily repaid to the Bank, the Bank's donors must replenish the IDA approximately every three years. These replenishments have become a major focus for the struggle to control the Bank, as interested parties seek to attach conditionalities to the Bank's funding.

Between 1992 and 1995, civil society organizations seized on the 10th replenishment of the IDA (referred as 'the 10th IDA' or 'IDA-10') to force reforms at the World Bank. TCSOs sought to reduce the size and influence of the Bank, change its approach to development, and create new mechanisms for outside oversight and accountability. The resulting campaign was arguably the first truly global civil society reform effort. While the term 'global civil society' was already in use in 1992, the studies which popularized the term generally depicted campaigns centered on small groups of US and European NGOs (see, for example, Lipschutz 1992). Although these groups had global spheres of operations and influence, their membership was largely limited to the citizens of industrialized nations. Local partners' involvement, where it occurred, tended to be ad hoc, focusing on mitigating the domestic impacts of a specific project (such as deforestation or forced resettlement) rather than the reform of a global policy. In contrast, campaigning on the 10th IDA involved CSOs from every inhabited continent, and its reform agenda impacted scores of World Bank borrowers. In many regards, the 10th IDA marks a key milestone for transnational civil society as an acknowledged international player in the modern era.

The case formed a turning point in the Bank's interactions with TCS. Many elements of the campaign were extremely successful. TCSOs succeeded in obstructing a significant portion of IDA funds. This funding cut forced the World Bank to recognize the importance of civil society actors in the international system and to create both formal and informal mechanisms for their continued involvement in Bank affairs. Following the cut in its IDA funding, the Bank's management invited TCSOs into policy consultations more frequently in an effort to fore-stall further attacks, giving TCS much greater influence over the institution's policies. The World Bank also made specific concessions, including the creation of a new information disclosure policy and the World Bank Inspection Panel, that facilitated future TCS impacts.

In the course of this research, inductive analysis of the IDA-10 led to a series of new, predictive hypotheses. These were then tested in a secondary, deductive phase of the research through two additional case studies: the 1994–96 campaign to cancel the World Bank's Arun III dam project in Nepal and the World Bank's adoption of borrowers' national systems for managing project procurement and finances in 2007–08. The cancellation of the Arun III dam project in Nepal was selected because it was one of the few TCS campaigns against the Bank subsequent to the IDA-10 in which changes in Bank behavior could be definitively attributed to TCS pressure. The campaign also utilized the World Bank Inspection Panel, an ombudsman function introduced in response to the IDA-10 lobbying, making it a logical follow-on case. Lastly, the international activism against the dam focused on a popular project in a democratic country and overlapped an election season in which the fate of the Arun III dam was openly debated among local political activists. Therefore the case provided a number of strong opportunities to compare international activist claims with local discourses and to examine the interactions between local government and TCSOs.

The second case selected was the World Bank's adoption of its Use of Country Systems for Procurement policy (UCS). Between 2007 and 2008, the World Bank changed its standards for project financial management and purchasing to begin allowing borrowers to use their own national systems in lieu of the World Bank's practices. The issue attracted significant attention from industry lobbyists, the International Labor Organization, and a number of concerned NGOs. These actors raised questions about the policy's potential impacts on competition, labor standards, aid effectiveness, and corruption. The resulting advocacy effort was relatively small and met with only limited success. However, the case provides an opportunity to examine outside engagement with the Bank post-9/11 and in the context of growing acceptance of a civil society role in global governance. The case also involved the Bank's Global Civil Society Team, which was introduced in 2003 to facilitate civil society engagement. Lastly, the

UCS case study was chosen because it is one of the Bank's most recent places of policy engagement with transnational civil society. As a result, the country systems policy change provides an opportunity to examine whether trends established in the early and mid-1990s continue through the present day.

How generalizable are the resulting findings? The Bank, after all, has a very unusual governance structure, funding model, mission, and scope of work. Yet the findings of the research suggest that the dynamics identified in Bank-TCSO engagement may be generalizable well beyond the Bank. As this book will show, many of the patterns of TCSO behavior identified in this research seem to result from factors internal to the TCSOs themselves or related to their funding environment, not their choice of institutional interlocutor. Additional findings on TCSO use of state power appear to be applicable in any institution in which the state members possess unequal power. In practice, this is most institutions. The findings of this research may be most robust as they relate to TCSOs and the World Bank, but the general patterns identified seem likely to be repeated in TCSO engagement with other global governance institutions.

Focus of the research

In examining TCS engagement with the World Bank, the intention of this work is to understand TCS impacts on global governance in empirical terms, rather than make normative claims. In so doing, this book takes two key steps. First, it seeks to establish a credible standard for assessing TCS's contributions to global governance. As the discussion above of TCS's supporters and critics indicate, no clear standard yet exists for determining whether TCS is making global governance more democratic. Without some standard of measurement, it is impossible to concretely evaluate TCS's impact on global governance.

Second, this book seeks to work from the origins of policy campaigns forward in establishing and examining TCS impacts, using individual TCSOs as its unit of analysis. Much of the research done on TCS takes what might be called a 'conclusion backward' approach. Researchers identify a key international campaign, usually one that has garnered significant attention or achieved noticeable impacts, and then trace it backwards to its origins. The origins are not ignored, but they circumscribed by the final conditions: researchers identify the TCSOs involved at the finale of a campaign and then investigate how they became involved in it, or look at the campaign's ultimate demands and examine their roots. The results yield something of a victor's history, in which TCSOs that exited the campaign or whose input was marginalized by more dominant members are ignored in the research and in which discarded demands and agendas go largely unexamined. This trend is particularly pernicious when researchers treat campaigns as monolithic wholes, rather than delving into the jostling organizations and interests of which they are composed. This book avoids these pitfalls by seeking to identify the actors involved at the start of each of the three campaigns it examines, and tracing their involvement forward in time through to the place where they either exit the campaign or the campaign terminates.

Two caveats should be specified. First, one must differentiate between democratizing World Bank policy and democratizing the World Bank's internal processes. A substantial body of literature exists examining how organizations themselves may be governed internally by representative processes, but it is not considered in this book. Creating internal democratic processes at the World Bank would do little to guarantee the balanced consideration of stakeholder interests. The Bank staff themselves are not the designated representatives of any group of stakeholders (although the president, admittedly, is chosen by the United States) and make most day-to-day decisions on a technical, rather than a political, basis. This is not to say that the Bank's decisions are apolitical; to the contrary, most are extremely political. However, the Bank's political nature comes from the constant external pressure exerted on it by the governments of its various stakeholders to promote their national interests. Given the Bank's technocratic internal environment and the high number of external inputs into its decisions, internal organizational democracy would do little to assure the equal representation of stakeholder interests or stakeholder control over policy decisions.

It is also important to note that the Bank has a significant history of engaging with local civil society in the course of project implementation. The Bank has long recognized that civil society involvement in development projects can increase the effectiveness and success rate of such projects. Consequently, the Bank has been regularly engaging with local civil society since the early 1990s. This involvement may have an admirable effect on democratizing local development (see Clark 1991; Long 2001). However, local, project-specific decisions rarely translate into transnational policies. Moreover, many of the civil society organizations involved do not meet the definition of TCSOs as their activities and connections are wholly local. For these reasons, this book focuses primarily on TCS engagement with the World Bank's Washington-based policy processes.

To determine whether civil society is democratizing Bank policymaking, this book poses seven sub-questions designed to ascertain how civil society contributes towards democratizing policymaking at the World Bank.

How should one evaluate the democratization of global governance?

Democracy itself is a term with multiple definitions. Moreover, most of these terms focus on democracy within the confines of the state. To evaluate TCS contributions to the democratization of global governance, one must define democracy and determine how TCS should be expected to advance or facilitate it.

Which TCSOs are involved?

The diversity of TCS is part of what enables it, in theory, to represent the global citizenry. However, as noted earlier, there is some disagreement among observers regarding whether transnational civil society is dominated by organizations from the developed world. Understanding which civil society organizations are involved in seeking to influence the Bank is necessary to verify TCS's diversity and is an important preliminary step in determining whether some organizations have disproportionate power or impact.

How do TCSOs interact with one another?

Literature on TCS has tended to focus on ad hoc campaigns in which the participating organizations hold very similar positions or has used a research approach that potentially overlooked dissenting TCSOs. In contrast, this book's study of policymaking at the World Bank features a greater diversity of views. By examining interactions between civil society organizations at the World Bank, this book aims to contribute to the understanding of how civil society organizations identify and handle differences and whether they engage in dialogue with each other. The presence or absence and nature of such engagement has important implications for depictions of TCS as an inclusive, participatory, or deliberative space, as well as the view that advocacy campaigns tend to represent broad consensus among the advocacy organizations involved.

How do TCSOs choose their policy positions?

A significant portion of the literature supporting TCS's capacity to democratize global governance posits that civil society advocacy arises from grassroots interests. Although it is not possible to test how well

TCSO policy positions represent the interests of grassroots stakeholders due to the lack of data on such interests, it is possible to investigate how TCSOs choose their policy positions. For instance, some authors claim that international organizations consult with local partners in constructing policy positions, whereas critics have implied that organizations based in the global North focus primarily on the demands of their Northern membership.

At the same time, several authors have suggested that funding concerns influence the activities of different organizations, especially NGOs providing development service delivery. In particular, critics indicate that some NGOs tailor their activities to curry favor with their major donors. If this is the case in policy advocacy, TCSOs may act as proxies for donor interests rather than as grassroots representatives. This sub-question explores whether TCSOs seek to include and represent marginalized voices in constructing their policy positions, and also explores the influence of funding on advocacy.

What impact has TCS had on the World Bank?

Verifying that TCS actually can influence World Bank policy is an essential part of testing claims made about TCS's democratizing capacity. Associating changes in Bank policy or behavior with the policy positions of specific organizations can help determine whether some TCSOs are more powerful than others and contribute to debates in the literature about equality of stakeholder influence.

By what mechanisms has impact been achieved?

Identifying TCSOs' mechanisms of impact is a key step in verifying their independence and agency. Examining which organizations can access the more impactful mechanisms and how they use such access also has bearing on the inclusivity of TCS as a whole and the distribution of authority among stakeholders. If the mechanisms by which TCS achieves its impact are accessible only to certain TCSOs, this finding might strengthen the contention, made by some critics, that a small number of elite organizations (generally from the developed world) dominate TCS influence.

What impact does TCS have on the power of developing country governments in transnational policymaking?

States may be an important means of representation for developing country citizens. Much of the concern about the democratic deficit in global governance focuses on the perceived marginalization of developing countries within the governance structures of international institutions. Research has already established that TCSOs may enhance government influence in some contexts (e.g. Raustiala 1997). However, while some TCSOs recognize states (particularly democratic states) as important partners, other TCSOs contest the legitimacy of states as popular representatives. Some researchers have indicated that TCS advocacy may further reduce the power of developing country governments in international policymaking. Explicitly examining the interaction between TCS and developing countries enables this book to address these issues and to develop a more nuanced and holistic picture of citizen input into transnational decision-making.

Argument and structure of the book

The case studies reveal that TCS is far more atomized than generally thought. Strong commitments to pre-existing missions, coupled with financial constraints, inhibit dialogue between organizations and make it difficult for TCSOs to respond to the concerns of grassroots stakeholders. TCS has abundant impact on the World Bank and some impacts, like improved transparency and accountability, have facilitated improved stakeholder influence over the institution. However, the most effective channels of influence, including partnerships with the Bank's powerful donor states, are accessible primarily by elite organizations based in the global North. In addition, TCSOs solicit the assistance of the Bank's major donors in ways that at times undermine the international influence of developing country governments. As a result of these issues, TCS not only fails to democratize policymaking at the World Bank, but may actually worsen the marginalization of some stakeholders. TCS seems unlikely to democratize global governance without significant changes in either the norms governing TCSO behavior or in the institutional contexts that shape its influence.

This book has eight chapters. Chapter 2 develops a framework for assessing TCS contributions to democratization, which is then applied throughout the work. The chapter begins by establishing a definition of democracy built around equality of access and popular control over governance outcomes. It draws on the work of Uhlin, Dingwerth, and Scharpf to divide democracy into input, throughput, and output components. The chapter then builds on these authors' contributions by identifying the different contexts and roles in which TCSOs can operate, ranging from undemocratic states to supranational policymaking, and shows how TCSOs must support different components of democracy in order to democratize governance in each context.

Chapter 3 is a chronology of the 10th IDA. It covers the interactions between TCS and the World Bank leading up to the IDA-10, highlights key events in the negotiations, and details the outcomes. The chapter identifies the key transnational civil society actors involved in the IDA, and shows that the actors formed two distinct groups with diverging policy interests, one supporting full IDA funding and one opposing it. This fracture within TCS allows the book to analyze TCS's motivations, impact, and representation via a comparative analysis of the two factions in subsequent chapters.

Chapter 4 examines the possible explanations for the divisions among the IDA-10 TCSOs. It explores the roles of Northern and Southern affiliation, mission, and financing. Mission appears to have determined the policy positions of most organizations, while financial incentives influenced their decisions to participate in or withdraw from advocacy. The chapter gives particular attention to the Charles Stewart Mott Foundation, which funded the activities of several key participants, and identifies a possible principal-agent relationship. Diverging financial interests are also found to lead to a lack of dialogue or compromise among the organizations being researched.

Chapter 5 analyzes the mechanisms by which TCSOs exerted influence over the World Bank. It explores the roles of transparency, accountability, and dialogue in increasing institutional responsiveness to stakeholders and shows how these elements were used during the 10th IDA. The evidence collected shows how the most effective tool used was financial leverage exercised via the US government. Such leverage was only available to US-based NGOs with strong political connections. This explains why the anti-IDA faction was able to carry its agenda over the objections of the numerically larger pro-IDA faction. These findings highlight the role of nation-states in facilitating TCS influence on global governance. They also indicate that although TCS may increase institutional responsiveness to certain stakeholders, TCSOs' use of powerful states to facilitate influence may undermine the cause of improved stakeholder equality.

Chapter 6 examines the impact of transnational advocacy on the capacity of states, particularly Bank borrowers, to act as representatives of stakeholder populations. It looks at the effect of transnational advocacy on the role of states in Bank policymaking, and at the effect of international campaigns on the internal policymaking processes of target countries. It also examines the role of local partners in transnational coalitions. The chapter finds that TCSOs weakened the bargaining power of borrowing state governments during the IDA-10 by challenging the credibility and authority of borrower governments in World Bank policymaking. The data indicates that the presence of local partners in international coalitions is no guarantee of their representivity and that TCS activity targeting borrower countries has the potential to negatively impact the self-governance of the national population.

Moving from inductive theory-building to deductive hypothesis-testing, Chapter 7 examines whether the patterns observed in the IDA-10 are repeated in the Arun III anti-dam campaign and the World Bank's adoption of country systems for procurement. The chapter finds strong support for TCSOs' reliance on state partners for influence in international policymaking, and strong indications that state assistance privileges better-connected actors. It also finds continued indications that TCSO involvement in policymaking is driven by a combination of financial and ideological pressures, and that dialogue among TCSOs is limited. The Arun III case provides particularly strong evidence of TCSOs ignoring the expressed will of local stakeholders and hindering national democratic practices.

Chapter 8 summarizes the findings of the book and examines the implications of the data from the World Bank research for our understanding of TCS and its contributions to democratic global governance. This chapter challenges claims of TCS representivity, and elaborates on the importance of North-South-North patterns of global advocacy, in which Northern TCSOs recruit Southern partners in order to convince international policymakers of the 'global' nature of the TCSOs' agendas. It suggests how the World Bank can channel TCS influence to produce more democratic policymaking processes and proposes some ways in which TCSOs themselves can enhance representivity through improved accountability, transparency, and interorganizational dialogue.

2
Context, Role, and Legitimacy[1]

Although TCS is frequently heralded as a key component of more democratic global governance, a noticeable gap has been observed between the hoped-for impacts of TCS as a normative construct and the real-world impacts of the organizations of which it is composed. A number of researchers have called into question civil society organizations' motivations, representivity, and democratic credentials (Bowden 2006; Cooley and Ron 2002; Foley and Edwards 1996; Nelson 1997b). Even among those authors that hold that civil society can contribute positively towards global governance, one finds a variety of competing and sometimes contradictory prescriptions for judging the democratic contributions of individual TCSOs or TCS as a whole.

Placing discussions of TCS within the larger context of discussions regarding democratic global governance, this chapter argues that TCS's democratic credentials should not be judged based not on wholly endogenous factors like transparency or participation, but rather on its impact on the democratic rights of the populations it impacts. This chapter clarifies the conditions under which TCSOs can contribute to creating or enhancing democracy by identifying the democratic needs of different political contexts and highlighting the role TCSOs play in contributing to democracy in each one. This chapter also highlights the dangers of confusing or conflating the role of civil society in national and international spaces, a problem that appears to occur frequently as civil society organizations expand their activities in the global realm. It thus establishes a standard of democratic legitimacy for use in the assessment of TCS activities.

This chapter divides the concept of democratic legitimacy into three parts: input (such as grassroots participation), throughput (such as transparency), and output (mainly impacts). As will be shown, the relative importance of TCS's input, throughput, or output varies in different political contexts. TCS's legitimacy is judged based on the contributions of the TCSOs involved in any given activity to the aspects of democracy most necessary in the political context in which they are acting.

To help highlight the impacts of context and the ways in which civil society can respond to it in a democratically legitimate way, I have used the language of 'roles'. Within the national context, civil society[2] (or a coordinated group of CSOs, like an advocacy network or campaign) can act as a *Revolutionary*, seeking to reform or replace an undemocratic regime and install a democratic one, or as an *Advocate* representing the interests of particular groups within a democratic system. In either the state or international context, a CSO can act as an *Agent* working on behalf of the state or international institutions. Finally, in the global context, civil society may also act as an *Authority* contributing actively to the creation and enforcement of global norms and policy. The reasons why each of these roles is associated with a specific context are explained below.

This chapter will proceed in five parts. It begins by examining the literature on TCS and identifying questions in need of clarification. Next, it disaggregates democratic legitimacy and discusses its various elements. Third, it identifies the four contexts in which civil society may act, and elaborates the rationale for judging democratic legitimacy differently in each context. Fourth, using insights from this analysis of contextual legitimacy, it highlights two important problems in the current analysis of the legitimacy of transnational civil society actors. It concludes by discussing the ways that a contextual understanding of legitimacy can contribute to the remaining questions in the literature, framing the examination made in the remainder of this book.

Researching and theorizing transnational civil society: A brief history

Academic writing on civil society and international affairs dates back over thirty years. As early as 1976, Mansbach et al defined 'the interstate non-governmental actor' as encompassing 'individuals who reside in several nation-states but do not represent the governments of these states', and included such actors alongside states and intergovernmental organizations as key players in the international system (pp. 39–40). Literature on TCS, however, did not reach critical mass until the early 1990s, when a more regular dialogue began on the role of TCS in global policymaking. Whereas earlier efforts were largely empirical, these new writings were prompted by a variety of theoretical, normative, and empirical interests. Since then, shifting foci within the field and a multiplicity of approaches have led to a fractured and at times meandering body of literature.

Some of the first contemporary references to TCS appear in articles published by Martin Shaw and Ronald Lipschutz in 1992. Lipschutz wrote that 'global civil society' was creating a form of transnational demos that would 'challenge, from below, the nation-state system' (Lipschutz 1992, p. 391). He embraced an explicitly normative agenda, calling for academics to 'undertake the reconstruction of world politics' to facilitate civil society's growing role (Lipschutz 1992, p. 420). Shaw took a slightly more cautious approach. He agreed that the growing power of TCS 'challenged the principles of sovereignty and non-intervention' at the heart of the state system (1992, p. 432). However, he did not think the 'global society perspective' would 'become central to world politics in the short or medium term' (Shaw 1992, p. 434). These articles were followed by a host of other writings, many of them arguing for the potential of TCS to revolutionize global governance. Some argued for civil society's democratizing potential (e.g. Held 1995; Payne 1996; Spiro 1995) whereas others simply emphasized its power and influence (e.g. Meyer 1997; Nelson 1997b; Willetts 1996).

Most of this writing reflected the effort, often led by constructivists, to break free from a state-based, realist depiction of international relations (cf. Wendt 1995). Constructivists and others contested the dominant materialist perspectives in international relations which depicted state power as the predominant explanation for international events and decisions. The influence of civil society and the existence of transnational networks were important proof that states were no longer the sole legitimate focus of study. TCS's power to create norms and influence policy indicated a locus of power outside the state and a means of power other than material dominance. The creation and adoption of international norms also indicated that, contrary to rational choice theory, states' interests could shift over time. Similarly, the idea of globe-spanning citizens' networks provided an alternative to the vision of international anarchy and isolated states favored by realists.

The focus on theory-building in the mid-1990s sometimes eclipsed empirical research. International relations writings about TCS often seemed to rely on media depictions of current events rather than carefully investigated case studies. At the same time, the case for TCS's potential to democratize global governance was more inferred than proven, sometimes from the precedent of the civil society-driven democratization of national governments in South American and Eastern Europe (Bowden 2006; cf. Lipschutz 1992; cf. Foley and Edwards 1996). The constructivist focus on norms and impacts left TCS advocates open to the charge of ignoring questions of agency by not specifying clearly the means by which TCS achieved its influence (Price 2003). Other critics challenged the relevance of national experiences to the global context (Bowden 2006; Goodhart 2005). A number of authors also suggested that early writing on TCS ignored the ways in which the complexities of global advocacy might inhibit genuinely democratic representation. They noted that effective global advocacy relied on coercive power available only to a minority of NGOs and that the political bargaining in which powerful NGOs engaged was neither transparent nor accountable to many of the people it affected (Foley and Edwards 1996; Nelson 1997; cf. Tvedt 2002). This new body of more critical writing marked a shift away from the discussion of TCS primarily as a homogenous, theoretical construct and towards a more empirical analysis of the observed behavior and impacts of TCSOs.

This wave of critique resulted in a number of strong, interdisciplinary works that combined constructivism with some elements of realist analysis. They focused on TCSOs' ability to upend the state system by introducing new norms while still relying on some state mechanisms to implement and enforce standards (Price 2003). Chief among these was Keck and Sikkink's *Activists Beyond Borders* (1998) which laid out the 'boomerang theory' of transnational advocacy, which depicted how CSOs facing local political blockages might enlist the aid of partners in powerful states who would exercise political leverage on their behalf. Other works contributed less theory, but improved the emphasis on detailed empirical data, often by including practitioner-authored case studies in edited volumes (e.g. Fox and Brown 1998b; Florini 2000; Edwards and Gaventa 2001).

These new works helped address some problems of theory and method but they did little to tackle growing concerns about the legitimacy of TCS. They also began the transition away from conceptualizing TCS as a global society and toward seeing it as a loose collective of autonomous actors. Questions remained about TCS's democratic credentials, particularly its accountability and transparency (Nelson 2000; Scholte 2004; cf. Ebrahim 2007). Authors challenged constructivist assumptions about TCSO autonomy from the state or material interests (Cooley and Ron 2002; Raustiala 1997; Tvedt 2002) and questioned whether civil society could function democratically outside the boundaries of the state (Bowden 2006).

One persistent concern was that civil society, particularly at the global level, was fundamentally dominated by elites. Research from both development studies (Nelson 2000; Murphy 2005) and political science (Anderson 2000) highlighted TCS's use of elite mechanisms. Some argued that TCS replicated and magnified existing power imbalances rather than remedying them (Woods 2000; Manji and O'Coill 2002; Scholte 2012; cf. McKeon 2010) or that global networks concentrated their benefits among actors with the 'resources, patronage or expertise' to participate in transnational discussions (Stone 2005). These concerns contributed to the continuing debate among academics and practitioners on the appropriate role for TCS in global governance.

Defining lines of argumentation

Numerous rifts exist within this body of literature. These rifts center on three main issues: the understanding of transnational civil society, the model of global governance, and the definition of democracy. Further complicating factors are the divisions between normative and empirical approaches and among various schools of academic research. Understanding the previous research is essential for assessing TCS's capacity to democratize global governance, but the challenge of addressing the democratic legitimacy of TCS is two-fold. First, most of the rifts are multilateral; none of the debates around TCS, global governance, or democracy can be neatly partitioned into two sides. Second, most authors manage to cross multiple fault lines as they write simultaneously about civil society, global governance, and democracy.

The most obvious debate centers TCS's membership, behavior, and motivation. Some authors maintain that TCSOs genuinely 'rescue the causes of marginalized or excluded groups' (Gryzbowski 2000, p. 442). Others insist that TCSOs pursue their own understanding of the public good (Florini and Simmons 2000; Nelson 1997b). Some focus on the diversity of organizations with TCS, reminding us that not all civil society is truly 'civil' – i.e. non-violent or interested in upholding the common good (Foley and Edwards 1996). The skeptics insist that civil society in its transnational form is highly parochial, with the tendency to promote rich-world policies for Southern or poor populations (Nelson 2000; Woods 2005). The most pessimistic of all insist that TCSOs are self-interested and driven by financial needs (Cooley and Ron 2002; Bob 2005) or even assist in an imperial agenda (Manji and O'Coill 2002).

A second debate is over the shape of global governance. Authors of the cosmopolitan school argue for the eventual dissolution of national governments or predict the rise of a global superstate (e.g. Korten 1998; Held 2004). Others argue for the enduring power and importance of states and institutions, including a role for states or international organizations in implementing the civil society agenda (Keck and Sikkink 1998; Risse 2000; Clark 2001). Again, a critical minority questions whether democratic global governance is even possible (Dahl 1999) and whether civil society is just a tool of the state (Raustiala 1997).

The definition of democracy forms another debate (cf. Näsström 2010). Bexell et al (2010) have observed that while normative democratic theory manifests a 'trichotomy' of separate representative, participatory, and deliberative models, writers on global governance feel free to sample from and combine these strands. Held's (2006) vision of cosmopolitan democracy, for instance, mixes elements of all three models. Nanz and Steffek (2004) take a more purely deliberative approach. An emphasis on participation is common among advocates for civil society participation in global governance (Payne 1996; Gryzbowski 2000), while others use accountability as a proxy for equal representation (Scholte 2004; cf. Nelson 1997b).

Over this fractured ground are layered other complicating factors. Some political theorists have created elaborate normative models, while empirical researchers have taken issue with the gap between TCS's idealized behavior and the reality of CSO conduct. At the same time, variations in approach among international relations, international political economy, development studies, and non-academic practitioners further complicate the literature.

A standard for evaluation

Rather than adding to the confusion by developing yet another set of unique standards, this chapter seeks to identify, organize, and address the underlying assumptions in previous work, building a framework for the systematic assessment of TCS's democratic legitimacy that facilitates, rather than inhibits, clear dialogue with previous research.

Defining democracy

The first step in this process is defining democracy. An appropriate definition must apply equally well to states, international institutions, and TCS, since these are all key players in global governance. Much of the literature on TCS and democratization is implicitly (or explicitly) a comparison of the relative democratic credentials of these three categories of actors. To fairly judge between them, the definition must apply to all three.

State-based democracy generally utilizes majority rule, in which some equally distributed measure of voice or authority is used by citizens to exercise control over the government (Dahl 1999; Näsström 2010). This understanding of democracy is not only embraced by state actors, but also a large number of practitioners, particularly those from the developing world (Naidoo and Tandon 1999; see also Mbogori and Chigudu 1999). If we acknowledge that majority rule can be achieved by methods other than voting, then majority rule can encompass the pluralistic or participatory standards of democracy typically used to identify democracy in non-state settings. This, in turn, allows us to engage with the evolving representative mechanisms of international institutions.[3]

In addition to being majoritarian, democracy must be representative. Representative practices are nearly universal in modern democratic states. As Dahl notes, 'in practice, all democratic systems, with the exception of a few very tiny communities, allow for, indeed depend on, delegation of power and authority; the citizen body delegates some decisions to others' (1999, p. 21). These designated persons are commissioned to represent or act on behalf of a particular population (Dahl 1999). Moreover, as noted, data suggest that much of TCS's impact is elite-driven. On its face, it is unrealistic to insist that in order to be democratically legitimate, TCS must function like an Athenian assembly, deciding positions on the basis of millions of individual views. However, we can ask whether individual TCSOs act as representatives of particular populations and whether the decisions made among such representatives reflect the will of the majority of stakeholders.

Finally, democracy includes the protection of citizen rights (Dahl 1999; Moravcsik 2004). Rights may be protected by either norms or laws allowing this definition to engage with constructivist, functionalist, and realist literature. Some of the 'rights' protected by civil society groups are quite controversial, so a specific list of the rights encompassed would be useful (see Dahl 1999, p. 20; Moravcsik 2004, p. 339). However, as Held has pointed out, the understanding of liberalism (and its constituent rights) has shifted historically (2006, p. 59). For the purposes of this book, it is more important to establish that democracy involves both popular sovereignty and the protection of rights than it is to enumerate those rights in great detail.

In summary, we can define democracy as a system of equal citizen authority or value expressed via some representative mechanism and resulting in government or institutional responsiveness to the will of the majority, but under which the government or institution is also constrained to protect the liberal rights of its citizens or stakeholders. The definition does not require that all citizens make use of their voice or actively participate, only that the mechanism of input (e.g. voting or otherwise) be equally accessible and provide for all participating voices to be equally valued. It also requires that the governance organization respond to the expressed will of the majority and protect commonly recognized rights.

Democratic legitimacy and TCS

As the history of TCS research reveals, TCS is discussed among academic authors as both a theoretical object and in empirical terms as the aggregate of some delimited set of CSOs. Studies examining civil society in empirical terms also often narrow their focus to a particular type of CSO or network or to a specific campaign. This book engages with civil society as a real-world phenomenon; it defines TCS as the aggregate of all TCSOs meeting the definition later out in the previous chapter. It also recognizes that all of the organizations constituting TCS are never all involved in the same campaign; indeed, smaller campaigns may involve just one or two TCSOs. Therefore this book develops a legitimacy standard applicable both to individual CSOs and to collective groups thereof, including campaigns and networks.

To build this definition, this book looks at both national and international contexts. Therefore it is useful, at least initially, to discuss the matter in terms of CSOs more generally before returning to the specific question of TCSOs. The democratic legitimacy of CSOs is judged on the basis of their contributions to the democratic well-being of the persons impacted by their actions. That is, the legitimacy of individual CSOs, and of collective endeavors such as campaigns and networks, are judged based on whether they contribute to a system of equal citizen authority, majority rule, and government responsiveness or the protection of basic rights.

Applying this standard requires dividing democratic legitimacy into several parts. In this regard, I follow on the work Anders Uhlin, who himself builds on the work of Sharpf and Dingwerth (Scharpf 1999; Dingwerth 2007). Uhlin (2010, p. 23) writes:

> In order to organize the various concepts related to democratic legitimacy, I find it useful to distinguish between input legitimacy (the relationship between the actor and its constituencies or people

affected by its activities), throughput legitimacy (the actual procedures for decision-making within the actor), and output legitimacy (the consequences of the actor's decisions and other activities).

Each of these elements presents a distinct agenda for investigation. Input legitimacy focuses on issues of representation and inclusion. It examines whether a state or non-governmental actor is representative of its constituents or stakeholders, whether stakeholders have equal voice in formulating policy positions, and, particularly in the case of advocacy organizations, to what extent they advance the interests of those populations they claim to represent. Throughput legitimacy examines transparency, accountability, participation, and deliberation. It asks how actors promote participation and discussion, whether they are transparent, and how and to whom they are accountable. Output legitimacy focuses on the consequences of actors' activities. It includes both the impacts of a successfully implemented policy and the ways in which activism can change the political system (Uhlin 2010).

Table 2.1   The components of input, throughput, and output

Input	Throughput	Output
Representation	Transparency	Policies/Impacts
Inclusion	Accountability	Structural change
	Deliberation	
	Participation	

Legitimacy and context

One logical implication of Uhlin's argument is that many of the apparent disagreements over the meaning of democracy in the literature on TCS are implicitly debates over the type of legitimacy most relevant to TCS and, in some cases, to civil society more broadly. The literature on civil society and democracy tends to describe CSOs as though they operate in a single, global context. Some authors distinguish between national and international civil society organizations, but organizations from these two contexts are frequently treated as equal parts of transnational networks. Although potential disparities between domestic and international actors are acknowledged (Keck and Sikkink 1998), their combined efforts are frequently treated as monolithic campaigns.[4] Moreover, transnational campaigns to change the national policies or practices of a single country (e.g. by stopping a dam or freeing imprisoned journalists) are treated as equivalent to transnational efforts to create new global policies (e.g. banning landmines or improving financial regulation). Finally, cases from specific national contexts, like the civil society-driven democratization of countries in Eastern Europe or Latin America, are used as models for the democratization of global governance.

Democratic legitimacy can be better understood if we think of CSOs as operating in three distinct contexts. First, they operate in undemocratic states. In recent history this would include places like Eastern Europe or apartheid South Africa. Second, they operate in democratic states, i.e. states that have some measure of liberal democracy and that are acknowledged as democratic by their peers. Historically this has included the US and Western Europe and, more recently, much of Latin America, Southeast Asia, and parts of Africa. Finally, they can operate in the international realm, where they are often beyond the control of any one state or institution. This is the newest of civil society contexts, but arguably the most powerful. It includes CSO lobbying of the UN, World Bank, or WTO, the development or implementation of aid programs, and campaigns working to construct new international norms or regimes.[5]

The different contexts should inform and shape our understanding of legitimacy. If the democratic legitimacy of civil society is judged by its success in developing or facilitating democracy, the goal of any organization wishing to be democratically legitimate must be to enhance the democratic rights of the entire population it impacts. This requires gauging the interaction between the CSO(s) and other structures (namely governments or institutions) which could or should grant enduring democratic rights and protections. These governments and institutions exist, they have impact, and, in many cases, they have better established democratic credentials than competing civil society actors. If CSOs claim to enhance the democratic well-being of their stakeholders, then the roles and impacts of governments and institutions must be taken into account. Insofar as the legitimacy and authority of these actors vary by context, so too will CSOs' interactions with them.

This book uses the language of 'roles' to describe the requirements of a given context. Each role defines the means by which civil society can address the democratic needs of a particular setting as determined by the presence or absence of other democratic structures. Therefore role, as used here, cannot be divorced from context.

The needs of each context create specific democratic legitimacy requirements for CSOs operating therein. Meeting these requirements leads to particular types of behavior. Roles encompass both the standards of democratic legitimacy and the resulting behavior. However, it is important to emphasize that these roles are used in an analytical sense, to assess democratic legitimacy, not as abstract descriptions of possible CSO activities. The roles are simply short-hand for the requirements of context. Thus, this book does not label a CSO as a 'revolutionary' simply because it is working to change the system or as an 'advocate' because it claims to be representing a certain group or interest. Civil society actors which do not meet the democratic needs of a given context are not said, on the basis of their behavior, to be fulfilling an alternative role. Instead, I would describe them as failing to meet the democratic legitimacy standards of their current context.[6]

The four roles

For civil society to be democratically legitimate in any given situation, CSOs must interact with other structures in a way that develops the democratic rights of the stakeholders affected by their actions. Each context presents one or two possible behaviors and a set of standards by which such behaviors may be judged. The behaviors and standards are summarized in the four roles. For the sake of clarity, each of the roles is described as it applies to a single civil society organization. However, the roles are equally applicable to multiple CSOs operating in a given context, including coordinated groups such as campaigns and networks, and to civil society or TCS as a whole.

In an undemocratic state, a CSO must be legitimated by its efforts to reform or replace the existing regime. In this context, it must play the role of *revolutionary*. It is important to note that efforts to create or enforce rights are commonly described as advocacy activities. In this context, however, such 'advocacy' is actually a form of revolution, insofar as it changes the system of government to make it more democratic via its recognition of rights. Non-revolutionary activities, such as educating children or providing healthcare may certainly be judged legitimate by any number of moral or technical standards, but they do not provide democratic legitimacy. Providing services or advocating on behalf of specific interests can have little enduring effect on citizens' control over government without a wholesale change in the mechanisms of governing. Service provision may prop up an undemocratic state, even as it mitigates its impact on its citizens. Advocacy that does not push for political reform may likewise legitimate the state. Even where CSO advocacy wins concessions, the CSO is reliant on an undemocratic regime to maintain them. Instead, a CSO must promote change in government, including the development of representative mechanisms and the recognition of basic rights.

In this context, a CSO's legitimacy should be judged purely on outputs. On the one hand, representation, participation, and transparency are meaningless if national democracy is not established. CSOs themselves might be internally democratic, but internal democracy will not succeed in obtaining democratic rights or protections for the country's citizens. On the other hand, if liberal democracy is established, new legal or constitutional standards will be developed to govern representation and protect rights. Thus a CSO in this context does not necessarily need to manifest these standards itself. Civil society is not the government; it is the means of reforming the government. Revolutionary CSOs, like Solidarity in Poland, are judged to be democratically legitimate when their efforts succeed in establishing a democratic state. Conversely, revolutionary organizations that act on hierarchical or otherwise undemocratic lines may be looked upon skeptically if they attempt to govern national affairs in such a fashion after national democracy has been established. ZANU, which morphed into the ruling party of an authoritarian Zimbabwe, is an obvious example but the democratic legitimacy of the more respected ANC in South Africa has also been threatened by complaints that it has created a one-party state and by its failure to protect the rights of mine workers during their 2012 strikes.

When acting within a democratic state, a CSO may play the role of *advocate*. Democratic rights are guaranteed by the state, and a CSO can enhance the democratic rights of a state's citizens by monitoring or facilitating state processes. It does this either by seeking to represent marginalized populations, ensuring that they are fully empowered within the political process, or by acting as a watchdog, ensuring that the government continues to function democratically and protect citizen's rights. In this role and context, a CSO is judged on either input or throughput. When acting as a representative, a CSO must be judged on both input and throughput. If a CSO claims to speak on behalf of a given population, then its claims must be verifiable. This requires both representation and a measure of transparency and accountability. Without these things, a CSO risks tipping the scales in favor of special or even imaginary interests or co-opting the causes of marginalized populations to achieve ends other than the ones desired by those populations. When acting as a watchdog, a CSO must be judged based on its throughput. A civil society organization can and should support the practices of transparency, accountability, and deliberation which enhance democracy, but in order to legitimately enhance them, it must also model them, creating a standard for the behavior citizens should expect from their government. A CSO operating within the democratic state context is not judged on outputs. Democratic governance is already provided by the state and, in a majoritarian regime, sometimes a CSO *should* lose, i.e. if it is representing an interest at odds with the will of the majority. One exception is when a CSO is attempting to enforce and protect the recognized rights of a particular minority. However, even in this case a CSO's legitimacy is not judged by its outputs, because a CSO ultimately has no control over the state. When a good-faith effort (input and throughput legitimate) to protect minority rights fails, it reflects negatively on the democratic credentials of the state, but not on those of the CSO involved.

In either the democratic national context or in the international arena, a CSO may act on behalf of a state or institution. When acting on behalf of an established authority, a CSO operates in the role of *agent*. Historically speaking, the agent role is a result of the neoliberal shift and 'hollowing out' of government observed in some states (e.g. the US and UK), whereby private actors were delegated responsibilities previously held by the state in the belief that such delegation would increase efficiency or diminish financial risk to the state. In particular, states have contracted CSOs to deliver foreign aid or domestic social services. Such operations feature heavily in some of the more critical literature on civil society, particularly from development studies. Identifying this type of implementation as a distinct role helps us understand how such critiques connect to the literature on civil society advocacy.[7]

When operating as an agent, a CSO must be judged by the democratic credentials of the state or institution on whose behalf it acts. If a CSO acts on behalf of a democratic state, it may be considered democratic; if it acts on behalf of an undemocratic one, it may be considered undemocratic because of the type of regime it is supporting. It is important to note that this must be examined differently in the national and international realms. In a wholly domestic context, in which a CSO is funded by the government on whose behalf it works, the principal-agent relationship is clear. Internationally, the situation is more complex. A civil society organization may be funded by one government, or a multilateral organization, for work in another polity. In this case, the will of the people in the polity in which the work is done must be considered, insofar as they will reap the benefits or suffer the consequences of the CSO's activities. Even in those instances in which a CSO's intervention is approved by a local democratic government, one must also consider whether the local government truly desires the CSO's services or whether those services have been forced upon it by more powerful states or organizations.[8] In short, a CSO acting as an agent may be considered democratically legitimate if it works under contract to a legitimate representative of the people impacted by its work, or if a majority of these people themselves approve that work. The choice of principal (including the alignment of interests between an external principal and the local will) may be considered a form of input. Therefore a CSO acting as an agent is judged based on input legitimacy.

CSOs as authorities

The first three roles occupied by civil society – revolutionary, advocacy, and agent – have been thoroughly examined in the literature. It is tempting to assume that the observations made about CSOs acting in these well-recognized roles and contexts transfers to civil society involvement in international policymaking. In reality, however, CSO involvement in international policymaking requires recognition of a new role.

When a civil society organization engages in global policymaking (either in a de jure way through formal participation in international decision-making or in a de facto way through the propagation of international norms), it is acting as an *authority*. The reach of both individual CSOs and networks of organizations frequently spans national boundaries, and transnational activism often results in the creation of international networks. Activists make broad claims of popular support. At the same time, the rise of global problems like terrorism and climate change has necessitated international collaboration to a degree unprecedented in political history. Technology has further facilitated multilateral collaboration, and international institutions like the UN, World Bank, and WTO have laid the framework for global governance. The proliferation of transnational issues, voices, and forums challenges states' claims to act as the sole voice of their citizens in the international realm. When CSOs operate across multiple national contexts (e.g. simultaneously coordinating local protests in a developing country, organizing a letter-writing campaign in Europe, and lobbying bureaucrats in Washington) in order to establish a new international norm or benefit a transnational group of stakeholders, they are operating in this de facto authority role.[9]

At the same time, the research of the past decade has demonstrated that CSOs have the power to change the international behavior of states and institutions, and to create new norms and regimes. Individual CSOs and networks of concerned actors have been credited with playing a significant role in expanding human rights and environmental norms, and even in nuclear disarmament (Clark 2001; Wade 1997; Evangelista 1999). CSOs were the driving force behind debt forgiveness and the Ottawa Convention banning landmines and have been a driving force on climate change (Busby 2007; Anderson 2000; Gulbrandsen and Andresen 2004).

CSOs, either independently or through campaigns and networks, have greater agency or reach in the international realm than many states or institutions possess: they can reach wider audiences, have greater credibility, and, within their core issue areas, often have better information and greater technical expertise. In international policy-making, CSOs are not acting to undermine states (in a revolutionary role) nor acting within them (as an advocate). And while partnerships or alliances with CSOs are often an important part of state success in international negotiations, the CSOs involved are rarely contracted agents of the state (Raustiala 1997; cf. Pallas and Urpelainen 2012). In truth, civil society has established itself as a new mechanism of citizen influence. CSOs are a part of contemporary global governance arrangements. Thus CSOs are best described as acting in the role of authority.

A CSO's democratic legitimacy when acting in this new role is determined by the international context. Currently, however, no enforceable democratic rights exist for global politics. Thus, as a participant in global governance, a CSO must be judged on the same criteria by which other international actors, i.e. states and institutions, have been judged: whether they provide for equal representation, respond to citizen control, and protect fundamental rights. These are essentially questions of input and output. Thus, in this context a CSO's legitimacy is judged on both input and output.

Clarifying debates in the literature

Theories of civil society are more complementary (or deviations between them take place on clearly identifiable theoretical grounds) when they are viewed through the lens of role and context. The litera-

Table 2.2   Roles, context, and legitimacy criteria

		Role & Context Requirements		
Role	Context	Input	Throughput	Output
Revolutionary	Undemocratic state			X
Advocate	Democratic state	X	X	
Agent	Democratic or Undemocratic state or International	X		
Authority	International	X		X

ture on civil society and national democratizations clearly reflects the standards of the revolutionary role (e.g. Bernhard 1993; Fatton 1995; Fioramonti 2005; Kopecky and Mudde 2003). Such literature describes undemocratic regimes and judges civil society, usually positively, for its role in contesting them. According to the standards presented here, organizations involved in national democratizations should be judged based on their output legitimacy. Studies of such organizations can be judged on the extent to which they recognize and theorize the importance of output legitimacy in determining CSOs' democratic credentials.

Writing on advocacy and interest groups and their roles in the democratic process should reflect the standards of the advocacy role. Again, much of it does (e.g. Berry 1999; Sabatier and Jenkins-Smith 1993). The context and rationale of the advocacy role explains why this literature focuses on the behavior of organizations or coalitions, their mechanisms of influence, and ways such behaviors and influence model or create democratic throughput.

Studies of NGOs as implementers of state policy come under the agent role. Here we find much of the development studies literature. The input legitimacy criteria of this category are reflected in the emphasis of much of this literature on principal-agent relationships and the impacts of foreign intervention on local representation and autonomy.

In short, this pattern in the literature supports the use of context and the disaggregated components of legitimacy in judging CSOs' democratic credentials. At the same time, however, it highlights the dangers of transferring a model from one context to another without sufficient study or adaptation. In particular, the four-role parsing allows us to identify two common flaws in the literature on TCS. One is the failure to recognize the significance of the international context and thus treating global policymaking (i.e. the authority role) as though it is taking place within an established state. The other is treating local policymaking (i.e. intervention by TCSOs in local political affairs) as though it is taking place within the global context.

Transnational policymaking

Misidentifying a CSO's role can lead to two errors when examining CSO involvement in international policy or norm formation. The first is to treat transnational civil society actors as though they are revolutionaries. This attitude is particularly common among practitioners, who are prone to interpreting the unwillingness of some global institutions to accede to a TCSO's demands as evidence of a democratic deficit at those institutions (Rich 1994; Udall 1998). Adherents of this view frequently push for the elimination of specific international governance mechanisms or for them to be reformed in a way that gives greater voice and authority to TCS. A TCSO is legitimated by its opposition to the perceived injustices of the current international system. The emphasis is thus primarily on outputs, i.e. how much change a TCSO can force on the current order. Representative inputs are largely assumed.

The alternative error is to judge a TCSO as though it is acting as an advocate, occupying that role as it does within established democratic states. This perspective is more common among academics (e.g. Keck 2004; Nelson 1997a; Risse 2000). This attitude presupposes that transnational civil society activism is legitimate as long as it is supporting someone or something, or working on behalf of marginalized populations. The emphasis thus is primarily on inputs, on a TCSOs' ties to its claimed constituents, clients, or ideas. Throughput is sometimes suggested as an additional measure of legitimacy, usually in the form of transparency and accountability to clients or constituents. It is not clear, however, that such throughput mechanisms always make TCSOs more responsive to the people they impact.

Both of these approaches ignore the consequences of the absence of a democratic, global superstate. In the absence of a global state (and without any realistic, near-term prospect for creating such a state), revolutionary or advocacy behaviors at the transnational level do little to enhance the democratic rights of citizens. As Bowden writes, citing Hegel, when civil society exists without the state 'the interest of individuals as such becomes the ultimate end of their association' (Bowden

2006, p. 163). TCSOs can act as effective interest advocates, but there is no state government which can subject individuals to the concerns of others who do not share their interests or needs. Similarly, there is no mechanism capable of enforcing democratic representation, nor any superior authority capable of protecting the rights of those stakeholders without a powerful interest group of their own. Walzer (1995, p. 23) writes regarding the synergies between the state and civil society:

> [A]cross the entire range of association, individual men and women need to be protected against the power of officials, employers, experts, party bosses, factory foremen, priests, parents, and patrons; and small and weak groups need to be protected against large and powerful ones. For civil society, left to itself, generates radically unequal power relationships.

This is indeed the problem with CSO activity in the transnational context: it is civil society largely left to itself. Whereas CSOs may be regulated and their influence counterbalanced within the confines of any given polity, transnational civil society activities transcend the authority of any state or supranational institution (assuming that the TCSOs involved have not contractually submitted themselves to state authority as agents). Because of its power in this context, a TCSO is a de facto authority and its democratic legitimacy must be judged based on its fulfillment of this role. Removing or reforming existing institutions only exacerbates the problems of the stateless context, particularly given that the reforms sought often give a TCSO or its allies more power in the policymaking process.

Acting as an advocate makes use of the situation without mitigating it, exploiting the absence of a superstate to advance the TCSO's own agenda. A TCSO functioning as an advocate may be accountable to those whom it claims to represent, but unless the TCSOs involved in creating or implementing a given policy are in some fashion accountable to everyone impacted by their work, the situation can easily facilitate tyranny and the abuse of power. To borrow from David Held, the result is a situation in which those who 'shout the loudest' win (2006, p. 307). Neither revolutionary nor advocacy behavior can be democratically legitimate in this context. Judging a TCSO as though it is occupying a revolutionary or advocacy role only serves to rationalize democratically illegitimate behavior.

For a TCSO to be democratically legitimate in the transnational context, it must rise to the standards to which states and institutions are held. Insofar as TCSOs themselves are part of global governance, TCSOs in the aggregate must seek to represent all stakeholders in any given policy, not just those to which the organizations are most closely tied, and to achieve outcomes that reflect the will of the majority while protecting liberal rights. Only in those cases in which TCSOs, campaigns, or networks ultimately determine and enforce majority rule of the protection of acknowledged rights can TCS's involvement in transnational policymaking be said to be democratically legitimate. Any analysis of the democratic legitimacy of civil society activity in the transnational context that does not recognize and grapple with the fundamental problem of statelessness is critically flawed.

Intervention in local settings

One must also be cautious when writing about the interventions of TCS actors in the domestic policies of a democratic state. Examples of such intervention abound. International NGOs or movements may apply direct pressure to a national government (via publicity campaigns, boycotts, lobbying, etc.). International actors may also apply pressure indirectly, for example by pushing donors to make aid funding conditional on specific policy changes. Outside donors or NGOs may create and fund 'local' CSOs (a phenomenon sometimes known as 'astroturfing'), establish and staff local chapters of an international organization, or fund existing indigenous movements, magnifying their influence. Such domestic interventions are a key means by which TCS actors or networks have impact.

Unfortunately, much of the writing on transnational advocacy has failed to delineate between such domestic intervention and TCSOs' involvement in international policymaking. There are several reasons the two have been conflated. First, the majority of TCS campaigns over the last thirty years have focused on problems and policies in the developing world. In developing nations, national decisions frequently involve some international component because many domestic policies or programs rely on international funding. Thus a decision by Brazil to build a rail line or an undertaking in Niger to prioritize primary-school education can easily be depicted as an externally-driven World Bank project (or an EU program or an IMF policy), rather than as a national decision. Second, the process of global norm formation can take place on both the national and international level. Transnational activists may promote an international norm of condemning torture or protecting children's rights, often working via the UN or other intergovernmental organizations, and then seek to have that norm applied to individual states. Its adoption by successive states, in turn, helps establish it as a global norm. Third, during the initial development of modern international civil society organizations and transnational networks in the 1980s and early 1990s, the majority of the world's population did not live in democratic states. Ignoring the role of the local state was easy because many states were perceived as illegitimate. Undemocratic states and undemocratic international institutions were easily tarred with the same brush, dismissed as mere obstacles in the pursuit of 'good' or 'democratic' policy.

The most significant change of the last fifteen years with regards to this trend is that the majority of the world's citizens now live in recognized democracies. This evolution has permitted more governments to function as the legitimate representatives of their citizens and has created an environment in which local civil society organizations can fulfill the advocacy role with its functions of watchdog and representative. As two civil society leaders from the global South have written (Naidoo and Tandon 1999, p. 9):

> The new political context that has emerged, marked by democracy and citizen participation, has increasingly led to more collaborative modes of relating [to government]. It is civil society's participation in political life, in that realm of public life in which societal decisions are made and carried out, that provides the conditions for sustainable development.

In such a context, it is imperative that academics and practitioners draw careful lines between national and international policies. For instance, it is helpful to distinguish between 'World Bank' projects like the Narmada Dam that are actually planned by national governments before receiving support from the World Bank, and policies like structural adjustment that are largely international creations.

When a TCSO is interacting with an internationally created project or policy, it occupies the authority role described earlier and is subject to the legitimacy tests described in the preceding section. However, when a CSO is working transnationally to influence a domestic policy, it must be judged by those standards that are applied to national civil society. Essentially it can act in either the revolutionary or advocate role and its legitimacy must be assessed accordingly.

It is tempting to treat transnational networks or campaigns as though they are above such considerations or as though their large international followings are an automatic source of legitimacy. Yet the non-local members of such campaigns are neither subject to the local polity nor part of the demos it governs. Allowing such international voices to overwhelm local democratic procedures is to give the members of international organizations or movements power on par with that of local citizens despite the fact that these global citizens have no allegiance to the country they are impacting and are unlikely to bear the immediate consequences of the plan they impose. International organizations or movements should not be presumed to be democratically legitimate simply because they are large.

Instead, as per the revolutionary and advocacy roles discussed earlier, the legitimacy of TCS intervention in local affairs must be judged by the degree to which it contributes to sustainable national democracy. A transnational actor, by definition, is not tied to a single country. When the international network leaves a dam cancellation fight in India to protest a dam in Pakistan, it leaves the local citizens behind. It is unable to offer them long-term democratic protections. If it does not contribute to the democratic functioning of the national state, then it has had no long-term impact on the democratic well-being of local citizens. It may have helped some of them win a particular battle, but it has done nothing to win the proverbial war. If the international intervention has promoted special interests at the expense of majority rule, the situation is even worse. In such a case, global activists may have actually undermined the function or legitimacy of the national regime responsible for ensuring most of the day-to-day democratic rights of local citizens and for providing them with social services and security. Granted, an exception may occur if an international campaign intervenes to protect minority rights against a tyrannical majority. In this sense it is supporting the 'liberal' portion of the definition of liberal democracy outlined earlier, provided that the rights supported rise to the level of internationally recognized liberal norms. However, if TCSOs' involvement merely swaps an oppressive local majority for an overweening global minority, it has done little to support long-term, sustainable democracy. To be democratically legitimate, TCSOs intervening in a local setting must either work within (and by the rules of) any existing local democratic system, or seek to replace an undemocratic system with a democratic one.

Conclusion

The input-throughput-output vision of democratic legitimacy used in this book establishes a series of roles in which CSOs must operate in order to achieve democratic legitimacy. Identifying the link between context and legitimacy helps explain similarities and tensions among different sub-sections of the civil society literature. The contextual legitimacy framework also has several implications for the core question of this book: whether TCSOs' net impact on policymaking at the World Bank supports the idea that TCS can democratize global governance.

First and foremost, the context and legitimacy framework presents a means of evaluating TCS's impact on democratizing governance at the World Bank. TCSOs engaging with the World Bank on transnational policymaking are generally operating in the authority role. As such, their impacts are judged based on their input and output. In order to be democratically legitimate, TCSOs must enhance stakeholder input, through improving either representation or inclusion, or both. Ideally TCSOs will represent stakeholders in an inclusive fashion and facilitate equal voice for all stakeholders in international policymaking. TCSOs must also improve democratic outputs. Although it is impossible to know whether any particular policy output is representative of a majority of stakeholders, outputs should reflect the stated interests of at least some group of stakeholders or otherwise increase citizen control over policymaking at the institution.

The authority standard is reflected in many of the questions posed in the previous chapter. For instance, examining how TCSOs interact with one another will help determine whether some organizations or views are routinely excluded from advocacy initiatives. By examining how TCSOs choose their policy positions, this book explores whether policy-setting arises from grassroots stakeholders or is constructed in a top-down fashion. It also examines whether some stakeholders have more influence than others. Exploring TCSO's mechanisms of influence allows us to examine whether those mechanisms of influence are equally accessible to all stakeholders.

To judge TCS's impacts, this book examines whether TCSOs, as a group, have been effective in creating new policy and whether specific changes in policy have increased the opportunities for future stakeholder input. This is examined both with regards to future input via civil society and future input by developing country governments. In this way we can assess whether TCS has created outputs reflecting the stated interests of least some stakeholders and facilitated increased citizen control over international policymaking.

It is important to note that TCSOs engaging with the World Bank can also impact national policies, particularly when TCSOs target Bank lending to a single country on the basis of particular objections about that country's proposed use of the funds. This is observed in the case of the Arun III dam, the second case study examined in this book. In this case, TCSOs simultaneously sought to create a precedent for the successful use of the World Bank Inspection Panel and obstruct a loan to Nepal because of specific objections to Nepal's development strategy. The former effort is clearly one of transnational policy and its impacts can be evaluated on the basis of input and output. The latter aspect of the effort, however, reflects an intervention in the national policy of a recognized democracy (as Nepal was at the time) and so is evaluated using the advocacy framework of input and throughput.

In addition to developing a standard for evaluating TCS's impact on governance at the Bank, this chapter identifies two potential flaws in some of the existing work on TCS and global governance. In particular, this chapter hypothesizes that it is inappropriate to judge TCSOs primarily by their democratic throughput when they are operating in an authority role in an international context. The framework presented in this chapter suggests that even TCSOs that enhance democratic throughput can actually inhibit democratization if they lack input and output legitimacy when operating in this context. Moreover, this chapter explains why, when working in a democratic state, TCS must be judged on its input and throughput legitimacy; otherwise civil society risks undermining the local democratic system. The data in subsequent chapters illustrate the importance of these considerations, and show how they must be incorporated into our understanding of TCS and the democratization of global governance.

3

Beating the Bank: Transnational Civil Society and the 10th IDA

The World Bank has a large policy footprint. Lending billions of dollars annually to scores to countries, its work has implications for everything from global environmental policy to human rights. As a result, numerous TCSOs have sought to influence the Bank in areas where its policies impact their activities or objectives. During the IDA-10, the attention of many of these groups converged to focus on a single issue of funding.

Understanding the synergies and conflicts which developed during the 10th IDA requires an examination of the history and agendas of the various actors seeking to impact the replenishment, as well as the events of the replenishment itself. This chapter begins by outlining the relevant trends in civil society activism in the decade preceding the 10th IDA negotiations. It then describes the events of the 10th IDA replenishment, beginning with the initial broad coalition formed among civil society actors and detailing the coalition's demise and the eventual outcome of the negotiations. The chapter concludes by demonstrating why the 10th IDA might be considered the first truly global civil society engagement with the Bank, and how its outcomes relate to the prospects for TCS-driven democratization of global governance.

1980–90: The origins of World Bank – civil society engagement

Modern TCS engagement with the World Bank began in the decade prior to the IDA-10, as the growing environmental movement began to tackle international issues and state governments began to rely more heavily on the NGO sector for aid implementation. From 1980 to 1990, TCS engaged with the World Bank through a combination of formal and informal dialogues, lobbying via member governments, and public advocacy campaigns. Engagement focused on two main themes: improving the Bank's development impacts and reducing its negative environmental effects. The development agenda focused on defining the Bank's mission more closely as one of poverty alleviation and pushing the Bank to mitigate the negative impacts some of its economic development practices had on the poor. The environmental agenda began with a series of campaigns against several Bank projects with well-documented, highly negative effects on both people and the environment. This soon evolved into an effort to promote more systematic policy reform within the Bank and to force greater accountability on key decision-makers. While the development agenda was promoted primarily by service delivery and social justice groups and the environmental agenda was advanced mainly by environmental groups, this was not exclusively the case. Individuals and organizations moved between the two strands as they identified causes of interest to their leadership or members.

Improving development impacts

The development agenda included a mix of 'do better' and 'don't do' items which combined to stress the Bank's responsibility to improve the lives of people in developing nations. The idea that the Bank should focus on poverty alleviation was not new. It was originally advanced by Robert McNamara during his tenure as Bank president (Kapur et al 1997, p. 374). A change in leadership, plus the commodities crises of the early 1980s, saw much of this focus lost. Nonetheless, a number of outside groups continued to press the Bank to make good on what they saw as its potential to be a poverty-fighting institution. They pushed the Bank to improve development via popular participation, forgive loans that had been made to previous corrupt governments in now-reformed states, revise its approach to structural adjustment, and use new sociological research to develop poverty-targeted interventions.

Initially some of this pressure was exerted in a somewhat collegial fashion. A pattern of *ad hoc* collaboration between the World Bank and non-governmental organizations on development projects led, in 1981, to the creation of the NGO-World Bank Committee. The Committee, composed of a rotating group of NGO representatives and senior members of Bank staff, discussed possible areas for potential collaboration and, in some instances, NGO reactions to Bank policy (Shihata 1991, pp. 239–241). Tensions over funding, however, disrupted this collegial atmosphere. The Reagan administration began seeking to reduce US contributions to the Bank in 1981 and eventually succeeded in 1984. Certain staff within the Bank believed that NGOs could help prevent future cuts. In internal discussions, Bank staff debated whether the role of NGOs was to assist the Bank as partners in development or to protect the Bank from political interference. Some staff began reaching out more aggressively towards NGOs and pressuring NGO allies to act as advocates on the Bank's behalf.

In this climate, members of the NGO-World Bank Committee sought to exert their independence from the Bank. In 1984 they established the NGO Working Group on the World Bank (NGOWG) to facilitate dialogue among the Committee's NGO members on issues of policy and advocacy. The NGOWG then used the Committee meetings to engage the Bank on issues of policy reform (Long 2001, p. 3). Development and justice NGOs outside the NGOWG also began engaging with the Bank via informal dialogues with Bank staff and, in at least one case, an organized letter-writing campaign (Mitchell 1991). Key issues included the following:

Popular participation

Popular participation focused on engaging stakeholder populations in dialogue and debate about the conditions and decisions affecting their well-being.[1] Techniques formalizing such practices grew out of a variety of political and cultural circumstances, including the Latin American liberation movements of the 1960s and 1970s. By the late 1970s, however, participation was being mainstreamed as a development tool. NGO pressure helped advance participatory practices at the World Bank, and by 1985 the Bank's Operations and Evaluations Department (OED) had issued a report documenting the link between popular participation and the sustainability of Bank projects (Long 2001, pp. 1–8). By 1990 the Bank had incorporated popular participation into the operational directives governing some of its social safeguards, but TCSOs continued to push to have stakeholders more broadly involved in Bank decision-making, especially project planning (Shihata 1991).

Debt relief

Concerns regarding the level of debt in Bank borrower countries became prominent in the early 1980s. Debt to the World Bank had been steadily accumulating for nearly two decades and in the early 1980s it reached the point where certain countries suffered from negative aid flows, i.e. the amount they repaid to the Bank each year exceeded the value of new loans received (Rich 1994, pp. 109–110). TCSOs like Britain's World Development Movement, an advocacy group funded almost entirely by church members, began monitoring the issue. By the late 1980s WDM and other faith-based groups were lobbying the Bank to give IDA funds as grants rather than as loans that would need to be repaid (Mitchell 1991, p. 155).

Structural adjustment lending

The early 1980s also yielded a World Bank program that would, rightly or wrongly, become one of the most notorious of the next two decades: structural adjustment lending. In the early 1980s a sharp decline in the world prices of many of the commodities, like copper and coffee, exported from developing nations led to significant budget shortfalls for the governments of those countries. The crisis was widespread and potentially persistent. To remedy it, the World Bank developed a system of Structural Adjustment Lending (SAL). Structural adjustment provided immediate financial relief in the form of new loans, but required that the government receiving the money reorganize government finances to bring expenditures into line with its new, reduced revenues. In theory, SAL would lead to greater efficiency, less bureaucracy, and reduced military expenditures. In reality, governments slashed social services, reducing access to medical care, education, and agricultural support. Structural adjustment also coincided with a decision by the US Reagan administration to use Bank lending to advance the administration's liberal economic philosophy (Gwin 1994, p. 40; cf. Manji and O'Coill 2002). This often meant that structural adjustment loans came with attached conditions mandating changes like the privatization of government-owned industries and the elimination of trade barriers. These rapid changes caused additional resentment and upheaval in recipient countries.

Not long after its implementation, adjustment began attracting critics. In borrowing countries, specific adjustment policies were sometimes met with forceful, even violent, grassroots opposition. Advocates from Oxfam and the World Development Movement (WDM) pushed internationally for a reconsideration of adjustment lending (Jolly 1991). Their concerns received substantial support in 1987 when UNICEF published its own report, *Adjustment with a Human Face*, challenging adjustment practices (see Cornia et al 1987). The report helped catalyze activism among development organizations, which pushed for the World Bank and the International Monetary Fund to reduce the frequency with which they employed structural adjustment lending and to restructure their lending to mitigate the human impacts of government cutbacks.

Poverty-targeted interventions

The idea that the World Bank and other development agencies should address poverty by attacking its key components, such as illiteracy, poor nutrition, or infant mortality, is currently a widely accepted idea. Objectives of these sorts, for instance, are embodied in the Millennium Development Goals. For nearly half of the World Bank's history, however, such objectives were entirely absent as Bank staff focused on macroeconomic impacts.

In 1980, however, the newly appointed head of UNICEF, James Grant, initiated a focus on infant mortality. To attract political attention to the subject, he used specific metrics, developing numeric targets for reductions in infant mortality (UNICEF 2012). He also collaborated with the US-based advocacy group RESULTS, which worked to increase public awareness of the child deaths in developing countries caused by preventable illnesses. In the late 1980s, RESULTS drew in the UK-based WDM to work with UNICEF on a world conference on child survival, which was finally held in 1990 as the World Summit for Children (Daley-Harris 2007; UNICEF 2012). Staff at Bread for the World who had previously worked with WDM also became involved, helping to shape Bread's agenda of poverty advocacy, and complementing the work of RESULTS and WDM. Together with UNICEF, these three organizations helped move poverty-targeted interventions (PTIs) into the political mainstream.

Preventing environmental disasters

Environmentalists' focus on the World Bank began in the early 1980s. During the 1970s, environmental activists from American groups like the Sierra Club, the Environmental Defense Fund, and the Environmental Policy Institute (which would later merge with Friends of the Earth US) had achieved a number of successes in the US, including new legal protections for the environment and the enforcement of federal environmental laws against corporations (Wade 1997).[2] A number of CSOs, like the World Wildlife Fund and Sahabat Alam Malaysia, were already addressing international environmental issues (Keck and Sikkink 1998, pp. 125, 130–131). However, it was a small group of American activists who would force the environmental issue on the World Bank.

In 1983 Barbara Bramble from the National Wildlife Federation (NWF), Brent Blackwelder from the Environmental Policy Institute (EPI), and Bruce Rich, then at the National Resources Defense Council (NRDC) but later with the Environmental Defense Fund (EDF), began working together on an international environmental campaign. Their goal was to create an international regime of environmental regulation mirroring the legal structures their organizations had used effectively in court battles in the US. They chose the World Bank as the target of their campaign not because it was the worst environmental offender but rather because of its prominent role and wide recognition in world affairs. A victory against the Bank, they believed, would lead to other victories elsewhere (Wade 1997).

Once Bruce Rich moved to EDF in 1985, EDF, NWF, and EPI (later Friends of the Earth US, or FoE)[3] formed the core of the new environmental campaign. Organizations from Germany, the Netherlands, England, Brazil, Malaysia, and Japan were also involved.[4] The organizations involved linked issues of environmental preservation to human suffering, for example by highlighting the ways in which poorly planned dam projects could spread waterborne disease or agricultural resettlement projects could lead to massive human rights abuses. Emphasizing the human element expanded their popular appeal.

Environmental activists largely eschewed the NGO-World Bank Committee and the NGOWG. They believed that the Committee was little more than window-dressing for the Bank and that the NGOWG was more concerned with continued aid funding than reform.[5] Instead, the environmentalists took a more adversarial approach. They began their work with an effort to expose the impacts of the worst World Bank projects and force their cancellation. Later they promoted the creation of new social and environmental safeguards at the Bank, including the creation of the Bank's Environmental Department. Finally, they sought ways to develop enforcement mechanisms that could help hold the Bank accountable to its environmental commitments.

Exposing problem projects

The group's first move was to request hearings in US Congress on the World Bank. These were held in June of 1983. The groups used the hearings to publicize the impacts of a series of World Bank projects, including a cattle ranching project in Botswana, an irrigation and hydroelectric dam project on the Narmada River in India, the Polonoroeste project in Brazil, and the Indonesian Transmigration Project, the latter two of which involved resettling poor citizens in less populated areas of the recipient country. These hearings generated enough publicity and Congressional pressure that the Bank was forced to respond with statements to Congress (Wade 1997, pp. 659–660). Follow-up hearings were held in 1984 and resulted in a series of Congressional resolutions calling for change at the Bank (Rich 1994, p. 119). Activists continued their pressure on the Bank with the pamphlet *Bankrolling Disasters: The Citizen's Guide to the World Bank and the Regional Development Banks* co-written by EPI and published in 1986. Through the Sierra Club's ties to the UN Environmental Program, the pamphlet was distributed worldwide.

Polonoroeste soon became the focal point of the environmental campaign due to its massive impact on the Amazon rainforest and the indigenous communities living there. Vigorous lobbying by organizations in the US, some of whom cultivated Brazilian partners, combined with the support of Republican Senator Robert Kasten, who had taken a personal interest in the campaign. At Kasten's request, Bank President A. W. Clausen, along with top Bank staff, held an unprecedented meeting with the Senator and US environmental representatives in January 1985 (Rich 1994, pp. 123–127; Wade 1997, pp. 664–667). Less than three months later, the Bank had halted disbursement of the remaining amount of the Polonoroeste loan. The cancellation of a project on environmental or human rights grounds was unprecedented in the Bank's history and provided significant encouragement for environmentalists as they continued their campaign (Rich 1994, pp. 126–127).

New safeguards and staff

Environmentalists saw Polonoroeste as an indicator of a more general malaise within the Bank. They believed that Bank staff as a whole failed to take ecological considerations into account when planning and implementing projects. Although the Bank had been one of the first multilateral development organizations to have an environmental staff, the Bank's Environmental Unit (also known as the Office of Environmental Affairs) was perceived to be toothless and undermanned (Wade 1997 pp. 618, 628, 640–641, 662–663). Civil society organizations charged that the Bank could not become an environmentally responsible institution without concrete safeguards and staff able to supervise and implement them.

In 1986, the Bank's new president, Barber Conable, moved to rectify these problems. He met with environmental leaders, acknowledged the legitimacy of their past grievances, and sought to move the Bank forward. In 1987 he announced a sixteen-fold increase in the Bank's environmental staff and between 1987 and 1990 the Bank introduced a number of significant new policies on environmental assessment and involuntary resettlement. Environmentalists, however, continued to campaign for the refinement and expansion of these policies and, above all, their proper enforcement.

Transparency and accountability mechanisms

Not trusting the Bank to enforce its own policies, campaigners sought means to monitor the Bank's behavior and hold it accountable to its commitments. Most efforts at monitoring and accountability worked via the US government. The Sierra Club, for instance, was instrumental in designing and developing support for the Pelosi Amendment, which promoted the use of environmental impact assessments. The amendment, attached to a 1989 bill on international finance, stipulated that the US executive director would be bound to vote against any Bank project for which the Bank's board had not been supplied with an environmental assessment.[6] The bill not only forced the Bank to create a comprehensive system of environmental impact assessments, it also fostered greater transparency and accountability. Previously documents like environmental assessments were viewed by the Bank as proprietary material belonging to the borrower. The Bank took the position that it could not disclose such documents even to its own board without the express consent of the owner. Consequently, the original Operational Directive on environmental assessments did not include a provision for the release of the data to the board.[7] By requiring the Bank to release environmental assessments well in advance of any board vote on a given project, the amendment expanded the board's access to information and enhanced its ability to monitor the actions of the Bank (Wade 1997, pp. 686–687).

Nonetheless, activists still worried that the Bank was largely unaccountable and had little incentive to effectively enforce its own safeguard policies. The need for an enforcement mechanism led to several proposals in the early 1990s for an independent appeals commission or ombudsman (see Bradlow 1993a; Clark 2003, p. 22). Such proposals gained the support of staff from the Environmental Defense Fund and the Center for International Environmental Law (CIEL); the appeals commission would become a central issue in later lobbying (Bradlow 1993b, p. 565).

1990–92: Convergence

Environmental and development concerns began to converge in the late 1980s. Environmentalists began to address some broader development issues, including structural adjustment. Even more importantly, development advocates began taking note of environmentalists' successes. Although development organizations had been working with the Bank for years, both through the NGO-World Bank Committee and through cooperation on various projects, their advocacy efforts had had only limited impact on Bank policy. In contrast, environmental NGOs had achieved their first major success, the suspension of the Polonoroeste loan, just two years after starting their campaign. Then, during the ninth replenishment of funds for the International Development Association (IDA-9) environmentalist threats to challenge donor funding of the replenishment had prompted the Bank to create a number of new policies reflective of environmental concerns. As a result, organizations like Church World Service (which, although faith-based, focused primarily on development) and Bread for the World recognized the effectiveness of environmental criticism and sought ways to use similar tactics themselves.

The political landscape was also changing as environmental successes made environmentalism more mainstream. Development organizations began including vaguely defined calls for 'sustainable development' in their policy recommendations and noting links between environmental preservation and human well-being. In 1990, after the Pope issued an address on the environment, the US Catholic Conference of Bishops became involved in environmental issues. Other faith-based organizations, like the World Development Movement, promoted both just development and environmental protection.

By 1992, as negotiations began for the IDA-10, the core of the environmentally-based Bank reform movement included EDF, FoE, and NWF, with some involvement from a number of other groups including Greenpeace, the NRDC, Rainforest Action Network, the Sierra Club, and the Center for International Environmental Law. These environmental NGOs saw the broadening of their coalition as an important strategic step and sought to develop alliances with development organizations both in other IDA donor nations and in the developing world.[8] To widen their appeal, they began discussing issues like debt relief and popular participation and developing their own poverty focus. An anonymous draft of a position paper on the IDA-10, circulated among these NGOs in January of 1992, noted that 'it is unrealistic to think that the South will cooperate in the development and execution of an environmental agenda in the absence of cooperation on development and execution of a social agenda'. The same paper recommended that poverty alleviation, changes in structural adjustment, and popular participation be included alongside existing environmental demands for improved accountability mechanisms, improved resettlement policies, and sustainable energy development.

The core environmental groups also began reaching out to potential allies by stressing overlapping objectives. In requesting Irish assistance with IDA lobbying, for instance, one representative of the US environmentalists wrote that 'though our opinions about the Bank and the various issues differ broadly, we all agree on the need for at least putting restraints on Bank activities'.[9]

Such diplomacy helped blur the lines between development and environmental issues. Irish service delivery organizations, anti-poverty advocates, and faith groups, for instance, integrated issues like transparency and environmental assessments into their lobbying agendas.[10] In other cases, disparate civil society organizations engaged in dialogue and joint advocacy. In one notable example, the Development Group for Alternative Policies (the Development GAP), a left-leaning development advocacy group with strong ties to the environmental movement, worked with Friends of the Earth, Greenpeace, Church World Service (CWS), Lutheran World Relief, Third World Network, and the European Network on Debt and Development to organize a 1992 forum on structural adjustment. The sponsors of the forum included the Environmental Defense Fund and the Rainforest Action Network; Caritas International and the World Council of Churches; and SWISSAID and several branches of Oxfam (Hammond and McGowan 1993).

1992–95: The IDA-10

The confluence of social and environmental interests was reflected in the initial lobbying surrounding the 10th IDA. The IDA replenishment was negotiated by a group of 32 IDA Deputies, each of whom represented an IDA donor nation. Borrowers were not allowed to send delegates or observers. The donor deputies were scheduled to meet five times in 1992, in January, April, July, September, and December. The agreed funds would then be appropriated by the negotiators' governments in 1993.

Earlier TCS campaigns had been sufficient to raise awareness of civil society concerns among member states and TCSOs won a number of initial victories without much additional campaigning. The US Treasury's objectives, drafted in advance of the January meeting, included strengthening 'key policy provisions' related to structural adjustment, energy conservation, popular participation, environmental action plans, poverty reduction, and gender in development. The draft noted that these were 'issues in which the US NGO community has expressed a particular interest'.[11] A more detailed position paper, written in April, outlined these concerns in greater depth.[12] Delegates from the Netherlands were also aware of civil society concerns and in the UK issues of popular participation and informational liberalization were debated on the floor of parliament.[13]

However, as the IDA deputies moved to prepare their draft resolution in July 1992, TCSOs worked together to apply more pressure. At the center of the networking effort was the Washington-based Bank Information Center (BIC). Established in 1987 using funding from the Charles Stewart Mott Foundation and other sources (see Keck and Sikkink 1998, p. 148), BIC was an information clearinghouse created to facilitate data-sharing among civil society organizations worldwide. Although BIC, in theory, worked with any and all organizations, its letterhead at the time described it as 'A Clearinghouse for Environmental Information on MDB Funded Projects'. Maureen Smyth, then the Mott Foundation program officer responsible for BIC's funding, recalled that the environmental focus was designed as a hook to attract more organizations to the BIC network.[14] The result was that BIC became heavily involved in environmental issues. Although it rarely engaged in direct lobbying itself, it worked closely with the DC-based environmental NGOs (including EDF, NWF, and FoE) at the core of the environmentalist campaign to reform the Bank.

DC-based NGOs were already engaged in the policy process through their connections with Pat Coady, then the US executive director for the World Bank. Coady was not part of the US IDA delegation, but he still had significant sway with the Bank. Many of the meetings with Coady were arranged by BIC, and Coady was very sympathetic to the environmental position. American NGOs were also in direct contact with the US Treasury.

Other organizations, like the UK-based Oxfam-GB, the Netherlands-based NOVIB, and the Australian-headquartered Third World Forum, were likewise involved through direct interaction with their countries' EDs and government representatives.[15] When the IDA deputies met in

Dublin in July to prepare a draft BIC, at the behest of unnamed 'US NGOs', recruited Andy Storey of the Catholic aid organization Trocaire to organize Irish support. Trocaire distributed leaflets provided by BIC at the IDA meeting, did television and radio interviews, and coordinated a joint statement from Irish NGOs on the IDA replenishment.[16] The statement included a blend of environmental and development proposals, including increased transparency, an independent appeals mechanism, popular participation, poverty reduction, and required environmental assessments, and was signed by twenty-one organizations, including Christian Aid, Oxfam in Ireland, Earthwatch, and the Irish Missionary Union.[17]

The civil society-run publicity campaigns and relationships between civil society organizations and several delegations made TCS demands an open topic of discussion during the negotiations. At the meeting in Dublin, several governments expressed concern about the legitimacy of the claims of the TCSOs involved; the German delegation even went so far as to state that 'Washington-based NGOs are not representative'.[18] In response to delegate requests, the World Bank organized a meeting between developing country civil society representatives and IDA deputies, held in Washington, D.C. in September.

At the September meeting, the CSO participants, from Africa, Asia, and Latin America, affirmed their support for much of the reform agenda. In particular, they emphasized poverty reduction, changes in structural adjustment, and accountability. They explicitly affirmed the overall intentions of Northern CSOs attempting to reform the Bank, although the Southerners were less categorically opposed to structural adjustment and less focused on environmental issues. Most importantly, they expressed disagreement with the proposal made by some Northern CSOs to use cuts in IDA funding to leverage change. The IDA, in the view of the Southerners, was too important to poor populations to be reduced.[19] This division over the fate of IDA would ultimately become a wedge, fracturing the reform coalition. The hammer driving it was the Narmada Dam.

The Narmada Dam: Testing the Bank's will to reform

Although some of the development organizations involved in the IDA negotiations, like CWS and Bread for the World, were interested in using donor funding power to leverage reforms at the World Bank, most civil society participants had no interest in actually decreasing the level of IDA funding. Instead they saw the IDA funding cycle as an opportunity to make reasonable demands that the Bank would be bound to accept. In this regard, their position was akin to that of many of the Bank's donors, who used the IDA funding rounds for negotiation and oversight. Almost universally, development organizations believed that the IDA and even the World Bank were necessary development tools delivering a net benefit to the world's poor.

Many of the Washington-based environmental NGOs, however, were far less certain. Some believed that the Bank's net impact on the world's poor was negative. The authors of an IDA-10 position paper noted, 'It is our position that safeguarding concessional flows to poor countries is unhelpful if those flows are not contributing to broad-based and sustainable development'.[20]

Debate among TCSOs over this issue was largely absent in the early negotiations surrounding the IDA. An emphasis on reforming the Bank, rather than limiting its operations, enabled environmental organizations to cooperate with development organizations like Oxfam or Bread that fundamentally supported the Bank's mission. Concerns about the Bank's capacity to change itself, however, were brought into sharp relief by the Morse Commission report on the Narmada Dam, published in June of 1992, and the Bank's subsequent handling of the commission's recommendations.

The Narmada Dam, also known as the Sardar Sarovar project, was actually a series of dams conceived by the Indian government in the 1960s. The dams were intended to provide drinking water, irrigation, and electricity in northwest India. The Indian government began finalizing plans for the dam in 1979, and by 1985 the Bank had approved the first Sardar Sarovar loan. By the late 1980s, the project had begun to attract international attention. The number of people to be displaced by the reservoirs from the dams was expected to reach approximately 250,000. Not only was the number extremely high, but many of the families to be displaced came from India's marginalized tribal class. The dam's rise to prominence also coincided with the birth of an international movement against dams, which accused large dams of destroying river ecologies and contributing to the spread of waterborne disease. The international attention focused on the Narmada Dam forced the World Bank to suspend disbursement of the Narmada loan in 1991. It then appointed an ad hoc independent review board, known as the Morse Commission after its chairman, Bradford Morse, to investigate claims that the Bank had violated its own resettlement and environmental policies in its funding of the dam.

The Morse Commission's report confirmed many of the critics' claims. It not only documented several key policy violations; it also implied that such policy violations resulted from systematic flaws in Bank practice. In the view of the commission, Sardar Sarovar could not easily be fixed. It recommended that the Bank 'step back' from the project (cited in Udall 1995, p. 216).

A number of the TCSOs involved in the IDA-10 viewed the Narmada as a clear test case of the World Bank's ability to reform. They also interpreted the commission's 'step back' language as a clear call for project cancellation. Instead of canceling the project, however, the Word Bank's board delayed making a final decision as the Bank's management and the Indian government rushed to assemble a remediation plan.

A board date to consider the project was finally set for October 1992. In anticipation of the board vote and management's attempts to defend the project, a group of NGOs took out full page ads in the *New York Times* and *Financial Times* opposing the project. The advertisements issued an ultimatum:

> If the World Bank does not withdraw from Sardar Sarovar it will confirm that the Bank cannot implement its own stated policies. Failing withdrawal, we will launch an international campaign to urge taxpayers, donor governments, and environmental and social organizations to oppose the $18 billion replenishment of the of the International Development Association.[21]

The advertisement, however, was not sufficient to sway the Bank's board. Although a number of donor country EDs, including the representatives of the US and UK, voted against the project, the board agreed to continue funding.

Anti-Bank and pro-IDA factions

The explicit threat to the Bank's funding triggered a sharp drawing up of sides between anti-Bank and pro-IDA groups. The anti-Bank faction encompassed those CSOs with a generally negative perception of the Bank who opposed its continued functioning in its present form. Environmental Defense led the charge, joined by the National Wildlife Federation, Friends of the Earth, the Sierra Club, and Greenpeace. Not all environmental NGOs, however, were anti-Bank. The World Wildlife Fund (WWF) wrote to the US Treasury early in the negotiations to note that they were not part of the larger DC environmental coalition,[22] and later sided with the pro-IDA faction. The NRDC, which was only somewhat involved in the IDA negotiations, would also take a more neutral approach. Development GAP, despite its strong connections to the environmental community and liberal bent, abstained from involvement. According to one source familiar with the organization, it felt constrained to heed the positions of its Southern partners, who opposed the attack on the IDA.

Southern CSOs within the NGO Working Group helped sway the organization toward a pro-IDA position. On October 30th the NGOWG published an open letter to World Bank President Lewis Preston:

> The NGO Working Group expresses its deep and abiding concern about the adequacy of funds on concessional terms being made available by the North to tackle poverty in the South ... The NGO Working Group is especially concerned about the possibility of cuts in real terms under the current round of negotiations for the IDA-10 replenishment.[23]

Although Preston himself had little direct control over the level of funding, the letter was an important public relations tool. In an implicit rebuttal to the environmental focus of many anti-Bank NGOs, the letter declared that 'measures to protect the global environment should not be at the expense of efforts to reduce poverty'.[24] Members supporting the statement represented thirty different organizations, many of them from the global South. They included religious groups like the Caribbean Council of Churches and the World Council of Churches as well as the DC-based development and relief group Interaction and the Dutch-based NOVIB. Many of the groups which had collaborated with environmentalists in Dublin, including Oxfam-Ireland, MISERFOR, and Caritas International, endorsed the letter.

The pro-IDA position was a fairly simple affirmation of the need for concessional aid for the poor, but the anti-Bank position was more complex. In the eyes of its members, the Bank had failed a crucial test in refusing to cancel the Narmada loan. Yet they were divided on how to deal with that failure. Within the group, there were two camps, referred to as 'abolitionists' and 'reformists'.[25]

For abolitionists, the Bank had proven itself unreformable. The combination of its intransigence on Narmada and its perceived record of environmental and social degradation meant that the Bank itself should be closed. Some abolitionists favored a new, smaller institution or a compensating increase in bilateral aid. Others questioned the value of development aid altogether (see, for example, Rich 1994).

Reformists took the position that although the Bank could not reform itself, sufficient external pressure might still yield changes. Yet reformists, like abolitions, still believed that the Bank had historically been a negative force in the developing world. They therefore favored sweeping reforms that would yield a smaller, less powerful institution that focused more on environmental preservation and service delivery to the poor, and far less on economic development. They were unwilling to see the Bank funded until this was accomplished. In many cases they called for non-specific additional changes in areas like transparency and popular participation in which the Bank was already making significant concessions. Such vagueness created challenges for the Bank because it gave few clear benchmarks for improvement beyond NGO say-so.

For the abolitionists, withholding IDA-funding was the first step in eventually eliminating the Bank. For the Bank-shrinking reformists, the withholding of IDA funds was a battering ram to be deployed to force the Bank to open and change. However, cuts in the IDA were more than just a means to an end. Withholding IDA funds and redeploying them via other channels or towards new objectives would have the desired effect of diminishing the Bank's power and reinforcing the alternative models of development. There are also indications that some of the groups with more abolitionist leanings took a reformist approach in public to avoid criticism. While ostensibly 'reformist', they sought to set the reform bar high enough to all but necessitate the cancellation of the IDA and thus diminish the Bank.[26]

The Wapenhans Report

In December 1992, the anti-Bank faction was inadvertently given an added boost by the World Bank itself after an internal evaluation commissioned by Bank President Preston was completed. The evaluation, 'Effective Implementation: Key to Development Impact', was known as the Wapenhans Report, after Willi Wapenhans, the Bank Vice President who led the evaluation task force. The report categorized over a third of the Bank's loans as non-performing and noted a significant increase in the number of non-performing loans between 1981 and 1991. More damningly, the report attributed the Bank's problems to an organizational culture that stressed making new loans rather than careful implementation of existing loans or the evaluation of completed projects.

The Bank's critics quickly seized on the report as evidence of endemic failure within the Bank and the need for wholesale reform or abolition. Representatives of the Environmental Defense Fund wrote a letter to the editor of the *New York Times* declaring:

> Before agreeing to provide $18 billion more to the [World Bank's] International Development Association, taxpayers in the United States and other donor countries should be aware that these problems are systemic and that without major reforms the money will continue to be wasted on environmental and social disasters ... To dump $18 billion into the lap of such an institution, without total reform and housecleaning from top to bottom, is financial folly.[27]

Wapenhans himself, by that point retired from the Bank, quickly responded with a letter of his own, charging that the EDF authors had 'misread' the report.[28] Despite his protests, however, the report would continue to feature prominently in discussions about the Bank.

The completion of the IDA negotiations

The donor deputies and the Bank concluded their negotiations in early December 1992 with an agreement to maintain IDA funding at IDA-9 levels, adjusted for inflation. The replenishment agreement reflected many of the concerns raised by various TCSOs. It included an agreement on behalf of the Bank to focus on poverty and to use poverty-targeted interventions to offset the impacts of structural adjustment. Deputies also stressed that adjustment itself should be done in such a way as to preserve social safety nets. The Bank committed that 50 per cent of new IDA expenditures would 'include specific actions to assist women', such as girls' education and family planning.[29] The Bank also committed to continuing to assist borrowers in preparing national Environmental Action Plans and to prepare Environmental Impact Assessments for new projects, although the commitment's language appeared to make some of this dependent upon the borrower's decisions. Popular participation was also stressed, as were transparency and accountability.

In short, the TCSOs involved in the IDA process received the vast majority of the concessions they had initially sought, including all core demands. However, the anti-Bank organizations influenced by the Narmada outcomes introduced new objectives. In addition to pushing for a reduction in the Bank's power or even its elimination, they also sought additional ways to control it. The anti-Bank faction increased the volume and scope of their transparency demands, calling for further improvements in the Bank's information policy. The creation of an independent appeals mechanism also became a high priority. This had been only a secondary issue during the earlier negotiations, particularly because development and justice-oriented organizations viewed it as a tool designed almost exclusively for the enforcement of environmental regulations.

US exceptionalism

To reduce the Bank's power and to leverage their new demands, the anti-Bank faction lobbied donor governments to cut or eliminate their IDA funding. This began in November, even before the final IDA agreement, and continued into early 1993. Parliamentarians in Canada and Britain debated the IDA's merits, and in Sweden a motion was even tabled to cut IDA funding. Only in Finland, however, was this attack on the IDA successful, resulting in a $14 million cut to the Finnish contribution (Udall 1995, p. 224).

IDA enjoyed broad support as the World Bank's primary poverty-fighting vehicle, but the failure of most of the political attacks on the IDA had a more systemic cause. Nearly all of the IDA's donor countries had parliamentary systems with combined executive and legislative functions. The party in power was both responsible for the IDA negotiation and the subsequent funding authorization; it was unlikely to inflict on itself a legislative defeat.

The major exception to this was the US. The US government was the IDA's biggest donor, with over $2.7 billion pledged, and traditionally had significant influence over the Bank. US funding depended on two different branches of government. The executive negotiated the agreement through the Treasury, while Congress appropriated funds. This provided two different opportunities for policy influence.[30] The US government was also particularly porous, allowing multiple entry points for lobbyists and activists. The organizations opposing the IDA therefore turned their sights toward the US.

The IDA fight in Congress

In Congress, IDA expenditures had to be approved in both the House and the Senate in a two-stage process. First Congress had to pass a bill authorizing the government to make the expenditures. Then a second bill needed to be passed appropriating the necessary money, without which the authorization would be meaningless. In each chamber these bills were discussed by the relevant subcommittees before being put to a vote by the entire chamber. In response to CSO pressure, the two committees responsible for IDA authorization and appropriation in the

House and the authorizing committee in the Senate all held public hearings in which CSOs were invited to participate.

NGOs including the Environmental Defense Fund, Friends of the Earth, the National Wildlife Federation, Greenpeace, and the Sierra Club used these hearings to lobby openly for cuts to World Bank funding or for a complete holdback in Bank funding pending large-scale reform.[31] Interaction, on behalf of a large number of Washington development and relief organizations, gave Congressional testimony calling for full funding for the IDA, as did CARE and Bread for the World.[32] Bread even went so far as to call for funding to be increased.[33] The Forum of African Voluntary Development Organizations (FAVDO), an umbrella organization representing a large number of African CSOs, also provided a representative who made an impassioned plea for continued funding.[34]

Lack of a permanent Washington presence or experience in DC-based lobbying excluded most non-American actors from direct involvement in the process. This included not just developing country CSOs, but even larger European actors like Oxfam-UK.[35] Besides FAVDO, only two non-US CSOs participated. Narmada Bachao Andolan (NBA), an Indian advocacy group which had previously supported the replenishment, submitted a letter through the Environmental Defense Fund calling for an elimination of the Bank and IDA. The Public Interest Research Group in India submitted a similar statement calling for complete cancellation of the replenishment.

The relative lack of developing country voices permitted those TCSOs who were involved to make broad claims to represent civil society in other parts of the world. These claims frequently conflicted. FAVDO and NBA, although both ostensibly speaking on behalf of IDA recipients, held diametrically opposing views. US-based groups, including Church World Service, Friends of the Earth, and the National Wildlife Federation all made claims to represent either local partners or unspecified developing country populations, yet held strikingly disparate positions.

Anti-Bank organizations, however, succeeded in framing the debate over the IDA as a referendum on the Bank itself. Prompted in part by EDF and Friends of the Earth, Congress discussed the costs of the construction of the Bank's new Washington headquarters, its staff salaries, and its co-ownership of a Maryland golf-course. The World Bank's spending was described as akin to that of the European Bank for Reconstruction and Development (EBRD), whose president, Jacques Attali, had been forced to resign after spending millions of dollars on private planes, a lavish Christmas party, and new marble for the EBRD's headquarters.[36] An amendment in the House designed to cancel all US funding to the Bank for the 1994 fiscal year was barely defeated on a vote of 210–216.[37]

Final outcomes

Ultimately Congress reduced US funding for the IDA by $200 million for the first year of disbursement. The appropriations bill, passed in September of 1993, stipulated that the US would pressure the World Bank to introduce an appeals mechanism and that the US Treasury would report back to Congress within six months on the Bank's progress.[38] Meanwhile the chair of the House authorizing subcommittee, Representative Barney Frank, negotiated an agreement to withhold authorization for one-third of the IDA's remaining funding pending further reform of the Bank's policies. This resulted in a holdback of $1.2 billion. He also lobbied key Bank staff personally, threatening to hold up all authorization unless there was rapid change at the Bank.

The Bank moved rapidly towards the creation of an appeals mechanism, the World Bank Inspection Panel, but was unable to overcome anti-Bank sentiment in Washington. In 1994, 50 per cent of that year's IDA funds, approximately $600 million, were also withheld. The appropriations bill stipulated that such funds would not be released until the US Treasury provided evidence of further improvements in the Bank's information disclosure policy, its resettlement procedures, and its response to the recommendations made to mitigate the flaws highlighted in the Wapenhans Report.[39] The Bank moved to further reform itself, but could not forestall all cuts. In 1995, the new Bank president, James Wolfensohn, joined by FAVDO, Oxfam, Interaction, and Church World Service, appealed unsuccessfully against further reductions (Lobe 1995). By early 1996, nearly the end of the IDA-10 cycle, total US cuts amounted to $934.5 million (Washington Office on Africa 1996).

In monetary terms, TCS opposition reduced the size of the total IDA-10 replenishment (1993–96) by approximately 5 per cent and the US contribution by approximately 35 per cent. The anti-IDA campaign also substantially eroded the independence of the Bank. The creation of the appeals mechanism and the liberalization of the Bank's information policy enhanced the Bank's transparency and public accountability by an order of magnitude. Both would greatly facilitate further TCS efforts to transform the Bank and curtail its actions. Moreover, by forcing the

Bank to deal directly with the US legislature, TCSOs undercut the Bank's tradition of dealing solely with member governments via their finance ministries. This created a new channel for civil society action against the Bank and also increased US power vis-à-vis other Bank members.

Conclusions

The activism surrounding the IDA-10 represents the first truly global civil society effort to reform the World Bank. Previous 'global' campaigns had been run largely by TCSOs based in the industrialized countries of the global North. Where they involved Southern actors, they tended to do so in a bilateral fashion with Northern CSOs, often from just one country, interacting with CSOs in a single Southern locale. In contrast, the IDA-10 campaign involved more than forty organizations from six different continents. Organizations from Latin America, Africa, and Southeast Asia took active roles, often independent of Northern partners. Previous campaigns often focused on project cancellation or the mitigation of a local or regional policy; where they did address global issues, they tended to focus on a single one, such as structural adjustment. In contrast, the IDA-10 activism encompassed nearly a dozen issues, all with global impact. Finally, the effect on the World Bank was unprecedented. The Bank increased participatory decision-making in a host of areas, opened its records and reports to the public, engaged its critics, and cultivated TCSO allies. The result was substantially magnified TCS influence in its policymaking.

In part because of its scope, the case raises a number of questions with regards to the democratic legitimacy of TCS. The forty-plus civil society organizations involved managed at times a striking degree of policy cohesion. At other times their positions were strikingly contentious. Actors formed alliances and broke them, acquired policy positions and discarded them. This raises questions regarding how TCSOs interact with one another, and how individual organizations chose their policy positions.

Examining how TCSOs chose to make or break alliances and whether they engaged in dialogue amongst themselves is important for understanding whether TCS can act to develop inclusive spaces for stakeholder input. Determining how TCSOs chose their positions, e.g. whether on the basis of power, ideology, money, or grassroots pressure, bears on the debate over the representivity of TCSOs. Both of these questions have relevance for TCS's input legitimacy (which involves representivity and inclusivity) and both address particular claims in the literature regarding TCS's democratizing potential. These issues will be explored in greater detail in Chapter 4.

The data discussed in this chapter also clearly confirm that TCS has the capacity to impact the World Bank. Civil society activism led the Bank to reinforce or improve the implementation of existing social and environmental safeguards, adopt poverty-targeted interventions, increase popular participation, liberalize the Bank's information policy, and create the World Bank Inspection Panel.

These impacts raise questions regarding the mechanisms and distribution of civil society influence. The IDA-10 case featured appeals to the public, like the *New York Times* advertisement; discussions with domestic politicians, like UK parliamentarians; negotiations with the international representatives of sovereign governments in the form of the IDA deputies and Bank executive directors; and direct discussions with leaders at the Bank itself. Which of these channels were most effective and why? Which CSOs used the most effective channels?

To the extent that TCSO activism led to the realization of stakeholder objectives or made global governance more responsive, TCS can be seen to be expanding the authority of the citizens of the Bank's member states over the policies impacting them, a democratic output. However, to the extent that TCSOs exploited existing imbalances in power between donor nations or donors and borrowers, or that some civil society actors used exclusive channels to advance the interests of some stakeholders over others, TCS activism may be seen as advancing political elitism and possibly undermining democracy. The fact that a small group of civil society actors ultimately managed to secure cuts in the replenishment over the objections of many other TCSOs makes this question particularly salient. These questions regarding the mechanisms and distribution of influence will be explored in greater detail in Chapter 5.

Lastly, the data presented in this chapter indicate the importance of examining TCS's impact on the power of developing country governments. By claiming to speak on behalf of the citizens of the Bank's borrower nations, TCSOs essentially claimed the traditional government role of representing citizen interests in international forums. The contradictory positions of many TCSOs raise questions as to how well TCS as whole filled this role. In addition, the use of US influence in the IDA-10 indicates that TCSOs may exploit power imbalances in the international system, utilizing powerful governments to marginalize weaker ones. These issues, and their implications for TCS's capacity to democratize global governance, will be explored in more detail in Chapter 6.

4
Principles and Paychecks: Positions and Participation in the IDA-10

Although a large number of actors had begun to develop a common policy agenda during the early days of the 10th IDA, this loose coalition quickly fractured during the post-Narmada controversy over whether to attack the Bank's funding. Nearly every civil society organization staff member interviewed for this research affirmed the presence of significant tensions and disagreements among TCSOs both during and after the IDA-10. One respondent described organizations as constantly 'competing for ... funding and publicity'. Another, from an NGO with a strong anti-Bank agenda, described the staff of more moderate NGOs as being plagued by an intellectual inferiority complex. A former staff member with one development organization recalled being excluded from meetings with colleagues from other TCSOs after he publicly disagreed with their position on the Narmada Dam. Instead of the consensual processes scholars often predict among civil society actors, divisiveness became common.

This chapter examines the divisions that formed between TCSOs during the 10th IDA around their policy objectives. In particular, this chapter uses the observed divisions to help identify how TCSOs chose their policy positions and the factors influencing the formation of alliances. These issues have relevance for TCS's capacity to improve representation and inclusivity, both key forms of democratic input, in international policymaking. They also have relevance for evaluating the claim, discussed earlier in this work, that TCS creates new discursive spaces and for engaging with current theories of network activism.

Much of the writing on TCS focuses on the behavior of NGOs and the impact of advocacy campaigns or networks. Relatively less attention has been paid to the means by which such campaigns have formed. North-South alliances have received significant scrutiny but

North-North and South-South cooperation are both under-researched, at least in those instances in which they presage global activism. The research on TCS networks, moreover, tends to begin by identifying a particularly prominent or successful campaign and working backwards. As noted in Chapter 1, this can lead to a kind of victor's history in which the history of the winning organizations becomes conflated with a history of the network or the issue.

Moreover, in such analysis data on the desires of affected populations are often provided by NGOs themselves. Many studies of global civil society treat NGOs as reasonable proxies for the grassroots interests of the stakeholders they claim to represent. This trend is exemplified by the incorporation of accounts written by NGO staff into academic texts (e.g., Fox and Brown 1998b; Pincus and Winters 2002; Walker and Thompson 2008). While practitioner accounts generally provide excellent detail and firsthand information, it is difficult to imagine that they represent a comprehensive sampling of perspectives. Combined with the tendency to sample only those NGOs involved in a winning coalition, this practice can erroneously create or magnify the impression that NGOs are reasonable representatives of stakeholder interests and that they help include new voices in transnational policymaking.

This chapter highlights the importance of avoiding such assumptions. During the activism surrounding the 10th IDA, mission and funding interests worked together to determine the policy positions espoused by different organizations and their decisions to participate in advocacy. The forty-plus organizations involved in the IDA-10 chose their policy positions largely on the basis of pre-existing missions and at the expense of genuine responsiveness to the borrowing country populations most affected by Bank policy. Organizational imperatives, particularly material needs, often drove the decision to participate in different aspects of the campaign and the formation of ad hoc alliances. Organizations participated when their participation was externally funded, supported by paying members, or when they expected a return on investment. Tensions over funding undermined incentives towards dialogue, enhancing factiousness within the civil society community. The most effective alliances occurred among organizations whose funders requested them to work together, thus magnifying funder influence. The result was that neither individual organizations nor TCS as a whole was particularly responsive to the majority of their claimed stakeholders.

To arrive at these conclusions, I examined the three explanations given by interview respondents for the divisions within the initial

IDA-10 coalition: values and mission; North-South tensions; and funding. This chapter explores each of these claims in turn and shows how a combination of mission and funding provides the most convincing explanation of TCSO behavior during the IDA-10. It concludes with an analysis of the impacts of these findings on TCSOs' claims to democratic legitimacy.

Values and mission

The idea of mission as a driver of the divisions between CSOs resonates strongly with the statements of the respondents interviewed for this research. CSO staff in particular were quick to associate the policy positions of their organizations with a particular set of values, such as the preservation of life, social justice, or environmental conservation. These values were reflected in the organization's chosen mission. When the intersection of values, mission and policy advocacy was not explicit, it was often implicit in the examples staff gave of either Bank malfeasance or positive Bank contributions to development or in the ways in which they contrasted their organization with other organizations.

Most TCSO leaders, along with outside observers including former staff from the World Bank and US government, described two main groups of TCSOs, identified by their mission: environmental and development organizations. Some also delineated a third group of faith-based organizations or justice advocates.

Environmental organizations

As described in the previous chapter, environmental NGOs formed the core of the anti-replenishment faction. These organizations varied in their strategies and the priorities they assigned specific issues but, in general, their environmentalism emphasized conservation. Their advocacy efforts focused heavily on preventing the depletion of natural resources, particularly woodlands. Ending the construction of coal-fired power plants and promoting improved end-use efficiency as an alternative to new power generation were also core elements of their agenda prior to the IDA-10. Some attacked hydroelectric power as well: Greenpeace, Friends of the Earth, Environmental Defense Fund, and others worked with the International Rivers Network (IRN) in opposing the Yacyreta dam in Argentina in September 1992. EDF and IRN also led international opposition to the Narmada Dam project.

Some of the organizations involved were ideologically opposed to the idea of development requiring industrialization and economic growth. In his book *Mortgaging the Earth,* published just after the peak of the IDA-10 campaign, Bruce Rich of EDF described economic development and industrialization as misguided efforts antithetical to most of human experience and concluded that 'primitive, non-Western modes of living are largely superior to modern ones' (Rich 1994, pp. 203, 240–241). This combination of environmental conservation and development skepticism was also shared by NBA, the sole Southern CSO to take an active part in campaigning against the IDA-10 replenishment.

Their value for conservation and their opposition to large-scale development made environmental organizations logical opponents of the IDA-10 replenishment. The International Development Association was the World Bank's primary means of lending to the world's poorest countries, many of which had large rural populations or relatively large amounts of wilderness. On the one hand, the IDA had a track record of supporting some of the projects most derided by environmentalists, including commercial forestry programs, power plant construction, and hydroelectric dams. On the other hand, it was an instrument of the Bank's overall agenda of development, which focused on economic indicators and had become increasingly neoliberal during the 1980s. Their suspicion of industrial development and their desire to protect the rights of the rural poor persuaded environmental actors to ignore claims from Southern governments or CSOs about the importance of Bank funding. Nonetheless, environmentalists recognized the popularity of the IDA and initially were reluctant to oppose it outright. Incremental reform seemed a better goal, until outrage over the Bank's refusal to cancel funding for the Sardar Sarovar project prompted a more radical course of action.

Not all environmental groups opposed the IDA-10 replenishment. The Bank Information Center stayed neutral despite its explicit environmental bent. However, this was not so much a contradiction of its environmental values as it was their subordination to another purpose. Although BIC was environmentally inclined, its primary mission was to act as a clearinghouse for information for all CSOs. It worked very closely with anti-IDA environmental NGOs, but explicit partisanship might have jeopardized its core mission. According to TCSO and government staffers, BIC did not itself engage in lobbying donor deputies or Bank executive directors, although it did arrange meetings for others to do so.

The Natural Resources Defense Council also demonstrated a similar pattern. The NRDC had worked closely with the Sierra Club on previous reform efforts and during the IDA-10 it partnered with EDF, National Wildlife Federation, and FoE. However, its core mission was the reform of the Bank's energy policies and forestry lending; broader issues of governance reform at the Bank were secondary priorities. Because US Treasury proposals for Bank reform reflected the NRDC's priorities, the NRDC agreed to support the full IDA replenishment if a reform agenda could be agreed.[1]

The World Wildlife Fund deviated more significantly from the line pursued by other environmental organizations. EDF, NWF, and FoE coordinated many of their lobbying positions and often borrowed from one another's research, particularly when one organization had a superior network among some project-affected population or better connections to potential overseas partners. WWF, however, maintained its own ground-level contacts, conducted its own research, and formulated its positions independently. While WWF promoted sustainability it did not support the anti-IDA agenda. To the contrary, David Reed, director of WWF's International Institutions Policy Program, wrote to the US Treasury that WWF felt that it was necessary to 'reinforce the contribution of IDA resources'.[2] WWF's position stressed poverty alleviation, public accountability, and changes in structural adjustment policy, with relatively little space devoted to environmental conservation. Reed's testimony before Congress in May 1993 reinforced this position. He noted that 'it is crucial to ensure the uninterrupted flow of IDA resources to alleviate poverty and to prevent further poverty-induced environmental degradation'.[3] Because it was a prominent environmental NGO taking a moderate position on the Bank, WWF was, in the words of one senior TCSO staffer, the 'biggest problem' obstructing a unified environmentalist position.

In short, the efforts of the majority of environmental actors to impede or eliminate IDA funding show a great degree of consistency, and strong logical links between values and the resulting policy positions. The core organizations involved shared a strong emphasis on environmental conservation, which led them to oppose many development initiatives. This trait was reinforced by a willingness to question the very concept of development. At the same time, however, not all environmental organizations developed anti-IDA policies. Some environmental organizations, particularly the World Wildlife Fund, shared some of the dominant environmental perspectives and values but instead chose neutral or pro-IDA positions.

Development organizations

Development organizations involved in the 10th IDA ranged from service delivery NGOs to advocacy groups. The most active were Bread for the World, Church World Service, Lutheran World Relief, Interaction, and Oxfam UK. These were joined by a host of other organizations, including US and European-based actors like CARE and NOVIB, and numerous parties from the developing world, such as the Malaysia-based Third World Network and the Inter-Africa Group.

The two values which seemed to be shared by all development organizations were a concern for poverty alleviation and a desire to empower the poor. The development organizations believed that poverty was real and objective, not just socially constructed or relative. Some had been involved in efforts to develop and popularize new metrics of poverty measurement. For the highly professionalized service delivery NGOs, identifying and addressing poverty was a core part of their organizational identity. For the representatives of Southern organizations, poverty was an inescapable reality of daily life in their home countries.

As a result, the overwhelming majority of development organizations supported full replenishment of the IDA. In October 1992 the NGO Working Group on the World Bank, on behalf of more than twenty development organizations, expressed its 'deep and abiding concern about the inadequacy of funds on concessional terms being made available by the North to tackle poverty in the South', a situation which would be exacerbated by 'cuts in real terms under the current round of negotiations for the IDA-10'.[4] This sentiment was echoed by those TCSOs testifying before Congress. CARE, a venerable and extremely large service delivery organization, described the IDA as 'the largest and most important single source of concessional development capital for the poorest countries'.[5] David Beckmann, president of Bread for the World, even used the opportunity of an IDA hearing to call for a general increase in US foreign aid.[6]

In general, support for the 10th IDA was more consistent among development organizations than opposition was among environmentalists. There were several development organizations that took an initial position calling for Bank reform, but never followed up with a clear position for or against the IDA replenishment. As noted in the previous chapter, some of those organizations that had called publicly for Bank reform also publicly supported the IDA once it was threatened. Only one development CSO, the Ireland-based Catholic group Trocaire, took a more aggressively critical stance. It issued several strong anti-Bank statements in July 1992. As with other Irish TCSOs, however, there is no evidence that Trocaire was involved later in 1993, when cancellation of the IDA was being discussed more explicitly.

Faith-based organizations

Numerous faith-based organizations were involved in the IDA-10 process. The Columban Missionaries, the Irish Missionary Union, and the Church of Ireland Bishops' Appeal all lobbied representatives of donor governments. The Aga Khan Foundation and the US-based Islamic African Relief Agency signed the NGO Working Group letter. Bread for the World and Church World Service, although grouped with development organizations above, also had strong faith-based values.

Faith-based groups tended to have a value set quite different from other TCSOs. In general, the driving principle of these groups was social justice, specifically a concern for the well-being of disadvantaged and marginalized people. A statement during the IDA discussions from the US Catholic Conference of Bishops, for instance, denounced structural adjustment on the basis that 'it is the poorest of the poor who suffer most' from its effects.[7]

Such concerns, however, do not seem to have manifested themselves in a consistent set of policy positions or consistent participation in the policy process. One respondent asserted that faith-based groups involved in the IDA aligned themselves with whichever of the two major camps, environment or development, was more persuasive. Presumably, this meant whichever side made a better case for the social justice benefits of its agenda. While environmentalists were successful in making this case early in 1992, the potential cancellation of the IDA funding changed the stakes of the game, pushing some faith-based groups to realign themselves with development activists. The only faith-based groups to hold consistent positions on the Bank and on IDA were those, like Bread for the World and Church World Service, with a standing interest in development.

A mission and values-based division?

A strong correlation exists between the categories presented here and the related organizations' positions on the 10th IDA replenishment, at least with regards to the environmental and development categories. The idea that an organization's policy positions should be driven by values and mission was also the perspective preferred by most of the respondents for this research, particularly for explaining their own actions. Moreover, the concept has a certain intuitive merit: environmental organizations should naturally care more about the environment, and development organizations should prioritize development.

Closer examination, however, reveals the pitfalls in this argument. Although values or mission may often predict an organization's policy preferences, they do not consistently predict its activities. Mission alone does not fully account for WWF's deviation from the environmental line. Values and mission also do not explain why so many non-US organizations in the development and faith categories ceased to participate later in the policy process, when their earlier behavior demonstrated that IDA advocacy was aligned with their organization's values. In short, values and mission do not explain all of the observed TCSO behavior.

To the extent that values and mission do drive policy formation, the findings cast doubt on organizations' representivity. The missions and interests discussed here, for most organizations, predated the IDA-10. Despite a mutually stated value for human well-being, development and environmental groups chose quite divergent positions on the most salient issue of the 10th replenishment, funding for the IDA itself. It seems likely that groups in each category viewed human well-being through a lens formed by their particular mission, with environmentalists believing that well-being could be best met through conservation and development groups believing it would be best met through Western-style development. It is difficult to know which understanding, if either, reflected the desires of the people most affected by the policies under negotiation.

North versus South

In 1992, FAVDO prefaced a pro-IDA statement by declaring that Southern NGOs had 'reached different conclusions from their Northern counterparts'.[8] Delegates to the IDA-10 negotiations expressed concerned about the representivity of Washington-based NGOs. Respondents from certain US-based TCSOs interviewed for this research suggested that Southern TCSOs held pro-IDA positions because of pressure from their governments. Statements such as these echo a common theme in the civil society literature, that Northern and Southern civil society organizations possess distinct outlooks and agendas. While such agendas may overlap, they are also potentially a cause for tension.

In order to evaluate any North-South division in the IDA-10, it is necessary to define the terms 'North' and 'South'. These terms are often used to delineate industrialized and developing states, but these categories of 'industrialized' and 'developing' can also be ambiguous. In discussing the World Bank, we can state more precisely that 'Northern' states refers to IDA donors, while 'Southern' nations refers to IDA borrowers. This is the definition used throughout this research, and it seems congruent with the intentions of the respondents referenced here.

A North-South divide on environmental issues was explicit at the government level in the early 1990s, with developing country governments strongly opposing nascent efforts on the part of bilateral donors to link development aid to environmental reform (Vidal 1992; Robinson 1992). However, this division was not clearly mirrored among TCSOs. Although Northern TCSOs were key players in the global environmental movement, TCSOs based in the global South were also involved. Greenpeace, prior to the Rio Earth Summit in June 1992, publicly exhorted developing nation governments to embrace environmental preservation (Reuters 1992). FoE joined Greenpeace in using the summit to attract attention to pressing environmental issues (Turner and Harding 1992). However, the Third World Network and the Forum of Brazilian NGOs partnered with Greenpeace and FoE in working to attract media attention to environmental concerns (Turner and Harding 1992). In June 1992, EDF and IRN lobbied against a hydroelectric project in Malawi, resulting in a 'no' vote on the project by the US representative on the World Bank's board (Crossette 1992b). In 1993, the India-based NBA issued strong attacks on the environmental impacts of another hydroelectric project, the Sardar Sarovar dam. Thus both Northern and Southern TCSOs were involved.

In discussions of development, the field was even more mixed. Development was not exclusively a Southern issue. The October 1992 letter on the IDA to Lewis Preston from the NGO Working Group on the World Bank closely echoed development versus environment sentiments previous articulated by Southern government representatives. However, it was signed by 18 TCSOs based in donor nations as well as 14 from developing nations. Northern TCSOs also displayed a mix of environmental and development priorities during the 1993 US Congressional hearings on the World Bank and 10th IDA. American organizations like FoE, EDF, and the NWF pushed for a reduction in the World Bank's power and funding, and stressed the Bank's negative environmental and social impacts. Yet other US-based organizations like Interaction, Church World Service, and CARE joined the Africa-based FAVDO in stressing the importance of the IDA for the development of poor countries and the welfare of their citizens.[9]

In short, there is no clear evidence of division between TCSOs along North-South lines on environmental or development issues. Although the environment was seen as a Northern issue in intergovernmental debates, some non-governmental actors from the global South supported environmental positions. At the same time, many TCSOs from the global North prioritized development over the environment. No other issue shows a strong North-South divide at either the government or civil society level. This lack of clear North-South divisions discredits the idea of geography as a consistent driver of TCSO policy advocacy during the 10th IDA.

Funding

A final possible parsing of policy positions offered by IDA-10 participants was material interests. Some respondents suggested that TCSOs selected their policy positions in accordance with their financial incentives. One indicated that the seeming divide between environmental and development organizations was, in fact, predominantly a divide between advocacy groups and service delivery organizations. The former, funded primarily by foundations or member donations, were able to take more radical, reformist positions than the latter, which relied on flows of aid funding. This opinion was echoed by several staff at environmental organizations, who accused development organizations of being motivated by financial gain. The data, however, indicates a more nuanced reality. Any organization wishing to survive and to continue in its activities requires funding to pay for staff, overhead, and operations. Evidence indicates that nearly all of the organizations involved in the IDA, including both service delivery and advocacy organizations, faced financial considerations that influenced their advocacy behavior.[10] In some cases, particularly among advocacy groups funded by foundations, donors made explicit indications of the policy positions they wished their funds to support, or facilitated the participation of TCSOs whose stated aims aligned with those of the foundation. In other cases, such as groups receiving funding from the government or members, there was less direct pressure to assume an explicit position. Nonetheless, the organizations had a strong interest in preserving the possibility for future funding or the loyalty of current donors. It is unclear that funding drove the policy preferences of most actors, although it may have been instrumental in defining the agendas of some. Rather, it appears to have been a key driver of participation, thus determining the matrix of organizations undertaking advocacy related to the IDA.

Correlating funding and policy

If funding-related organizational imperatives and advocacy are correlated, one would expect that TCSOs involved in the IDA would fall into three general categories based on the variety of funding models: organizations dependent on funding from governments or intergovernmental organizations (IOs), that back government or IO positions or advocate greater IDA funding; foundation-funded organizations which back the aims or agenda of the foundation(s) funding them; and member-supported organizations whose positions reflect the desires of the majority of their members. Such a categorization matches almost perfectly with the divisions observed in IDA-10 lobbying. Organizations like Oxfam, CARE, and the World Wildlife Fund, which received some or all of their funding from bilateral and multilateral aid, gave unanimous support to the IDA-10. Organizations like EDF, FoE, NWF, and the international advocacy arm of the Sierra Club had all received foundation funding for international environmental advocacy and the reform of multilateral development banks; all organizations with such funding opposed the IDA. Member-funded organizations divided according to the interests of their members: Greenpeace, Rainforest Action Network, and NWF (which received more funding from members than foundations) were supported primarily by American environmentalists and took anti-IDA pro-environmental positions. NBA was funded by dam opponents in India and opposed the IDA, which was helping fund the dam. Bread for the World, along with the US Conference of Catholic Bishops and other faith groups, had members interested in social justice and supported IDA funding as a means of helping the poor.

Claims of causation

The idea of a causal relationship between organizational funding and position-taking was elaborated upon by several respondents. One environmental leader used funding to explain the divisions among environmentalists, noting that 'the big project-oriented CSOs like World Wildlife Fund, Nature Conservancy International, and Conservation International ... looked to the Bank as a funder for their projects and that kind of thing. So they were never particularly strong advocates [for reform]'. Another noted a perennial tension between his organization and groups focused on ensuring that sufficient money is given for development. Organizations who received funding from aid were thought to oppose the cuts even if they did not receive direct funding from the World Bank, because they believed IDA cuts could precipitate a more general decline in US aid levels. According to one respondent:

> These groups were afraid to criticize the World Bank, even though they might have lots of criticisms ... they were reluctant to come out publicly and say critical things about the World Bank, or be too critical because they were afraid that would play into the hands of the right wing, the Reaganites, etcetera who didn't like foreign aid.

Although some of these claims came in the form of critiques from anti-IDA activists, they were validated by aid organizations and their allies. InterAction represented over 150 development and relief organizations during the IDA-10. It sat on the NGOWG and had worked with World Bank staff in 1990 on the reform of the Bank's participation policies. Its representatives were also invited to meet with US legislators and to testify in Congressional hearings. Yet according to a source involved with the organization, the most commonly held concern among its members during the IDA-10 time period was maintaining financing for their activities.

At the same time, the anti-IDA activists who speculated on the financial motivations of service delivery organizations were themselves subject to financial pressures. One respondent described environmental activists, including the core groups opposing the IDA, as continually 'competing for money, funding, and publicity'. The resulting conflicts never became public, but they could escalate to the point where activists sought to co-opt the support of their competitors' donors and draw away their funding. Another TCSO member noted that foundation donors rewarded vigorous advocacy. A certain anti-IDA leader, the respondent joked, seemed to be 'paid by the column-inch' for the press coverage they generated.

In the case of member-funded organizations, the advocacy agenda was decided or affirmed by members. NBA was supported by Indian donors, although the organization itself admits that these were not necessarily the project-affected people in the Narmada valley it claimed to represent.[11] NWF and Bread for the World had annual meetings at which members could vote, as well as regular correspondence with members. Greenpeace did not have such democratic agenda-setting processes, but its very public position-taking created a clear brand that members chose to support. Faith-based organizations were also member-supported, either directly by congregants or individual donors or indirectly via a denomination. They had a clear brand identity of their own: an adherence to faith tenets which set them apart (in either principle or practice) from secular organizations (cf. Pallas 2005).

The Charles Stewart Mott Foundation

The Charles Stewart Mott Foundation had a particularly strong effect on the IDA-10. Mott provided funds to all of the core anti-IDA campaigners, including EDF, the NWF, NRDC, the Sierra Club and FoE, as well as to the Bank Information Center, which arranged meetings and disseminated information on the others' behalf. Typically advocacy organizations initiate contact with potential funders, seeking grants to support the advocacy organizations' existing agendas. In this case, however, Mott sought out these environmental actors.

According to Maureen Smyth, who served as the program officer for these grants during the IDA-10 and is now a senior vice president at the foundation, Mott developed its strategic vision for environmental reform in the late 1980s. The foundation was engaged in a planning process for its environmental program and hired a consultant to examine the program's direction. The consultant identified a window of opportunity in international environmental policy, particularly with certain American environmental NGOs which were beginning to realize that they could influence the international environmental agenda by influencing the World Bank. Mott concurred with this belief that influencing the Bank could influence global environmental policy.

Acting on this conclusion, Mott initially provided funds to EDF, the NWF, NRDC, the Sierra Club and FoE. All of these organizations were putting pressure on the World Bank to stop funding projects that had negative environmental and social impacts. These NGOs had already begun lobbying the Bank on their own, but Mott was an early supporter of their efforts. According to Smyth, 'We saw that putting some early foundation money in this area could make a difference'.[12]

Mott funds also helped develop the support of non-US actors for MDB reform. Three grants to FoE, given in 1991 and 1992, specify that the money is to be used to 'strengthen multilateral development bank campaign activities in Japan' and for 'outreach to Third World groups'.[13] EDF was likewise given funds to 'empower Third World nongovernmental organizations to monitor, influence and change internationally financed development projects'.[14] The NWF, which received strong support from members, also passed some of its Mott funding on to overseas partners. Relatively few groups outside of the US environmental movement opposed the IDA or took strong reformist positions, but it seems that the activities of some of those who did were facilitated, cultivated, or amplified by Mott funding.

A principal-agent relationship?

There is no doubt that Mott funding supported a substantial portion of the anti-IDA activism during the 10th IDA or that Mott was pursuing its own strategic agenda. The key question is the extent to which Mott funding influenced the behavior of the groups involved. Several of the groups involved insist that Mott had little control over their actions: 'they had no influence whatever on [the Mott-funded environmentalists]', asserted one senior staffer, because 'the people working on these issues [were] strong-willed and professional'. Nonetheless, there are several indications that Mott had a principal-agent relationship with its aid recipients, leading them into behaviors they would not have undertaken on their own in order to facilitate the outcomes Mott favored. These include coordinated policy-setting on the part of grant recipients and the initiation of new activities in response to Mott requests.

Coordinating policy

All of the TCSO respondents interviewed for this research were asked about their relationships with other nongovernmental actors and the extent to which they coordinated policy positions or lobbying activities with like-minded organizations. Only the core group of environmental activists, EDF, NWF, NRDC, FoE, and the Sierra Club, reported regular meetings to coordinate policy and tactics. The groups shared information among themselves and would allow the members best informed about a particular policy or project to influence the position of the coalition as a whole. The groups used coordination to magnify their political footprint. For instance, when Bruce Rich of EDF spoke before the Senate hearing on the IDA-10 replenishment in June 1993, he spoke on behalf of the Sierra Club and NWF as well. He began his testimony by reminding the senators present that these three organizations combined 'have more than 5.7 million members and supporters nationwide'.[15] In an earlier hearing he testified on behalf of EDF and the Sierra Club, while noting that his testimony was 'congruent' with the positions of NWF and FoE.[16]

This coordination was a direct result of Mott influence. Maureen Smyth, overseeing the Mott grants, strongly suggested that the

Mott-funded organizations coordinate their activities. When Mott began working with the organizations, each group had a niche area but their agendas overlapped. Smyth believed that the groups could do more if they coordinated. One staffer who worked on the NRDC effort described the organization's partnership with the other four major IDA opponents by saying that 'some of that [partnership] was by design', a result of Mott's influence. At least one respondent indicated that his organization would not have participated in such meetings without Mott's influence. Tellingly, such regular coordination has largely ended since the related Mott funding ceased.

Initiating activities

As noted, Mott sought out the five TCSOs it funded for World Bank work. According to a staffer at one recipient organization, Mott 'liked this international financial institutions work' and gave money specifically for such work, rather than because of any broader relationship with the organization. The foundation's funding led its grant recipients to undertake activities they would not otherwise have undertaken. 'Mott was the major contributor', according to another staffer, 'if it hadn't been for Mott, the whole community wouldn't have been able to do what it did'.

Mott's influence was most clearly demonstrated in the creation of 50 Years is Enough, a loosely organized campaign for the intensive reform or elimination of the World Bank and IMF, inspired by the two institutions' fiftieth birthdays in 1994. The campaign began organizing in 1993 and announced a platform in 1994. IRN, Development GAP, FoE, EDF, and Oxfam America were key participants. Although the campaign, which still exists, describes itself publicly as the spontaneous creation of energized activists (50 Years, undated), it resulted in part from pressure by the Charles Stewart Mott Foundation. In 1992 the Development GAP coordinated a forum where a variety of CSOs discussed their agendas with potential foundation funders. The forum highlighted the potential synergy between environmental groups and others which, like the Development GAP, had some sort of economic justice agenda. Mott approached the Development GAP and asked that a new, coordinated campaign be developed, and the Development GAP agreed. In June 1993, Mott provided the Development GAP with $130,000 for work on 'global economic justice'. In early 1994 it provided IRN, which was already receiving Mott funding for 'General Purposes', $90,000 dollars for the 'Media Outreach Project of the '50 Years' Campaign'.[17] The campaign became a major source of negative publicity for the Bank over the rest of the decade, influencing policy-makers' opinions of the World Bank in the crucial 1992–95 period during which the US cuts to its IDA-10 contribution took place.

Funding, policy, and participation

The data indicate a clear link between funding and activism. Organizations pursued the positions which they had a material incentive to pursue, aligning their activities with their financial interests. These findings parallel work by Cooley and Ron (2002). Looking at NGOs engaged in service delivery, they find that a broad set of organizational imperatives, particularly the need to pay staff and overhead costs and to compete with other organizations for scarce funding resources, causes most NGOs to prioritize economic concerns over mission, values, or other aspects of identity. The IDA-10 findings indicate that this dynamic also holds true for TCSOs in an advocacy setting.

The accusations of some actors notwithstanding, however, it seems unlikely that the majority of TCSOs involved in the IDA-10 chose their policies on a purely mercenary basis. Although many organizations chose positions that supported their financial goals, causality in this area is difficult to prove. Organizations' pre-existing missions seem to have had a stronger impact on their policy preferences.

The pattern of participation indicates that the significance of funding (as opposed to mission) increases as the costs of activism increase. Numerous organizations with an interest in IDA-10 related issues, such as poverty alleviation or debt relief, were involved in low-cost ways early in the IDA process. Many smaller faith-based organizations and developing world TCSOs signed the NGO Working Group letter, or other similar position statements. However, organizations only engaged in sustained advocacy when their activities were likely to be expected by paying members, when they believed that the policies being negotiated would affect their future revenue, or when outside funding subsidized the costs of activism.

The influence of the Charles Stewart Mott Foundation further demonstrates the impact of funding on participation. Mott funded the core group of American TCSOs opposed to the IDA, and its funding may have helped them cultivate the support of overseas partners. Mott chose its partners for their pre-existing agendas, but it induced them to modify their existing behavior. In response to Mott influence, Mott clients initiated new advocacy activities and coordinated their policy positions in ways that increased their political impact.

In short, during the 10th IDA time period, funding appears to have had an important influence on advocacy activity. According to participants in the process itself, funding interests may explain the seeming contradiction between the mission of certain TCSOs, such as the World Wildlife Fund, and the positions they espoused. Similarly, it helps explain the choices organizations made to participate in or withdraw from different advocacy activities. The role of Mott is particularly significant because it implies that the majority of TCSOs opposing the 10th IDA were functioning as the clients or agents of a single entity, rather than representing the interests of a diverse group of stakeholders.

CSOs and stakeholder input

One of the most striking elements of TCSO participation in the 10th IDA is the sharp divisions that manifested themselves over the question of continued funding for the IDA. Participants in the process noted these divisions themselves and explained it as a function of differences between environmental, development, and faith-based missions and values, Northern and Southern interests, or the result of organizations' concerns with funding. However, only divisions over mission and over funding correlate with the divides observed in this case.

Funding strategies appear to serve an organization's pre-existing mission and values, rather than determining them. However, it is important to note that consistency in values or mission may also be a form of branding: a public identity shaped for the market of potential funders. The funding environment is highly competitive for all types of organizations, whether they are seeking to win the attention of foundations, the contracts of aid providers, or the loyalty of members. In such an environment, defining and maintaining a clear mission is a necessary part of establishing a value proposition for potential donors. Telling donors the benefits of their donation implicitly requires telling them what they are gaining with one's organization that cannot be gained elsewhere. This is not to say that TCSO staff develop or evolve their organization's mission with money in mind. Instead it seems probable that the perpetual process of applying for grants, bidding for contracts, and advertising for members has an inescapable impact on TCSOs, with their missions being honed and shaped by the need to compete. Thus staff could genuinely seek only that funding reflective of their organization's present mission, yet their actions could still be explained and predicted in terms of financial imperatives, because the public mission which they are using as their compass has itself been adjusted to reflect the donor-influenced characteristics of the funding market.

Even if organizations remain independent in selecting their values and mission, this by no means guarantees their responsiveness to the populations affected by their activism. To the contrary, an organization's focus on a particular mission may lead it to reinterpret the stated desires of a people impacted by a given policy, or even determine such peoples' 'needs' without reference to their stated desires. Although most organizations claim to be acting for the good of certain stakeholders, it may not be a good determined by those stakeholders themselves. This is a crucial distinction because such action, while possibly morally legitimate by some standards, cannot be considered democratic.

Furthermore, if TCSO participation in a given campaign is facilitated by donor funding, money and related organizational imperatives are the proximate cause of TCSO action. Thus, rather than representing a cross-section of stakeholder interests, a campaign will represent a sampling of financial incentives. The role of third-party donors in structuring those incentives may be particularly significant, leading to international campaigns that primarily reflect wealthy populations or funding bodies. In the case of the 10th IDA, policy-makers were given the impression that five prominent TCSOs had each chosen to engage on the issues surrounding the World Bank replenishment. Yet EDF, NWF, the Sierra Club, FoE, and the NRDC arguably did not represent a consensus of five independent actors so much as they represented the agenda of a single entity, the Charles Stewart Mott Foundation, which had carefully selected its agents and incentivized them to work collaboratively.

The democratic credentials of TCSOs

Chapter 2 of this book describes democratic legitimacy as having three parts: input, throughput, and output. Input legitimacy is concerned with the relationship between an actor and its constituencies. What this chapter shows is that identifying such constituencies is not always easy. TCSOs engaged in advocacy generally have a specified, *nominal* constituency. These are the persons on whose behalf they claim to work. At the same time, the data in this chapter indicate that TCSOs also have an *authoritative* constituency. These are the persons to whom the organization is directly reliant for its continued functioning or existence, such as members, funders, and staff. The two groups overlap, but the authoritative group is often smaller than the nominal one.

Academics and practitioners imply (and sometimes explicitly state) that the nominal constituency is authoritative, that is, that international advocacy is initiated by the grassroots and guided by clear signals from the interested stakeholders. The reality can be quite different. As seen, TCSO advocacy can exist primarily in response to organizations' pre-existing missions as determined by staff and, in some cases, members. Decisions to undertake advocacy are also constrained (and occasionally prompted) by financial imperatives, giving donors a particular type of power. The disparity in influence between the nominal and authoritative constituencies challenges the inclusivity of TCSO advocacy. When TCSOs grant disproportionate power to their authoritative constituency in determining organizational agendas, they hinder the development of an open and participatory decision-making process involving all of their nominal members.

These power dynamics also undermine TCSOs' representivity. Individual organizations pursuing pre-determined goals seem likely to ignore or reinterpret local needs. Collectively, TCSO activism on an issue will reflect the financial incentives linked to the campaign. Organizations with financial incentives for their involvement will participate, while those hampered by limited resources may drop out. Neither individual TCSOs nor TCS as a whole can be shown to represent those persons they claim to represent. The lack of representivity and inclusivity directly impugns the input legitimacy of TCS.

In addition, this chapter's findings challenge TCSOs' throughput legitimacy, particularly when looking at TCSOs as a group. TCS may lack any meaningful interorganizational deliberation. If organizations must continually pursue or maintain funding in order to operate, organizations may be unable to engage in significant compromise or collective decision-making. For most environmental advocacy actors involved in the 10th IDA, meaningful compromise with development organizations would have resulted in a violation of the fundamental interests of their donors (e.g. as in the case of Mott-funded CSOs) or their members (e.g. in the case of NWF or NBA). By the same token, for development service delivery organizations, advocating for cuts in World Bank funding had the potential to result in the loss of broader political support for funding for their activities. Respondents for this research were well aware of these tensions, with several indicating that they chose not to engage opposing TCSOs in dialogue because they perceived that the financial interests of their opponents resulted in rigid policy positions. Such dynamics clearly inhibit deliberation or consensus-building around key issues. This is a particular challenge for those theories promoting TCS involvement in global governance as the key to deliberative democracy in transnational decision-making.

The same dynamics that inhibit TCS's ability to produce a consensus position also inhibit majoritarian outcomes. First, financial barriers to involvement in policymaking may limit the cross-section of stakeholders represented. Second, even if a representative group of organizations is present, financial pressures as well as ideological drive may inhibit them from entering into majoritarian or pluralistic decision-making processes. Instead, each organization may use the best means at its disposal to pursue its own interests. Thus, while a particular position or set of voices may seem to dominate TCS advocacy on a given issue, it would be unwise to consider such a position representative of all or even most TCSOs or of their nominal stakeholders.

The previous chapter indicates that some TCSOs were able to significantly impact World Bank policy and operations. This chapter shows that these impacts were achieved in spite of sharp divisions amongst TCSOs and the lack of any overwhelming TCS consensus. This naturally raises the question of how successful TCSOs achieved their impacts and the consequences for democracy. The next chapter explores this issue.

5
Mechanisms of Influence and the Distribution of Authority

This book has thus far identified the TCSOs involved in the IDA-10, determined their impacts, and explored their agenda setting and their interactions with one another. This chapter explores their mechanisms of influence. TCS advocacy has limited the Bank's technocratic independence and forced it to consider certain stakeholder demands in its decision-making. Yet in the IDA-10 engagement, certain TCSOs were noticeably more successful than others in achieving their desired impacts on the World Bank.

As noted in Chapter 2, in order for TCS to achieve democratic legitimacy, it must foster both democratic input and democratic outputs in transnational policymaking. In practical terms, democratic outputs require citizen control over government, while democratic inputs require mechanisms of influence that are equally accessible to all stakeholders. TCS's influence at the Bank suggests a new level of citizen control over a previously technocratic institution. Yet the fact that the small group of anti-IDA activists was more influential than the much larger pro-IDA group suggests that power was unevenly distributed among the TCSOs involved.

This chapter addresses these issues by focusing on two questions. First, how did TCSOs advance their agenda and which of their methods were most successful? Research on civil society advocacy has yielded a number of typologies of influence, yet it seems many claims of influence are more inferred than proven: TCSOs act, their targets take new action, and the activists' recent tactic is assumed to be cause. Sometimes this can be misleading, particularly when activists are eager to declare victory. This chapter therefore seeks to go beyond inference or one-sided claims to establish more reliable evidence of TCS influence and to identify which tactics are, in fact, the most influential.

Second, this chapter asks whether new channels of influence pioneered by successful TCSOs are equally accessible by all the Bank's stakeholders. Breaking down the autonomy of an authoritarian or technocratic institution may be a key step in democratizing it, but if influence over the institution is not distributed in an equitable fashion, autocracy or technocracy may be replaced with aristocracy or plutocracy. Therefore this chapter examines which TCSOs were able to use the most effective mechanisms of influence.

The research finds that while TCSOs used a wide variety of tactics in their attempts to influence World Bank policy, few of them can be shown to have had direct impact on policymakers. During the IDA engagement, the most effective tactic was to apply financial leverage by attacking the Bank's funding. Employing this tactic required a partnership between TCSOs and the Bank's donor states, particularly the US. The tactic was primarily available to a select group of TCSOs with established connections to relevant American policy makers or strong domestic political clout. As a result, access to this channel was restricted to a minority of TCSOs. These TCSOs used the channel primarily in pursuit of their own missions and even played a gatekeeping role in which they excluded competing TCSO voices. The findings suggest that to the extent that TCS power employs partnerships with states, that power may be unequally distributed within TCS.

Enhancing citizen control

From the early 1980s through the period of the 10th IDA, TCSOs engaged with the World Bank in a number of ways that enhanced citizen control. This book divides such engagement into three categories: transparency, accountability, and dialogue.

Improved transparency

The idea that TCSOs exert influence by gathering testimony, disseminating information, or monitoring projects is common in discussions of TCS, but such activities are typically subsumed under a broad label, such as Keck and Sikkink's 'information leverage'. In establishing the impact of mechanisms of influence, however, a more detailed parsing is useful. Data on TCS engagement with the World Bank indicates that information-related activities have taken three main forms: information transfer, information creation, and information liberalization. Because all of these activities expose the Bank's policies and actions to public scrutiny, they are grouped here under the heading of improved transparency. These various types of transparency decrease the autonomy of international organizations by providing outside actors with the information necessary to evaluate, monitor, or direct the actions of international organizations. These activities are by no means mutually exclusive; the same transnational campaign may promote multiple forms of transparency and improved transparency may also overlap with the other types of governance reform discussed later.

Information transfer

Information transfer goes beyond merely publicizing abuses or disseminating information. It is most accurately described as the provision of actionable information to third-party agents with the capacity for influence, such as government representatives or an interested public. This activity contributes to informed decision-making and breaks elite monopolies on information.

In the case of the World Bank, information transfer began in 1983 when American environmental NGOs began opposing certain World Bank projects in Brazil and Indonesia. Their efforts resulted in seventeen US Congressional hearings between 1983 and 1986 on multilateral development banks and the environment (Keck and Sikkink 1998, p. 139). During these hearings the NGOs presented information from independent researchers and local civil society organizations in the project-affected areas. The hearings brought World Bank practices to the attention of both the general public and Congressional decision-makers, laying the groundwork for a series of US-driven environmental reforms at the World Bank. In 1987, the Charles Stewart Mott Foundation and several TCSOs sponsored the creation of the Bank Information Center (BIC) as an independent clearinghouse for information about World Bank activities and a repository for leaked Bank documents (see Keck and Sikkink 1998, pp. 148–149). During the IDA-10, BIC played a key role disseminating information to NGOs and Congressional staffers. TCSOs also testified at three Congressional hearings related to the IDA and information provided by NGOs, including leaked World Bank documents, surfaced in British Parliamentary debate.[1] TCSOs sponsored the full-page advertisements on opposing the Narmada Dam project in the *New York Times* and *Financial Times* and prepared briefing documents for a significant number of the World Bank's executive directors. These actions fomented a combination of public awareness and informed decision-making on the part of public officials that significantly eroded the Bank's independence, enhancing the possibility of citizen control.

Information creation

Information creation expands the amount of data available on international organizations. It can include independent research, monitoring and evaluating the implementation of new policies or projects, and the creation of new reporting requirements. Logically, information creation should precede information transfer. Chronologically, however, most TCSOs have engaged in the business of information creation only after initial successes in information transfer.

As a result of resource constraints, independent research has also been relatively uncommon among TCSOs. American environmental NGOs involved in the IDA-10 were prone to accepting the accounts of local partners at face value or adopting the charges of other American environmentalists as valid and accurate. Nonetheless, TCS engaged in some independent research. The Canadian NGO Probe investigated the World Bank's Narmada Dam project in India, and Probe's findings were used in the advocacy campaigns against the project. Human Rights Watch and the NRDC also published an investigation on logging in Malaysia with implications for World Bank policy.[2]

TCSOs also forced new reporting requirements on the World Bank itself. These requirements mandated that the Bank evaluate and report on the consequences of current or planned actions. These evaluations provided decision-makers with the information necessary to effectively oversee the Bank's activities and provided activists with the information necessary to hold the Bank accountable. One of the earliest examples of this is the Pelosi Amendment, written by Congresswoman Nancy Pelosi in collaboration with representatives of the Sierra Club. Attached to a 1989 funding bill, the amendment mandated that the US executive director automatically vote against any World Bank project for which an environmental impact assessment had not been conducted and released to the board.

Information liberalization

The greatest source of information on the World Bank is often the Bank itself, which authors dozens of reports on its own activities each year. Some of these reports are surprisingly critical and leaked reports have provided some of the strongest substantiation for the charges leveled by civil society. Therefore it is unsurprising that TCSOs have long sought access to this trove of data.

When TCSOs first began lobbying the World Bank, the Bank was so secretive that even its phone book was confidential. Starting in 1989, the Bank began to revise its information policies, largely in response to

NGO pressure (Shihata 1991, pp. 250–274). TCSOs found these revisions to be insufficient and continued lobbying for greater disclosure. In 1993, during the IDA negotiations, the Bank again revised its information policy. According to a senior Bank staff member who helped draft the new policy, the staff team working on the revision found itself split between two factions. One favored a conservative information policy in which only those documents that could be proven necessary to release would be made public. The other faction favored a significantly more liberal policy, very much akin to the American Freedom of Information Act, under which only those documents which it could be proven necessary to restrict would be withheld. The conservative faction won out in team deliberations, but members of the more liberal faction persuaded the team to attach the alternative policy as an appendix to the final proposal submitted to the Bank's board for approval. A member of the team then leaked the report to the civil society community, which lobbied influential executive directors to push for the alternative policy presented in the appendix. This strategy was successful and the liberal policy, unique among international organizations at the time, was adopted.

Accountability

Improved transparency lays the foundation for organizational accountability. Once external actors have sufficient information on an organization's activities, they can move to punish or reward it for the actions it takes. Accountability can be defined thus, as the establishment of consequences for another's actions. In a democratic society it is most often exercised through the vote, by which a wayward or under-performing politician or party is not reelected or loses its majority. Beyond the ballot government actors are held accountable by the rule of law and by the oversight of independent ombudsmen. Similarly, in the case of international institutions, TCS has helped create both public accountability and structural accountability. TCS has also, via government allies, exercised financial accountability. These three levers have increased outside control over international organizations by creating clear consequences for these organizations' actions.

Public accountability

In public accountability, TCSOs exercise influence via attacks on an organization's reputation and legitimacy. During the negotiations surrounding the IDA-10, for instance, the Bank was subject to regular public critique. Provocative demonstrations against the Bank by

Greenpeace and others were a staple of the 50 Years is Enough campaign, which generated ample negative press. In one notable example, a protestor unfurled a banner reading 'World Bank Murderer' behind Bank president Lewis Preston during a speech in Madrid; the moment was captured by the press and created a defining public image (Mallaby 2004, pp. 61–62). Protestors gathered regularly in the park outside the World Bank headquarters in Washington, DC to shout their disapproval. By the mid-1990s, the Bank was receiving thousands of complaint letters each month (Mallaby 2004, p. 87).

In the case of international organizations, however, the effectiveness of such actions is limited by the fact that institutions like the Bank have little statutory need for public legitimacy. Their position is secured by international agreements among national governments which are not easily revoked or abridged. Thus protestors must rely on an organization's concern for its reputation.

A number of Bank staff and civil society activists interviewed for this book opined that the World Bank is very sensitive to criticism and thus susceptible to public pressure tactics. Nonetheless, this form of accountability met with only limited success. There is no clear evidence that such public pressure forced major changes during the IDA-10. Looking more broadly, Fox and Brown conclude from a review of major Bank policy changes from 1980–95 that public pressure is among the least effective means of accountability exercised by civil society (1998a, p. 497). At the same time, discussions with Bank and TCSO staff make clear that the Bank undertook significant charm offensives and public relations initiatives both during and after the IDA-10 to build bridges with TCS and mollify critical elements. These may have been a low-cost alternative to more substantive policy reform. Public pressure is dramatic and is perhaps reputation-building for TCSOs. However, because of the lack of public authority and the possibility of defending an organization's reputation without real change, it constitutes a weak form of accountability.

Financial accountability

When an international organization is reliant on regular infusions of cash from donor nations, TCSOs can pressure donors, often using local political channels, to withhold funding or to conditionalize its disbursement upon organizational actions. In cases where those infusions are perceived to be essential to the completion of a core mission or to the long-term survival of the organization, such tactics can be extremely effective.

This is exactly what happened in the IDA-10. Beginning in the late 1980s, a number of TCSOs concluded that financial pressure was the one type of accountability to which the Bank readily responded. Their attack on Bank funds during the tenth replenishment was instrumental to the success of numerous reforms, including the liberalization of Bank information policy. The initial reductions made by the US Congress in the American IDA commitment, combined with hold-backs, conditions, and additional cuts, led to rapid concessions from the Bank. Financial pressure also had an impact on individual Bank projects. TCSO pressure was linked to the Japanese withdrawal from the Narmada Dam project in India and to other, smaller changes in the bilateral aid often given in conjunction with Bank projects.

Structural accountability

Certain TCSOs used the IDA-10 to push for the creation of an independent monitor, funded by the World Bank itself, capable of judging organizational actions, identifying breaches in ethics or policy, and detailing appropriate remediation. Where such monitors are sufficiently independent and endowed with a reasonable ability to enforce their decisions, they can provide the kind of checks and balances provided by independent agencies in many democratic governments (Scholte 2004, pp. 221–222).

In 1992, the World Bank created an ad hoc inspection group to investigate claims that the Bank had violated its own environmental and social policies in planning the Narmada Dam project in India. The Morse Commission's highly critical findings, described in Chapter 3, helped energize the nascent proposal then being discussed between TCSOs and American policymakers to encourage the Bank to create an independent ombudsman. The Inspection Panel, created in 1994, formed a means for direct citizen appeals against the Bank. The Inspection Panel guidelines allow any group of two or more citizens living in an area affected by a planned or current Bank project to file a claim with the panel. The panel will review the claim and, if it deems it valid, request permission from the Bank's board to conduct a full-scale investigation. Although the panel can evaluate only the Bank's adherence to its own policies, the proliferation of environmental and social safeguards, particularly in response to TCS pressure in the late 1980s, has meant that the Bank's policies, at least 'on the book', are very stakeholder-friendly. The history of Inspection Panel appeals indicates that it has been effective at increasing outside control over the Bank.

Dialogue

Deliberative democracy theorists in particular hold that dialogue is an essential element of democracy. Many scholars, particularly cosmopolitan theorists, have suggested that civil society currently contributes to such dialogue or may so contribute in the future (Held 2004, 2006; Korten 1998; Nanz and Steffek 2004). Such discussions vary in their focus, emphasizing either inter-CSO dialogue or stakeholder-international organization dialogue. As noted in Chapter 4, inter-CSO dialogue was uncommon during the IDA-10 and research indicates that even in recent times, truly inclusive dialogue among TCSOs is quite rare (Nelson 2000; Murphy 2005; Woods 2005; Scholte et al 2009). Therefore this book focuses on the second category of interaction: dialogue between stakeholders and institutions.

TCS has helped create two types of dialogues between stakeholders and international institutions: project consultations and policy consultations. Both of these have been used by civil society actors engaging with the World Bank. Such dialogues may force disparate organizations to develop compromise positions, but more importantly they allow direct citizen input into the activities of international institutions. Like accountability, successful dialogue relies on TCS's accomplishments in building transparency. Detailed information can make citizens critical and independent participants and keep dialogues from rubber-stamping institution proposals. Unlike the Inspection Panel, ombudsmen, or other forms of accountability, dialogue can, in principle, permit citizens input into planning processes, allowing stakeholders to actively guide future organizational actions rather than just reacting to punish past errors.

Project consultations

Project consultations occur in international organizations that undertake discrete projects. At the World Bank, project consultations began in the early 1980s in response to data gathered by practitioners and social scientists indicating that development projects could be made more effective if the stakeholders who were supposed to benefit from any given project were consulted on its design and implementation (see Long 2001). Local stakeholders were deemed to be better informed about their own needs and conditions than outside development agents and the process of consultation was also expected to increase citizen ownership over any given project (Long 2001; cf. Clark 1991).

The World Bank created the NGO-World Bank Committee in 1982 in part in response to staff interest in popular participation as a development tool. Such interest was limited, however, and other members of staff sought to co-opt NGOs as allies in defending the Bank's budget (Covey 1998). However, there were some notable dialogues, including discussions between World Bank staff and members of Arch-Vahini, an Indian NGO, and Oxfam-UK in the late 1980s. These discussions, regarding the resettlement of tribal peoples in Gujarat to be affected by the Narmada project, resulted in drastic improvements in the terms of their resettlement (Patel 1995, pp. 185–187).

Around 1990, the Bank began sponsoring more poverty-targeted interventions (PTIs), projects aimed at improving specific social indicators like poverty or infant mortality, rather than general economic development. The move towards PTIs necessitated the hiring of more non-economist social scientists (or 'nessies' as they were known) who believed in the value of local civil society as a development tool (see Kapur et al 1997, pp. 373–375; cf. Ibrahim 1998). This shift arrived concurrently with a push by InterAction and other development actors to increase popular participation in Bank projects. This pressure, begun just before the IDA-10 and continuing through the IDA negotiations, helped make popular participation a standard and expected part of most subsequent Bank projects.[3]

Policy consultations

Policy consultations refer to dialogues between institutions and stakeholders on issues of broader organizational policy. This is potentially a more powerful aid to democratization insofar as it can have more wide-reaching effects than discussions limited to a single, geographically isolated project. Although the Bank generally resisted policy input from the NGO-World Bank Committee during the 1980s, in 1990 the Bank formed the Learning Group on Participatory Development with civil society leaders to discuss the future of popular participation in Bank projects (Long 2001, p. 27). This helped feed into the evolution in popular participation policy mentioned above. In the late 1980s, Bank President Barber Conable also consulted with US environmental NGOs about environmental reforms at the Bank. In September 1992, during the 10th IDA, the Bank hosted six civil society leaders from developing countries in a meeting with donor representatives to discuss the replenishment of the 10th IDA.

These examples, however, highlight two of the challenges of policy dialogue. The first is that the Bank only seemed to invite TCSOs into dialogue when there already existed significant interest within the

Bank in a policy change. Thus dialogue could help expand or shape a policy, as in the area of popular participation, but it was not an instrument of creating new policy. Second, the Bank's location in Washington, DC created a barrier to access for organizations in other countries, particularly those from developing nations. The meeting between Bank staff, IDA deputies, and Southern CSOs arose largely out of deputy concerns that Washington-based NGOs did not represent an accurate cross-section of civil society.

The distribution of authority

Although each of the aforementioned mechanisms created a means of potentially enhancing stakeholder control over the World Bank, such authority was not equally distributed among stakeholders prior to and during the IDA-10. The most effective mechanisms relied on assistance from donor governments or even the Bank itself. Among the means of transparency improvement, information liberalization relied on government pressure, as did the more notable forms of information creation, particularly the Pelosi Amendment. Even information transfer was most useful when the information was being transferred to public officials with some form of authority over the Bank. Likewise, the only form of accountability not requiring third-party assistance, public accountability, was the weakest form. Financial accountability required donor action and institutional accountability required a combination of donor pressure and Bank consent. Dialogue too, while sometimes prompted by public accountability campaigns, occurred largely at the Bank's initiative or in response to donor pressure.

As a result of these trends, power was concentrated among those TCSOs with the greatest degree of support from donor governments for Bank engagement. Because government policy toward the Bank was shaped by political processes, power redounded to those actors with the greatest domestic political clout. This was particularly true in the United States which, uniquely among Bank donors, had a two-part funding process in which any funding agreement negotiated by the executive was subject to review and revision by the legislature.

The victories achieved by TCS early in the IDA-10 process, prior to the schism over the Narmada Dam, resulted largely from a combination of Bank acquiescence and government inclination. According to a Bank staffer familiar with these issues, in some areas such as increased popular participation or debt relief the Bank had already been considering action prior to the start of negotiations and so conceded willingly to demands for policy change. In other areas, like poverty reduction or the consideration of gender in development, donor governments had adopted the TCS positions before the start of the negotiations. Such adoption reflected professional decisions by donor government staff rather than a reluctant response to TCS pressure. In particular, the US Treasury staff responsible for developing Treasury policy toward the World Bank were themselves experts on the policy issues being addressed and they created their own reform agenda based on their assessment of the Bank's performance.

The remainder of the TCS successes, particularly the funding cuts, information liberalization, and structural accountability were achieved by the anti-IDA faction after the Narmada schism. These successes are more directly attributable to TCS influence, but they reflect the efforts of a handful of TCSOs that used their domestic political clout to persuade US lawmakers to apply pressure to the World Bank.

Triangulating the Bank

As noted in Chapter 3, the World Bank's decision to continue funding the Narmada Dam project galvanized Bank skeptics. Although the Bank had made substantial concessions in the areas of development practice and environmental policy during the IDA-10 negotiations, the Bank's continued support for the project signaled to certain TCSOs that the Bank still fundamentally supported environmentally destructive, industrially-oriented projects that focused on macroeconomic development to the detriment of individuals. These groups included the Environmental Defense Fund, National Wildlife Federation, and Friends of the Earth, as well as the Sierra Club and the Natural Resources Defense Council. Greenpeace, Rainforest Action Network, and others played smaller roles.

By this point in late 1992, the IDA deputies had already negotiated a preliminary agreement. To all appearances, this document reflected a substantial 'win' for TCSOs. It included an emphasis on poverty reduction, mitigation for the impacts of structural adjustment, and popular participation. It also featured substantial increases in environmental protection, including requirements for new environmental assessments, a ban on IDA funding for rainforest logging, and an emphasis on energy conservation.[4] Consensus among respondents for this research, including both environmentalists and development advocates, was that TCSOs had gotten nearly everything for which they initially asked. With few grounds on which to press for a renegotiation of the agreement, Bank-skeptics took their case directly to donor governments.

Leaving aside the international negotiations, the new anti-IDA coalition worked at the national level to press donor governments to refuse to fund the agreement negotiated by those governments' deputies. The coalition's success in most cases was extremely limited. In most cases, parliamentary governments seemed unwilling to inflict a political defeat upon themselves by overruling the recommendations of their own negotiators. Finland opted to withdraw funding from the IDA, but the Finnish contribution was only a small fraction of the whole. In the UK, the issue was debated in Parliament, but to no effect.

In the US, however, the situation was different. IDA negotiations had been carried out by the US Treasury, an arm of the executive branch. Funding had to be approved by Congress, a separate, legislative branch. For a significant portion of the IDA-10 replenishment round, these branches were controlled by different political parties, adding to their Constitutional division.[5] Moreover, Congress had a history of using its fiduciary power to intervene directly in Bank affairs, in spite of the Bank's own mandate to deal only with the finance ministries of its member countries. In 1979, Congress used its control over IDA funding to successfully pressure the Bank to commit not to fund projects in Vietnam (Kapur et al 1997, p. 1150). In the 1980s, the US Congress was instrumental in the Bank's environmental reform. Bank President A. W. Clausen even agreed to meet directly with Senator Robert Kasten, Jr. and the environmental NGOs with whom he had allied himself in order to negotiate concessions. Bank staff resisted such interactions, believing that they violated the Articles of Agreement on which the Bank was founded, but they continued nonetheless (Wade 1997, p. 665).

Some of the same actors who had worked on the environmental reforms, including Bruce Rich of EDF, Brent Blackwelder of FoE, and Barbara Bramble of the NWF, were leaders in the anti-IDA campaign. According to a source at FoE, their experiences in the 1980s had led them to believe that genuine Bank reform could only result from financial pressure. Through years of lobbying they had also developed significant expertise at lobbying Congress and solid networks of contacts. As the IDA-10 agreement moved towards donor ratification, these leaders moved to attack the IDA at the level of Congressional funding. Thus pressure would flow from these organizations to Congress and then to the Bank.

Limiting competition

The shift in venue to the United States had the effect of excluding most non-US TCSOs from participating in the final stage of the IDA process. With the exception of FAVDO, which had been provided office space by InterAction, most non-US TCSOs with an interest in the IDA lacked a permanent presence in Washington, DC. Not only did they lack the staff and facilities necessary to lobby Congress in a sustained way, but their lack of presence deprived them of much of the necessary expertise and contacts. When asked how Oxfam-UK and other non-US development organizations participated in the IDA process once it moved to the US, a source who had worked for Oxfam at the time said simply, 'We didn't'.

The absence of most non-US TCSOs changed the demographics of the group facing Congress. Most developing country organizations involved in the IDA were in favor of full replenishment, but now their voices were largely absent. Other respected and venerable actors from donor countries, like Oxfam-UK and NOVIB, also withdrew from participation. Pro-IDA organizations had originally outnumbered anti-IDA organizations five to one; now the ratio of pro- and anti-replenishment TCSOs engaging with Congress was roughly one to one.

Building on experience

The core group of anti-replenishment campaigners had significant experience in Washington, DC. Lori Udall of the Environmental Defense Fund came from a political family: Morris Udall served fourteen terms in the House of Representatives and Stewart Udall had been Secretary of the Interior under President Kennedy. Other members of the family held prominent political positions at the state level. At least one informant for this research noted that Udall's family history had given her significant expertise in Washington.

Rich, Bramble, and Blackwelder had been lobbying Congress since the mid-1980s and had cultivated noteworthy political ties. Representative Barney Frank, who chaired the House subcommittee responsible for authorizing Bank funding, was among their supporters. In late 1992, before Frank had even been appointed to head the subcommittee, the Bank Information Center contacted him on behalf of the Working Group on Appointments to the International Financial Institutions, an ad hoc group composed almost exclusively of US environmental NGOs[6] to begin planning work on 'on issues relating to multilateral development banks'.[7]

Access and gatekeeping

By mid-January, BIC had arranged the first of a series of meetings with Frank. BIC described these meetings as discussions between the Congressman and 'Washington NGOs'. BIC's initial list of invitations, however, featured fourteen environmental CSOs and only three development organizations.[8] Not all of the organizations invited were involved in the IDA-10, but among those that were, opponents of the replenishment outnumbered supporters five to three. At the actual meeting, only two of the thirteen organizations present were development organizations,[9] and staff from organizations opposing the replenishment outnumbered staff from supporters seven to two.[10]

Frank responded enthusiastically to the January discussion and requested that TCSOs submit a list of issues they wanted to 'discuss at Hearings'. The compilation of the list was again organized by BIC, which contacted nearly the same mix of environmental and development organizations asking them to contribute.[11] On February 3rd, BIC presented to Frank 'a list of issues NGOs would like to see discussed at Congressional hearings'. The top priority was the IDA-10 replenishment, with specific reference to the Narmada Dam project, the Wapenhans Report, the 'need for an independent appeals mechanism' and 'better implementation of environmental safeguards'. The second priority was 'Environmental and Social Impacts of IBRD Lending', including environmental impact, popular participation and information policy, 'sustainable forest management', 'Indigenous People's Policy', and resettlement.[12] In March, even before he had held public hearings on the Bank, Frank invited civil society organizations to meet with him to 'prepare a legislative options paper'.[13] Again BIC facilitated the meeting and chose the participants.

Anti-IDA NGOs enjoyed access at other levels, sometimes through BIC and at other times on their own. BIC developed a relationship with the staff advising representatives and senators on multilateral development bank issues and invited some to the Early Warning meetings, a monthly dialogue between USAID, Treasury, and US NGOs on the MDBs, that the Sierra Club had helped establish and which BIC now co-chaired.[14] The anti-IDA campaigners also arranged a meeting with Representative Bill Orten, another member of Frank's subcommittee. These same NGOs had substantial access to US Executive Director Pat Coady who, although not directly involved in the IDA legislation, was still the major US voice at the World Bank.

Among pro-replenishment organizations, only the World Wildlife Fund seemed to enjoy similar contact with US legislators. After Representative David Obey, a Bank supporter, held his own hearings on the World Bank in March, WWF corresponded with him to press the case for continued IDA funding and to explicitly dissent from the views of the US environmental organizations that had testified before Obey's subcommittee.[15] However, there is no evidence of other pro-IDA organizations taking similar steps or gaining direct, independent access to policymakers during the Congressional discussion of the replenishment.

In short, close relationships between environmental actors and politicians allowed environmentalists to filter participation in meetings between members of Congress and members of TCS in such a way that the environmental viewpoint was vastly over-represented. Among US environmental NGOs, only the World Wildlife Fund was an active supporter of full IDA replenishment, whereas the others were either opposed or neutral. Although some development organizations that supported the IDA were also invited, the result was that opponents of the IDA consistently outnumbered its supporters. Ultimately, the hearings set to discuss the IDA, particularly those chaired by Frank, reflected closely the agenda of the anti-IDA faction.

Setting the record

Between March and June 1993, Congress held three hearings on World Bank funding. Two were held in the House of Representatives and one in the Senate. Representatives of the EDF, NWF, FoE, and the Sierra Club testified at all three hearings. No pro-IDA actor was represented at all three of the hearings. InterAction testified at two, including once via a surrogate from FAVDO. Church World Service, Bread for the World, and the WWF each testified once. No other pro-IDA organizations testified in person.[16]

The anti-Bank actors used their predominance to depict themselves as the legitimate representatives of developing world stakeholders. FoE submitted a statement to Congress declaring that 'grassroots groups in the Third World' had chosen as their Northern counterparts 'not traditional development NGOs, but environmental and indigenous rights groups'.[17] Lori Udall of EDF submitted statements from NBA to support her claim to work on behalf of grassroots groups.[18] Barbara Bramble testified that opposition to Bank activities 'is an extremely broadly based problem ... brought to us by the affected people'. She claimed that NWF had 'consulted with hundreds of partner organizations in the south ... that have asked us year after year, Why aren't you taking a stand on this?'.[19] By the end of his hearing on the IDA, Barney Frank was asking Bramble, 'What is the Asians' position on the utility of the IDA, and why do they have that position?'[20]

Domestic politics

As Congress began deliberations on Bank funding, TCS opponents of the replenishment used local political pressure to advance their agenda. The Sierra Club had significant DC clout due to its political action committee and close ties to many members of Congress. NWF also had a huge grassroots base, the largest of any organization participating. Its base was organized into local chapters with a track record of successfully lobbying their senators and representatives. A source at NWF indicates that this gave NWF considerable influence.

EDF and FoE developed a populist anti-Bank message. During the IDA-10, the World Bank was in the process of building a new Washington, DC headquarters. Staff from anti-Bank organizations circulated details of the project's $250 million budget and terrazzo floors to legislators.[21] These revelations coincided with Jacques Attali's disastrous tenure at the European Bank for Reconstruction and Development, during which staff flew in private aircraft, the existing marble in the headquarters lobby was torn out and replaced with a more luxurious grade of marble, and $78,000 was spent on the staff Christmas party. The new building at the World Bank was easily conflated with the EBRD's needless renovations and general profligacy, and raised the ire of many members of Congress.

This tactic was extremely successful in developing Congressional opposition to World Bank funding. Although it did not immediately result in a backlash against the IDA, it did result in other attacks against Bank funding. Concurrent with the IDA replenishment, the World Bank had also negotiated capital contributions for the IBRD, which lent to middle-income countries. When the Foreign Operations appropriations bill, which included the IBRD and IDA funding, was introduced on the House floor in June 1993, Representative John Kasich offered an amendment calling for a complete cancellation of US funding for the IBRD in fiscal year 1994. Kasich and his allies made specific reference to statements by EDF, NWF, FoE, and the Sierra Club on the Bank's record of environmental destruction and forced resettlement, and also referenced the cost of the Bank's new building. His amendment was opposed by both Barney Frank and David Obey, but garnered significant support among House members; it was defeated 210 to 216.

Final outcomes

In the United States, Congressional spending decisions must pass through two phases. First, the expense must be authorized, with the government agency responsible for the actual disbursement, such as the US Treasury or USAID, being given permission to spend the money. Second, money must be appropriated for the expense, usually in the budget of the upcoming fiscal year. David Obey's subcommittee, which was responsible for World Bank-related appropriations, yielded to anti-Bank sentiment by cutting the IDA appropriation for fiscal year 1994 by $200 million. Barney Frank's subcommittee, which was responsible for authorizations, authorized only two-thirds of the remaining IDA amount, holding back the third tranche pending reform. This was a major break from previous US practice, in which authorization had always been made for the full three-year IDA period. It was hotly resisted by the US Treasury, the agency which was being authorized to disburse the money to the Bank. In the Congressional elections of 1994, the Democrats lost control of the House of Representatives. Republican politicians, with whom the anti-IDA environmentalists had consistently cultivated ties (Kasten and Kasich were both Republicans), initiated further cuts in the IDA disbursement.

Frank also played a key role in advancing the two major policy initiatives that the Bank skeptics had added to the agenda. As noted, most of the initial reforms requested by IDA campaigners had been included in the IDA agreement. However, following the Bank's Narmada decision, the EDF, NWF, FoE, the Sierra Club and their allies had determined that the Bank was in need of more serious reform. In addition to the Bank-shrinking exercise of cutting funding, these NGOs pressed for the creation of an independent appeals mechanism at the Bank, along with a huge increase in information access. According to sources familiar with these events, they believed that these reforms would help consolidate previous gains, particularly improvements in the Bank's environmental and social safeguards.

These changes were strongly resisted by the Bank, as well as most of the Bank's borrowers. However, Frank insisted that the Bank make commitments to change before he permitted the authorization of any of the IDA funding. In the summer of 1993, in violation of the Bank's standard policy of engaging only with the treasury administrations of member governments, Ernie Stern telephoned Frank to contest the Congressman's position. Stern was the Bank's long-time managing director and, having outlasted several presidents, was possibly the most powerful person at the Bank. During the conversation, which Frank shared with the anti-IDA environmentalists and which became widely cited in the community, Stern protested that the reforms Frank had requested were too difficult to implement in the time Frank had allowed. The Bank was like a large boat, Stern said, taking time to change course. Frank responded that he was faced with a busy legislative session and that if Stern was too busy to make the necessary changes at the Bank, Frank might find himself too busy to authorize the Bank's money. By the end of 1993, changes in the information policy and the creation of what would become the World Bank Inspection Panel were well underway.

Democratization delayed

In its engagement with the World Bank in the decade leading up to the 10th IDA and during the IDA itself, TCS created or reinforced a number of channels of stakeholder influence that made significant contributions toward citizen control of global governance. TCS activism helped improve knowledge about the Bank's activities and created new norms for transparency, accountability and dialogue. Its actions resulted in some specific reforms, such as the liberalization of World Bank information disclosure or the creation of the Bank's Inspection Panel, which facilitated future activism or gave stakeholders guaranteed access to key policymakers. These new norms, policies, and structures served to empower stakeholders and increase their authority in Bank decisions.

However, the biggest changes in Bank policy relied on government influence. The broad reform agenda, focusing on participation, poverty-targeted interventions, and structural adjustment, and which was widely embraced by TCSOs early in the IDA process, succeeded because it was supported by the IDA deputies of powerful donor nations. Later reforms, including information liberalization and creation of the World Bank Inspection Panel, resulted directly from US influence. Cuts in the Bank's funding also resulted from donor decisions.

This use of national power meant that TCS influence mirrored the power imbalances among the Bank's member nations, rather than correcting those imbalances. TCSOs exploited the dominance of powerful actors. The use of state power, in turn, facilitated imbalances within TCS. Those organizations with the strongest national connections had a significant advantage in advancing their agendas, whereas those without a strong presence in the relevant donor countries were effectively excluded from deliberation.

Playing to win

TCSOs were more than willing to use their advantages in undemocratic ways. The NGOs lobbying for cuts in the Bank's funding, as well as informational liberalization and the creation of the Inspection Panel, exploited insider access to key US policymakers. The Bank Information Center acted as a strategic gatekeeper, filling meetings with a disproportionate number of anti-IDA TCSOs. It also vastly favored environmental organizations over development organizations.

As a result of these early connections and efforts, Bank skeptics enjoyed a significantly more prominent role in Congressional hearings than IDA supporters. Once present, the Bank skeptics depicted their positions as representing the majority of TCS and the majority of stakeholders, despite the fact that the former was untrue and the later unverifiable. They encouraged lawmakers to accept their statements by emphasizing their domestic political influence and exploiting populist grievances with little relation to the IDA itself. They succeeded in gaining cuts in Bank funding that were anathema to most other TCSOs involved in the process and used the Bank's resulting vulnerability to push through policy reforms designed largely to support their environmental agenda.

The consequences of undemocratic mechanisms were magnified by a lack of internal democracy, or even much dialogue, within TCS. Each TCSO or ad hoc alliance pursued its goals individualistically. Political access and influence created the ability to achieve policy impacts without generating overwhelming support within TCS. This seems to have created a disincentive towards dialogue or coalition building; why engage in the inevitable compromises of building a broad coalition when one could achieve one's agenda without it? The new channels of citizen control over the Bank were thus dominated by a select group of powerful TCSOs.

The role of the state

Of particular relevance in this regard is the role of state influence. The data indicate that some of TCS's most powerful mechanisms of influence, including financial accountability, required the assistance of powerful states. This enhanced the power of TCSOs with strong connections to those states. In the case of the IDA-10, once US Congress became the most significant venue of debate, policymaking was dominated by those organizations with existing ties to Washington legislators, experience with US legislation, and domestic political influence. This advantage was further magnified by the architecture of the Bank itself, which gave certain states, namely Bank donors, significantly more power than borrowers.

The importance of state influence suggests that international policy-making is not a bilateral duel between civil society and international institutions, fought wholly in the realm of public opinion and new norms. Rather, states continue to have significant influence over international institutions, sometimes exercised in very material ways, such as financial pressure.[22] At the same time, TCSOs are more than just the tools of states. Through their access to information, domestic political connections, and ties to key policymakers, TCSOs can influence state behavior in line with an independently formulated agenda. The data at the Bank thus supports combining constructivist and realist thinking on TCS and global governance in a way that reflects both TCS' ability to independently propagate norms and the state's enduring role as the codifier and implementer of such norms. The fact that TCS can act via the state, often through domestic political activity, also suggests that the modeling of international policymaking (including TCS's place therein) should be multi-layer. Similar to Putnam's (1988) model of two-level games in international relations, it should consider both domestic and international dynamics and the connections between the two.

In terms of the larger question of democratization, TCS's collective contributions to Bank policymaking were, interestingly, both democratizing and anti-democratic. As argued in Chapter 2, TCS is an authority in international policymaking and thus must be judged on both its inputs and its outputs. The data in this chapter indicate that TCS has some genuine independence and agency. Thus, insofar as TCSOs can be assumed to represent at least some stakeholders, their impacts at the Bank indicate the creation of a new, independent mechanism of stakeholder input. Moreover, TCSOs created new means of stakeholder control over the World Bank through promoting new policies of transparency, accountability, and dialogue. The net impact was broadly enhanced stakeholder control over the institution. These results may be considered democratic outputs.[23]

At the same time, TCS advocacy seems to have exacerbated the inequality among the Bank's stakeholders by concentrating power in the hands of a minority of TCSOs, many of which seem closely connected to the populations of wealthy, powerful states. Because the net impact of TCS is not improved stakeholder inclusion or equal representation in Bank policymaking, it cannot be said to enhance democratic input. Indeed, it may worsen it. This finding casts doubt on TCS's capacity to democratize the World Bank. The next chapter explores the idea of input further by examining TCS's impact on local representation.

6
Transnational Civil Society and Local Representation

At this point in the discussion it is necessary to consider in more detail the impact of TCS on the role and influence of state governments in Bank policymaking. There are several reasons for this. As noted in the previous chapter, the data demonstrate that states continue to play an important role in Bank policymaking. Also, the preceding chapters indicate that TCS as a whole is not a democratic representative of many of its stakeholders due to the unequal distribution of authority among TCSOs. Lastly, many TCSOs are unaccountable to their claimed stakeholders and likely to pursue agendas defined by their own pre-existing mission and interests.

Governments form an important avenue of representation for their citizens in international policymaking. This is particularly true for democratic governments, insofar as they have some measure of accountability to the national population. Democracy, as noted throughout this book, requires equal citizen authority or value expressed via some representative mechanism and resulting in institutional responsiveness to the will of the majority. Therefore the impact of TCS on governments' ability to act as representatives of their citizens has direct impact on whether civil society engagement with the World Bank indicates a capacity to democratize global governance.

This chapter investigates the relationship between TCS and the governments of the World Bank's member states. It focuses in particular on the relationship between CSOs and borrower country governments because, as noted in Chapter 1, the Bank's democratic deficit results primarily from the under-representation of the interests of citizens from these poorer states. It finds that data from the IDA-10 reveal a direct conflict between many TCSOs and the governments of many Bank borrower nations. During the IDA, claims by TCSOs to represent the interests of borrower state populations constituted a challenge to the traditional state role as representative of its citizens, particularly when TCSO claims about the needs or desires of state populations conflicted with the claims of state governments. In addition, several Northern TCSOs directly contested the right of borrower states to represent their own citizens. They challenged the representivity of certain states and often acted to undermine the influence of developing country governments in international policymaking. TCSO claims to representivity were unverifiable, and did not seem to be improved by partnerships between Northern TCSOs and Southern TCSOs. The net impact of TCS advocacy was to diminish opportunities for stakeholder representation via government structures, without replacing this channel with a more accessible or democratic one.

This chapter also illustrates one of the hypotheses advanced in Chapter 2, that TCS intervention in domestic policymaking risks undermining local democracy. This risk is particularly great in developing nations. Many of the most influential TCSOs are headquartered in the global North and are not subject to the local laws or regulations of developing countries, except perhaps for those actions taking place within those countries' borders. As seen in Chapter 4, the connections of TCSOs to populations outside their membership or funding base may also be tenuous. Moreover, TCSOs may seek to privilege those portions of the local population that support the organizations' international agenda. To the extent that such interventions may overturn decisions made by democratic governments, they undermine the function of the local democratic system and impinge upon the representation of the majority of citizens. In investigating the interactions between TCSOs and governments, this chapter also examines the domestic ramifications of TCS activism.

Contesting state authority

During the IDA-10, TCSOs' capacity to contest borrower authority arose from several sources. One source was structural. The architecture of the Bank empowered donor nations while granting borrowers only marginal power and input. As a result, TCSOs with access and influence in donor governments enjoyed significantly more power than those tied to borrower governments. Second, TCSOs encouraged the proliferation of loan conditionalities that enhanced the Bank's power vis-à-vis its borrowers. These conditionalities also had the effect of magnifying the power of donor states and affiliated TCSOs. Third,

TCSOs from the global North directly contested the legitimacy of borrower governments, seeking to undermine their credibility in international fora. Fourth, TCSOs promoted the development of structural changes that formalized the authority of TCSOs to challenge donor government policies and practices.

Authority and structure at the World Bank

The World Bank has a board of twenty-four executive directors, but over 150 member countries. Representation is assigned to members primarily on the basis of the number of shares a country holds of the Bank's capital stock. In 1990, the US had a 15.1 per cent voting share in the International Bank for Reconstruction and Development and a 17.2 per cent voting share in the International Development Association (Gwin 1994, p. 55). For the case studied in this book, the IBRD board was responsible for ratifying changes in overall Bank policy, such as information liberalization, whereas the IDA board was responsible for IDA-specific decisions, such as the suspension of the Narmada Dam project. However, the boards have the same structure, and countries that are members of both the IBRD and the IDA are represented by the same executive director on both boards. Therefore the difference between the two in terms of political pressures and policy-making dynamics is marginal, and Bank staff generally refer to a single entity, 'the board', when describing administrative decisions and their impacts. This book follows that model.

As a result of the voting share system, donor countries have hugely disproportionate power in Bank decision-making. During the Bank's 1996 fiscal year (1 July 1995–30 June 1996), which marked the close of the IDA-10 period, the US, Japan, Germany, France, and the UK were the Bank's most powerful members. Together they controlled 35 per cent of the board vote on IBRD decisions and 42 per cent on matters pertaining to the IDA.[2]

Donors also had a disproportionate voice in board discussions. Each of the five major donors appointed their own executive director to the board. In contrast, the next most powerful executive director (Walter Rill of Austria), had to balance the interests of ten countries, all of whom together commanded only 5 per cent of the IBRD vote (and 4.3 per cent of the IDA). Bangladesh, Bhutan, India, and Sri Lanka all shared a director and just 3.6 per cent of the IBRD vote. Benin, Burkina Faso, Cameroon, Cape Verde, Central African Republic, Chad, Comoros, Congo, Côte d'Ivoire, Djibouti, Equatorial Guinea, Gabon, Guinea-Bissau, Madagascar, Mali, Mauritania, Mauritius, Niger,

Rwanda, São Tomé and Principe, Senegal, Togo, and the Democratic Republic of Congo (then called Zaire), also shared just a single voice on the board. In fiscal year 1996, only five of the twenty-four directors themselves came from countries poor enough to be eligible for IDA funds.[3] In short, borrowing countries had both limited power and limited opportunities for input.

This situation was magnified in the IDA negotiations themselves. In 1992–93, only donors to the IDA were permitted to participate in the negotiations.[4] Participants included nineteen European countries, plus South Africa, Brazil, Mexico, Saudi Arabia, Korea, Kuwait, and Turkey. Of these, only Korea and Turkey had ever been IDA-eligible, and they had graduated from the program in 1973. None of the participants in the negotiations would themselves be subject to the IDA rules they were writing, because they would never (or never again) qualify for IDA loans.[5]

Multiplying conditionalities

Whatever marginal power developing countries enjoyed they exercised at the project level. Bank projects were collaborative efforts between Bank staff and country governments. While Bank staff sometimes ran the show, many projects genuinely originated with developing country governments and responded to government-identified needs. Country influence was potentially enhanced by the professional aspirations of Bank staff who, as the 1992 Wapenhans Report revealed, felt that career success rested on making large loans. Favorable relations with borrowers made it easier to suggest new projects and develop further borrowing.

Multiplying conditionalities, however, restricted staff's technocratic freedom and narrowed the autonomy of borrower governments even in planning their own projects. Particularly during the era of structural adjustment, beginning in the early 1980s, borrowers were required to cut government spending, remove trade barriers, or make other economic changes in exchange for loans. By the late 1980s and early 1990s, borrowers were also required to conduct environmental assessments, limit resettlement, or earmark funds for social services. Structural adjustment limited governments' spending options, forced the privatization of national industries and was widely blamed for increases in poverty. The environmental reforms advanced by US and European campaigners inhibited borrowers' freedom to calculate their own trade-offs between the environment and development. These limitations were viewed by many Southerners as hypocritical given the ways Northern states had exploited the environment to facilitate their own development.

Outside of their frequent critique of structural adjustment, many TCSOs encouraged the proliferation of conditionalities. Environmental efforts were the most noticeable, but the IDA agreement included specific earmarks for anti-poverty spending designed to determine how borrowers used Bank funds. David Reed, director of the WWF's International Institutions Policy Program, argued that 'we cannot pass a country through a filter and see [if] it is democratic or not ... but we can assure that the benefits go to the sector that needs it most'.[6]

Certainly some conditionalities may have been beneficial to certain stakeholder populations. Bank social safeguards, for instance, sought to limit the ability of borrowers to ignore the rights of minorities or to forcibly resettle restive populations.[7] Regardless of their ultimate impact on the ground, however, the increasing number of conditionalities sent a clear signal to the Bank's staff: the Bank's future would depend on pleasing donors, not cultivating borrowers.

Southern governments and the IDA-10

Not surprisingly, most borrower countries opposed the various conditionalities imposed via the initial IDA-10 agreement, as well as subsequent lobbying on information disclosure and the Inspection Panel. Environmental conditionalities were a contentious issue even prior to the start of the IDA-10 negotiations. In discussions at the Earth Summit in Rio in June of 1992, developed nations raised the idea of making aid contingent on environmental preservation. As, Kamal Nath, India's minister of environment and forests recounted (Robinson 1992):

> They [developed countries] say, 'Yes, we are the major polluters, so we must pay. But now that we pay, we must dictate also' ... That is the ridiculousness of it. I don't think you can shove the environment down anybody's throat.

Jessica Ocaya-Lakidi, permanent secretary at the Ugandan environment ministry, echoed that sentiment, noting that, 'We don't yet have the big industries. We are lagging so far behind that we don't talk of industrial pollution. Finance is the most important thing to us' (Robinson 1992).

Northern TCSOs were perceived by many Southern governments to be fomenting North-South tension. Environmental campaigners themselves acknowledged that their priorities were not necessarily shared by the governments which would be impacted by environmental reform (Crossette 1992a). However, they were quick to depict Southern governments as autocratic and unrepresentative, illegitimate regimes whose will could be easily dismissed (Crossette 1992b). Thus it was unsurprising that India, when faced with the civil society-driven cancellation of the Narmada Dam project 'viewed the criticism by environmentalists as an affront to its sovereignty' (Holmes 1992).

This sense of tension was also highlighted during the IDA-10 by the Congressional testimony of Lisebo Khoali-McCarthy of FAVDO. Contrasting her statement with that of the Northern organizations also testifying, she stated that 'African NGOs ... want an openness, we want to work with our governments'. She warned that efforts to funnel more lending through private voluntary organizations would 'undermine the legitimacy and impact' of African governments, and asked that African leaders be allowed to decide the economic affairs of their own countries.[8] CARE, in its Congressional testimony, supported her statement.[9]

Attacking borrower legitimacy

Sentiments like those of FAVDO and CARE were in the minority among those expressed by TCSOs during the IDA-10. A much larger group of TCSOs attacked the legitimacy of borrower governments. One joint statement given by the Sierra Club and EDF decried 'gross negligence and delinquency on the part ... of the Indian government' and denounced South Africa for giving aid to the dictatorial regime in Malawi.[10] NBA, writing about the Indian government, opined that 'the elite in our own country are bent upon promoting projects that are highly centralized, that lack people's participation, and those that benefit are only the elite'.[11] The WWF argued that even in the democratic nations of the developing world, decision-making that WWF would consider legitimate 'doesn't happen very often'.[12]

Some of the TCSOs involved did not base their accusations of illegitimacy on a lack of functional democracy. Instead, many indicated that democracy was a moot issue. Bruce Rich, in his writings, indicated that even democratic governments might mistreat their citizens (Rich 1994, pp. 116, 289–291). Church World Service and Lutheran World Relief contended that the IDA and IBRD should 'begin to shift lending toward countries with the most effective and consistent pro-poor policies'.[13] New conditionalities would pay no attention to whether countries were democratic or not. In the words of Glenn Prickett of the NRDC, 'the Bank can't make decisions on political grounds and that has been interpreted to mean that it can't look at a country's form of governance and then decide how it loans to that country'.[14] All borrowers would need to be directed and supervised.

Guiding borrower development

In addition to promoting conditionalities that would restrict borrower behavior, TCSOs involved in the IDA-10 sought to develop a watchdog role for themselves and to create a new accountability mechanism, the World Bank Inspection Panel.

TCS as watchdog

Certain organizations proposed a watchdog role that would codify TCS involvement in future policymaking processes, especially decisions impacting developing nations. Whereas groups like Bread spoke only of a need for greater ownership and participation for grassroots populations, FoE stipulated that reforms 'ensure that affected people and *knowledgeable NGOs* are involved in WB projects from the earliest planning to monitoring after construction' [emphasis added].[15] Carol Capps of Church World Service and Lutheran World Relief opined during the May 5th Congressional hearings that the Bank 'should ensure that affected populations and *interested nongovernmental organizations* are involved in all stages' of country poverty assessments [emphasis added]. Other organizations advocating expansive roles for TCS included EDF, the Sierra Club, and Greenpeace.

This was in keeping with an outlook that depicted TCSOs as natural representatives of the public interest. For instance, Church World Service and Lutheran World Relief reinforced their calls for new policies with the declaration that 'for too many years donors, NGOs and the people of borrowing countries have settled for minor reforms in IDA lending'.[16] A group of primarily Northern TCSOs submitted to Congress an 'International NGO Statement Regarding the 10th Replenishment of the IDA'. The signatories of the October 1992 *New York Times* advertisement denouncing the Bank claimed to be speaking on behalf of Indians. Other examples are discussed in the previous chapter. Thus, even as they questioned the right of developing country governments to represent their citizens, TCSOs arrogated that right to themselves.

The inspection panel

The ultimate manifestation of the trend to delegitimize borrower governments and substituting civil society as an alternative representative was the World Bank Inspection Panel. The panel, which was heavily supported by Barney Frank and US environmental advocacy NGOs, was created in 1994 as part of the Bank's bid to ensure that the US released the one-third of the IDA funds that Frank's committee had withheld. The panel's rules stipulated that any group of two or more citizens in a borrower country could, under certain conditions, make an appeal for the review of a World Bank project.

Governments were ostensibly the originators and the implementers of any given project in their territory. Thus while the panel allowed citizens to explicitly question the Bank's performance, it was a de facto means of citizen appeal against government approval of any given project and government performance in implementing it. Democratic and undemocratic governments alike would be subject to it.

At the same time, the panel legitimated TCS involvement in project monitoring and evaluation. Although the panel specified that claims be made by two citizens, this was a minimum number. In practice, claims would turn out to be made by organized groups, with Washington-based NGOs being very involved in the appeals process. This pattern was not unanticipated. Two senior TCSO staffers present during the IDA-10 negotiations who were interviewed for this research indicated that the US environmental NGOs supporting the panel viewed it as a means of enforcing the policies those NGOs had promoted, rather than as a means of empowering local populations. In effect, TCS was given a permanent mechanism for policing the Bank and its borrowers. The panel was compelled to give each case preliminary consideration (although a full investigation required a board vote) and the criteria upon which the Bank would be judged would be its staff's adherence to the various rules and safeguards for which some of the IDA-10 TCSOs had been lobbying for a decade. The panel's sponsors among the IDA-10 organizations were seemingly unconcerned with the potential for such a system to be used by minority groups or a political opposition to bring extra-national pressure to bear on a local government affairs or to use such pressure to overturn the policies of a democratically elected government.

Civil society, governments, and representation

Civil society campaigners involved in the IDA-10, with only a few exceptions, actively challenged the role of developing country governments as representatives of their citizens' interests in international policymaking and sought to use the replenishment to implement a number of policy changes that diminished borrowers' authority over their own development. This behavior was manifest across the civil society spectrum. Member-funded faith-based organizations and government-funded development service providers pushed for a greater emphasis on pro-poor spending and popular participation, while member- and foundation-funded environmental NGOs pushed to strengthen environmental safeguards. TCSOs countered borrower government opposition to conditionalities by questioning the legitimacy of borrower governments and presenting TCSOs as alternative representatives of borrower citizen interests. NGO-driven activism by donor governments forced Bank staff to prioritize placating donors over cultivating relationships with borrowers. In addition, after the Narmada Dam fallout and the schism between more radical reformers and moderates, the Bank-skeptic faction pushed through changes in the information policy and the creation of the Inspection Panel, policies that helped ensure civil society input into future policymaking.

Determining how these events impacted the representation of borrower citizens requires comparing the relative merits of TCSOs and governments as means of representation. As noted previously in this book, the representivity of any actor in international policymaking is difficult to prove. However, one can observe the impact of TCS activism on the functioning of democracy and the international influence of democratic states.

Undercutting existing democracies

Challenging the legitimacy of developing country governments may have seemed justified in 1992–93 when many of the Bank's borrowers were non-democratic nations. Yet within five years the majority of the Bank's borrowing population would be living in democratic states, as countries like Mexico, Brazil, Indonesia, and Ghana became more fully democratic. Practitioners from the global South have themselves stated that most citizens now live under democratic governments and that the spread of democracy has altered civil society-state relations (Mbogori and Chigudu 1999; Naidoo and Tandon 1999). The state has become a potential ally and collaborator for many civil society organizations in developing nations. Governments may fall short of ideal democratic performance, but they pass a certain threshold of real-world democracy at which they may be considered legitimate (cf. Moravcsik 2004; Schedler 1998).

Within a democratic state, it is natural for competing factions to seek influence. Broad claims to representivity, such as those made by US

NGOs claiming to speak on behalf of all Indians or Asians, can undermine democratic debate by obscuring the identity of the faction for which the organization is actually speaking. More importantly, attacking the government is counterproductive, insofar as the government itself provides the arena in which competing claims can be contested and balanced. Thus one developing country activist (Marschall 1999, p. 173) states:

> 'We the people' type of claims ... are not only false and misleading; they can also undermine a CSO's credibility and seriousness. In addition, these claims suggest that politicians and public officials do not act 'on behalf of the people' and that they en bloc are morally inferior to citizen activists. Although we all know of corrupt and immoral public officials, the generalization is false and unjust.[17]

Because of the ambiguous democratic credentials of many of the IDA-10 borrowers, it is difficult to know whether the IDA-10 activists challenged the authority of democratic states. However, the type of behavior manifested by TCSOs during the IDA-10 does appear to be, at the very least, unhelpful to the development and functioning of democracy.

Devaluing democratization?

Significantly, the majority of TCSOs involved in the IDA-10 seemed unconcerned with whether their activities helped or hindered the development of democracy in borrower states. Instead, many of the most influential TCSOs involved in Bank negotiations assessed government legitimacy based not on democratic credentials, but rather on government agreement or disagreement with TCSO positions. Even those TCSOs without radical advocacy agendas were unwilling to acknowledge the legitimacy of borrower governments. Instead, the majority of TCSOs lobbied for targeted aid, strong conditionalities, and even the use of nongovernmental agents as service providers or watchdogs.

If TCSOs were replacing the unrepresentative borrower governments with some more representative voice, TCS could reasonably be said to be promoting representation. However, the IDA-10 TCSOs used sweeping language and vague imputations that did little to facilitate the representation of specific populations. Indeed, the TCSOs themselves seemed to care little about the democratic rights of the people they claimed to represent. TCSOs challenged the legitimacy of democratic and undemocratic governments alike, explicitly excluding democracy as a criterion of government legitimacy. They also used the Bank's authority to impose in a top-down fashion policies that might otherwise have been the subject of vigorous local debate. The heavy-handed imposition of policy, so derided in the area of structural adjustment, proved perfectly acceptable to many TCSOs when employed to alleviate poverty or prevent environmental degradation.

As stated throughout this book, democracy in the transnational setting requires a combination of democratic inputs and outputs. It is theoretically possible that TCSOs involved in the IDA-10 achieved the latter, in that the net impact of TCS activism may have reflected the will of the majority of stakeholders. The tension between Northern and Southern actors suggests that this is unlikely. More importantly, the way in which TCSOs pursued their agendas suggests that the long-term impact of TCS advocacy may not be the creation of a system of assured, equitable stakeholder representation or majoritarian control. To the contrary, during the IDA-10 the net systemic impact of TCS advocacy seemed to be the transfer of power away from borrower governments that were at least nominally accountable for representing their citizens to TCSOs, donors, and Bank bureaucrats with no formal accountability to most stakeholder populations. Our faith in this as an improvement over the previous, government-centered system depends entirely on the extent to which we believe that TCSOs, particularly the most dominant and influential organizations, correctly understand and represent the will of the stakeholders they claim to represent.

Local civil society and citizen representation

Much of the advocacy done during the IDA-10 was conducted by TCSOs based in the global North. One common means by which such TCSOs bolstered their representative claims was to associate themselves with organizations from developing countries. InterAction stressed its connections to African organizations by inviting FAVDO to testify on its behalf before Congress. EDF included statements from NBA along with its testimony. The NGO Working Group on the World Bank drew credibility from its mix of Northern and Southern members. Policymakers themselves seemed to give preference to Southern CSO input; IDA deputies skeptical of Northern NGO demands, for instance, arranged a meeting with members of Southern organizations in the expectation that these NGOs would be more representative than their Northern counterparts.[18]

There are a number of reasons to be skeptical of this preference for Southern voices, especially when Southern CSO views are presented via a Northern CSO partner. Some of the civil society organizations in developing nations with the strongest ties to international processes are, in fact, those that have been created by outside donors, such as foundations, Northern governments, international institutions, and well-resourced NGOs (see Howell and Pearce 2002, pp. 12, 89–93; also Scholte 2012, p. 190). Such donors may give the most emphasis to the voices they like best (Howell and Pearce 2002, pp. 118–122). Such manufactured or astroturf organizations are not wholly lacking in agency, but donor involvement may encourage them to cultivate favor with funders rather than developing a strong, grassroots base (Kopecky and Mudde 2003; cf. Howell 2000; cf. Brown et al 2012).

Even where strong local organizations originate indigenously, international NGOs and global networks may cherry-pick their local partners, choosing those that best suit the agenda or operating style of the international counterpart (Bob 2005; Pallas and Urpelainen 2013). In South Africa, for instance, international partner involvement has resulted in a situation 'favouring elite-based and mainly urbanized civil society organizations, and almost completely excluding smaller organizations with rural constituencies' (Fioramonti 2005, p. 78).

Efforts to build genuine partnerships between Northern and Southern CSOs have met with limited success. In the area of service delivery, the proliferation of objectives and reporting requirements set by the funding organization has rendered many Southern service-providers de facto subcontractors (Simbi and Thom 2000). In advocacy situations, Northern TCSOs running a supposedly global campaign may feel free to ignore the input of developing country partners in order to maintain a consistent political agenda (see Nelson 2000; Atkinson 2007, p. 68; cf. Scholte 2012, pp. 188–191).

The Sardar Sarovar project

In the context of the IDA-10, the challenge of determining who represents the populations affected by transnational policymaking is demonstrated by the activism surrounding the Sardar Sarovar project. The TCS campaign which began against the project in 1989 also illustrates some of the ways in which TCS can challenge the authority and independence of national governments. The project, which funded the construction of a series of dams in the Narmada River Valley, was heavily influenced by both local activists and, later, an international civil society campaign. As noted in Chapter 3, the Bank's decision to continue funding for the project in the face of activists' protests helped catalyze the decision of certain TCSOs to oppose funding for the IDA-10. The perception of Bank wrong-doing in the project, reinforced by the findings of the Morse Commission, also provided justification for the creation of the World Bank Inspection Panel.

It is not possible to judge conclusively the representivity of the Indian CSOs involved with Sardar Sarovar or the North American and European CSOs that sought to assist them, nor of the Indian government. Instead, my goals are to demonstrate that claims to representivity, even when made by TCSOs based in the global South, must be critically assessed; that drawing local actors into transnational advocacy campaigns may further obscure representivity or subvert local interests to an international agenda; and that TCS can successfully challenge the authority of sovereign states in global policymaking.

Origins of the project: 1946–85

The idea for a series of dams in the Narmada Valley was conceived by Indian leaders in 1946, just prior to independence. Planning for the project began in 1965. The project was designed to provide drinking water, irrigation, and electricity for the inhabitants of India's northwest, especially in the state of Gujarat (Fisher 1995, pp. 12–13). The government planning the project was internationally recognized as a democratic one. Jawal Nehru, India's first prime minister, recognized that the project would negatively impact some of the indigenous people living in the project area. However, he believed the development would be for the good of the country (Mehta 1994). Moreover, the governments of each of the affected Indian states – Gujarat, Maharastra, and Madya Pradesh – were involved in project planning (Fisher 1995). The government finalized its plans in 1979, and in 1985 the World Bank approved funding for the project.

The major problem with the project was that it would displace up to 250,000 people as the dams flooded sections of the valley and irrigation canals were dug across farmland. Although the scale of displacement was truly massive, the Bank had been involved with other projects involving forced resettlement. In the case of the Narmada project, however, the government initially made no plans to resettle the majority of the citizens forced out by the project. The Indian government had retained a British colonial act under which the colonial government had expropriated all forest land; the majority of the project-affected people lived on such timberland. Although their presence on the land predated the British act, the Indian government used the forestry law to declare the Narmada Valley inhabitants 'illegal encroachers' who were not entitled to resettlement (Patel 1995, p. 180; cf. Fisher 1995). The situation was compounded by the fact that most of the valley residents were tribal people (or 'tribals') who were already socially and politically marginalized.

Indian civil society: 1985–89

Arch-Vahini, an Indian development NGO working in the area, began hearing about the problem from local residents in the early 1980s. For Arch-Vahini, the issue was essentially one of human rights, particularly pursuing the recognition of the property rights of the valley tribals. In 1983, Arch-Vahini contacted the World Bank on behalf of the so-called encroachers and other valley residents. The Bank commissioned a study of the tribal situation, and the resulting report was very critical of the Indian government's treatment of the tribals. In 1984, tribals in Gujarat and Maharastra held a protest against the project, which attracted massive press attention in India. Arch-Vahini also enlisted the help of Oxfam-UK, which acted to lobby the World Bank directly on behalf of the valley residents. Participants from both Oxfam and Arch-Vahini agree that, in this instance, the agenda was driven by the grass-roots. However, there was also no international advocacy campaign. Instead, most activism took place within India, supplemented by careful and somewhat collegial efforts by Oxfam staff to lobby the Bank. As a result of these efforts, the final loan agreement for the project, signed in 1985, included resettlement provisions for these previously unrecognized peoples. The late 1980s and early 1990s were spent using the Indian legal system and administrative appeals to enforce the resettlement provisions. The struggle was extremely difficult and contentious, but ultimately largely successful. For instance, among the Gujarat displaced persons (or 'oustees'), all men over a certain age were promised plots of arable land, making the formerly illegal squatters landowners (Patel 1995).

Through the late 1980s, the emphasis of most of the activism was on pursuing favorable terms of resettlement. In 1988, however, a new, anti-dam agenda emerged as other organizations became involved in the lobbying. EDF and its local partner, Narmada Bachao Andolan, were at the forefront of this movement. NBA, like Arch-Vahini, was a professional NGO from outside the river valley. However, it was more ecologically oriented and enjoyed support from members of India's intelligentsia and urban middle-class. As it began its work in the

Narmada Valley in 1986, it sought to 'challenge the underlying assumptions and validity of the project', rallying villages into direct opposition (Udall 1998, p. 395). It was led by veteran activist Medha Patkar. In 1987, one of the founders of the Indian NGO Lokayan (Voice of the People) contacted his friend Bruce Rich of the Environmental Defense Fund to discuss the project. Rich visited the Narmada Valley and toured the dams' submersion area, guided by Patkar. Patkar requested Rich's help in attracting attention to the project.[19] Rich, working with Lori Udall, another key EDF staffer, began building an international campaign.

Transnational activism: 1989–93

The international campaign, led by environmentalists, fundamentally changed the nature of the Narmada struggle. Instead of fighting for a just resettlement, Northern TCSOs and their Indian partners fought to stop the project. TCSOs working in World Bank donor countries enlisted the aid of their governments in pressuring the Bank to cancel the project. Some of the organizations involved, including EDF, were already involved in a long-term effort to reform the Bank; EDF had already received a five-year grant from the Charles Stewart Mott Foundation for the reform of multilateral development Banks. Following the pattern set in the earlier international protests against the Bank's Polonoroeste project in Brazil, TCSOs turned the project into a referendum on the World Bank's behavior. Unlike in Brazil, the Bank had been one of the primary advocates for the rights of the people to be displaced by the project, pressuring the Indian government to adjust its plans in order to accommodate them (Patel 1995). Nonetheless, the Bank was depicted as a primary culprit for the project.[20]

As the international campaign flourished, it seemed to become further and further removed from the people living in the Narmada Valley. Indian observers agree that the majority of locals were more interested in reasonable resettlement terms than stopping the dam (Gill 1995; Patel 1995; Mehta 1994). NBA itself was originally focused on the resettlement terms as well. Only after its partnership with EDF did it announce total opposition to the dam (Patel 1995, p. 912; Udall 1998, p. 396; Gill 1995, p. 239).

By 1989, Patkar was insisting that the people in the valley would rather drown than move from their homes (Udall 1998; Rich 1994). This statement was extremely surprising: even NBA's allies recognized that the organization had had to work to develop local interest in its anti-dam, ecologically-oriented approach. Patkar herself later admitted that not all valley-dwellers were fully committed to a radical approach, with some supporting dialogue with the government (Patkar 1995, p. 164). Meanwhile, the majority of oustees, the Gujaratis working with Arch-Vahini, had accepted the resettlement terms offered by the Indian government (Patel 1995).

To prevent a collapse in local support for the anti-dam movement, NBA cordoned off the areas in Maharastra state that would be inundated by the dam construction. No government officials or consultants were permitted into the area. This inhibited the government's ability to survey the villages to be submerged and make plans for resettlement, but it also gave NBA primary control over contact between government officials and the villages. When government officials sought to visit the villages to hear villager demands and negotiate resettlement, they were detained by members of NBA and, in some cases, threatened or beaten (Gill 1995).

Meanwhile, NBA declared itself the sole representative of a large group of Maharastra oustees, more than thirty villages. The oustees had earlier requested to be resettled on government land in the Taloda forest. After much negotiation, including pressure from the World Bank, this land was released by Indian forestry officials to be used for resettlement. Yet when NBA was informed of the arrangement in 1990, it unilaterally rejected the offer (Patel and Mehta 1995, pp. 403–404). EDF and international allies joined NBA, declaring that the oustees did not want the Taloda land (Patel 1995, p. 193). It took almost two years for the tribals themselves to learn of the offer. When they did, in April 1993, they denounced NBA's representation and chastised the Maharastra government for allowing the organization to speak on their behalf (Patel 1995, p. 196; Gill 1995).

Despite the ambiguous position of the oustees, EDF and its allies still claimed in their October 1992 newspaper advertisements that the Narmada Valley dwellers would rather die than be resettled. In 1993, NBA joined American environmentalists in vehemently denouncing the World Bank. In a letter addressed to Barney Frank and entered into the record during the hearings held by his Congressional subcommittee NBA wrote of the 'intense feelings that are brewing in India and, in fact, in the whole third world about the World Bank' and urged Frank to 'respond to the voices of millions of poor and disadvantaged all over the world' by eliminating the IDA and the IBRD.[21]

Loan cancellation: 1992–93

Pressure from Indian and international activists eventually forced the World Bank to initiate a review of the project. By 1991, civil society protests had convinced several key decision-makers at the Bank that a review was necessary (Fox 2003, pp. xi–xxxi; Udall 1995). The final decision was catalyzed by NBA and Medha Patkar. After an NBA-organized protest was prevented by police from occupying a dam site, Patkar began a hunger strike. She insisted that her strike would not end until a comprehensive review of the dam project was promised. The protest and hunger strike forced the Bank into action, and an independent review as promised.

US NGOs played a significant role in selecting personnel for the Independent Review. Bradford Morse, the nominal head of the review, was in poor health and most of the work would be done by his deputy. US-based environmentalists helped ensure the selection of Thomas Berger, a Canadian lawyer with a strong record of supporting indigenous rights (Wade 1997).

Some of those involved with the review on the ground saw other signs of environmentalist influence. Arch-Vahini complained that they were never invited to meet with the reviewers, despite the organization's longstanding involvement in the project (Patel 1995). In contrast, representatives of the US-based NGOs EDF, FoE, and BIC, along with the Canadian group Probe and the Indian organization Lokayan (which had introduced Rich to Patkar) all met with the review in Washington, DC, in August 1991, a month before it had even begun its official work (Udall 1995). The final report, released in June 1992, was extremely negative and seemed to call for a halt in the project. Arch-Vahini, however, questioned the report's methodology and its findings claiming that, 'far from being impartial, the Report of the Independent Review has gone out of its way to 'prove' or 'establish' facts that show the projects in a negative light' (Patel and Mehta 1995, p. 413).

When the report was released in June 1992, the Indian government and Bank staff fought to preserve the project. They were supported by other developing country governments. During the October board vote on the project, the board voted to preserve the loan despite calls from the executive directors representing the US, Germany, Japan, and several other developed countries to suspend the project (Udall 1995). Six months later, however, it was clear that the project had failed to meet benchmarks included in the remediation plan developed by the Bank. Rather than face cancellation at the hands of the board, the Indian government voluntarily cancelled the remaining installments of the Sardar Sarovar loans. A *New York Times* account of the cancellation noted that 'The Indian government has viewed the criticism by environmentalists as an affront to its sovereignty, and an example of

Westerners telling a developing nation how to run its affairs' (Holmes 1992).

Analysis

It is impossible to know with certainty which organizations best represented the valley dwellers affected by the project. Both NBA and Arch-Vahini were professional NGOs and outsiders in the valley area. Both had international partners with the potential to influence them. Nonetheless, Arch-Vahini's credibility seems somewhat sustained by the fact that the project-affected Gujaratis, who constituted the majority of those displaced by the project, accepted the deal it negotiated and that the oustees from Maharashtra also sought its help (Patel 1995). In contrast, at the height of its power, NBA found itself denounced by a significant number of the groups it claimed to represent and found its coalition of Indian partners wavering (Patel 1995; Mehta 1994).

Northern TCSOs were key to the policy work of both organizations. Arch-Vahini's link to policymaking at the World Bank was via one of its funders, Oxfam-UK. Although Arch-Vahini met with some Bank staff and consultants in India, Oxfam also negotiated with Bank staff on Arch-Vahini's behalf.[22] NBA's international influence was significantly bolstered by EDF and North American organizations allied with EDF.

Oxfam's influence on Arch-Vahini is unclear. Although the relationship was one of donor and recipient, sources from both organizations suggest that Arch-Vahini determined the agenda.[23] NBA and its international partners also claim that NBA led the campaign, but it is clear that NBA's agenda shifted as it became involved in a powerful international campaign, and that the new agenda reflected more closely the agenda of its donors than it did NBA's original objectives. The anti-resettlement agenda it adopted, while actively promoted by EDF and its allies, seems to have been instrumental in its loss of local support.

In short, the project featured two strong, locally-based TCSOs, both with reasonable claims to represent project-affected people. Although initially allied, the claims of the two organizations became directly opposed. Each claimed to represent the whole of the persons being displaced in the valley, yet one stressed fair resettlement (and the continuation of the project) while the other insisted that the project be cancelled. It is true that in the short term Arch-Vahini and NBA were both effective in helping to protect the rights of the Narmada Valley dwellers and holding the Indian government accountable to its promises to the World Bank. The push for just resettlement was also successful in securing land tenure for many oustees. Following the loan cancellation, however, India continued to construct the dam without World Bank funding. In the long term, the only clear benefit of the cancellation campaign was for NBA's Northern partners, who used the Narmada issue to great effect in attacking Bank.

Conclusions

TCSOs participating in the IDA-10 strongly contested the right of developing country governments to represent their citizens in international negotiations. TCSOs encouraged powerful states to use their authority with the Bank to advance TCSO agendas over the protests of borrowing country governments. In particular, TCSOs encouraged the proliferation of conditionalities that limited borrower control over development decisions and aid projects in their own territory. Moreover, many of the TCSOs involved in the IDA downplayed the importance of national democracy and challenged borrower authority wholesale, encouraging a donor-driven approach to development that privileged TCSO-influenced ideas of global best practice. At the same time, key TCSOs encouraged changes in Bank policies in ways that would ensure continued TCSO input and influence in the future.

Even as the net effect of TCS advocacy has been to reduce borrower government authority at the World Bank, TCS has yet to offer borrower country citizens an equivalent means of representation. North-South partnerships do little to ameliorate concerns regarding the representivity of individual TCSOs or collective advocacy efforts. TCSOs from developing countries are often linked to international networks by funding or other forms of material support. Research, much of it from development studies, indicates that externally funded civil society organizations may lack strong grassroots support. This is not to say that all developing country CSOs lack independence. Many genuinely grassroots organizations exist in the developing world and even some that are donor-funded retain significant agency. However, well-funded TCSOs coordinating international campaigns, may select local partners purposively to support pre-existing goals. Such local counterparts may also be treated as junior partners and freely ignored by more powerful organizations if their ideas conflict with established objectives. The Sardar Sarovar case illustrates the difficulties of establishing the representivity of an advocacy effort, even when locally-based TCSOs form an integral part of transnational activism.

Democratic legitimacy

In short, the data from the IDA-10 raise concerns about the marginalization of developing country governments and about inequalities in North-South interactions with TCS. However, the data also demonstrate civil society's potential for positive impacts. The tension between these two observations highlights the importance of the context-based 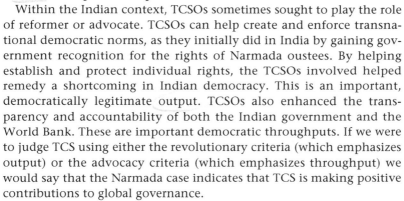 criteria developed in Chapter 2.

Within the Indian context, TCSOs sometimes sought to play the role of reformer or advocate. TCSOs can help create and enforce transnational democratic norms, as they initially did in India by gaining government recognition for the rights of Narmada oustees. By helping establish and protect individual rights, the TCSOs involved helped remedy a shortcoming in Indian democracy. This is an important, democratically legitimate output. TCSOs also enhanced the transparency and accountability of both the Indian government and the World Bank. These are important democratic throughputs. If we were to judge TCS using either the revolutionary criteria (which emphasizes output) or the advocacy criteria (which emphasizes throughput) we would say that the Narmada case indicates that TCS is making positive contributions to global governance.

However, the rather than simply holding the state accountable to democratic principles in the Narmada case, campaigners used international pressure to overturn the domestic policy of the Indian government. The TCSOs involved in the cancellation acted in spite of Bank efforts to protect oustee rights and, in most cases, without reference to the interests of India's broader, national population. The fact that TCS activists were able to overturn the decisions of a democratic government supports the concerns raised in Chapter 2 regarding TCS interventions in domestic affairs and also the importance of judging TCS on its role as an authority.

The rest of the data from this chapter emphasize TCS's authority role. As occurred in the IDA-10, TCSOs may compete with developing country governments for the power to speak for their citizens in international policymaking processes or work to undermine local government authority for the sake of advancing organizations' agendas. TCSOs' success in their advocacy reinforces the idea of TCS as an independent force in the international realm, capable of engaging with both governments and states.

Viewed through the lens of the authority criteria, the data in this chapter reinforce the pattern observed in Chapters 4 and 5: TCS engagement with the World Bank produces some democratic outputs but, in the aggregate, TCSO activities also obstruct democratic inputs. The data here are more ambiguous than in previous chapters. Not all governments have equally valid democratic credentials and, although TCS cannot be proven to represent any given group of stakeholders, it cannot be conclusively proven *not* to represent them either. Instead, this chapter emphasizes the importance of a nuanced approach to evaluating TCS's impact on the democratization of global governance, including a careful consideration of those TCS activities that impact domestic policy and the continued exploration of North-South dynamics.

Inverting the boomerang

One particular area meriting additional research is the roles of Northern and Southern civil society actors in initiating activism. In their landmark work on global activism, *Activists Beyond Borders*, Keck and Sikkink (1998) present their boomerang theory of influence. According to the theory, CSOs stymied in their local efforts circumvent local government obstacles by enlisting the aid of foreign partners who rally international support. Because of this pattern, transnational campaigns typically begin in the South, move to the North, and then return to the South bearing increased power and influence.

The details of the 10th IDA, however, indicate that an 'inverse boomerang' is also possible. TCSOs in the global North selected Southern partners whose work or positions supported (or could be adapted to support) pre-existing Northern agendas. Northern organizations then used this Southern support to bolster and legitimate their claims to represent large stakeholder populations, thus lending credibility to their policy goals, particularly in their discussions with policymakers during the US Congressional hearings. The pattern of influence thus moved from the North (where the agenda was formulated) to the South (to acquire partners and legitimacy) and then back to the North (in the form of political pressure on key policymakers). This pattern, and its possible implications for TCS's capacity to democratize global governance, will be discussed in greater detail in this book's conclusion.

7
Beyond the 10th IDA

Based on the events of the IDA-10, this book identifies a number of key dynamics governing TCS's influence on World Bank policy. Individual TCSOs appear to work to advance their ideological goals without consulting many of the stakeholders impacted by their actions, particularly borrowing country populations. Financial interests play a key role in determining which organizations participate in a particular campaign or policymaking dialogue, giving funders disproportionate influence over the make-up of the campaign or the chorus of voices participating in the dialogue. Moreover, TCSOs often make use of the influence of powerful states in advancing their international agendas. Such assistance, in turn, is prompted by domestic political pressure or national concerns. The result of these dynamics is that TCSOs with good connections in powerful states tend to have disproportionate influence. Such elite organizations have little incentive to conduct meaningful policy dialogue with other civil society actors, particularly when conflicting financial incentives between organizations make compromise unlikely. Partnerships between elite organizations in the global North and partners based in the South also seem to have limited impact on the behavior of the more powerful actors or on the representivity of a larger group or coalition.

As a result of the pressures and incentives facing individual organizations, the collective influence of TCS may do little to enhance stakeholder representation. Civil society's net effect may be to create or enhance transparency, accountability, and dialogue, and it has used such channels to impact particular policies and projects. However, the control of such channels is distributed in a highly unequal manner. Well-connected or well-resourced organizations dominate TCS impact. In the case of the World Bank, TCS has eroded the World Bank's independence, increasing stakeholder control over the institution. However, TCS has done little to improve the equality of authority among stakeholders themselves, to ensure that Bank policies are representative, or to improve the accessibility or inclusivity of Bank policy-making. Indeed, TCS may magnify existing imbalances in power between the North and South by attacking Southern governments in international policymaking negotiations. These findings challenge the suggestion that TCS is democratizing global governance.

Engagement after the IDA-10

The question remains, however, as to whether the patterns observed in the 10th IDA are replicated in other interactions between the World Bank and TCS. TCS engagement with the Bank has evolved since the early 1990s. First, large-scale advocacy campaigns have become less common and perhaps less impactful. Other IDA replenishments have attracted civil society attention, but at nowhere the level of the IDA-10. Some specific project loans have attracted the attention of protestors, but most of the resulting protest campaigns have had a fairly narrow membership. The largest campaign to engage with the Bank, the Jubilee 2000 debt campaign, began its engagement with the Bank after the Bank had already begun building a debt relief strategy. Because Jubilee was encouraging a trend already present in the Bank, its real impact is difficult to assess. Moreover, Jubilee itself was skeptical of its degree of impact on the Bank, and focused much of its attention on the IMF and the G8 (Barrett 2000). One former Bank vice president also claimed that after September 11, 2001, the volume of aggressive attacks by NGOs against the Bank had substantially diminished. He suggested that for a public confronted by the specter of violent terrorism, the idea of a development institution posing a serious threat to human well-being lacked credibility. Regardless of the reason, the raucous protests that once seemed to permanently reside in the park opposite the World Bank's main Washington office are now largely a thing of the past.

In my discussions with TCSO staff, I found that they consistently agreed that no subsequent campaign had involved as many actors as the IDA-10 or produced such significant results. The lack is not a manifestation of satisfaction: many of the organizations originally involved in Bank reform still have Bank-focused elements in their agendas and newer organizations also press the Bank for change. However, Jubilee 2000 notwithstanding, an equivalent number of TCSOs have yet to gather around a single Bank-related issue. Several of the TCSO staff involved in the IDA-10 who were interviewed for this research suggested that the Bank reform movement has lacked a core group of coordinated activists since the Charles Stewart Mott Foundation began redirecting its funding to other areas in the mid-1990s.

Second, new TCSOs have arrived on the scene. Gatherings like the World Social Forum and Davos have given some organizations from less developed countries a more prominent, international voice, if not necessarily more influence. At the same time, many erstwhile development groups, most notably Oxfam, have been expanding their advocacy operations and launching global and regional campaigns. The combination of significant resources, ground-level networks, and a stock of credibility and public goodwill have made these implementation groups formidable advocates.

Lastly, the Bank itself has changed. The Bank itself came away from the 10th IDA much more interested in dialogue with TCS, even if some of that interest was driven by the Bank's need to protect its funding. Dialogue with TCSOs was given a major boost by the presidency of James Wolfensohn (1995–2005). Wolfensohn, seeking to learn from the mistakes of his predecessors, sought to engage personally with the Bank's major TCSO critics, even inviting Washington-based NGO leaders to his house for dinner. During his tenure, staff also codified procedures for ground-level consultations with local purely civil society in the Bank's borrower states and regional staff began engaging with CSOs in their areas (Pallas 2005). The combination of Wolfensohn's influence, interest from within the Bank and the Bank's member governments, and growth in the number of CSOs seeking to engage with the Bank led the Bank to begin to consolidate and strengthen its efforts to engage with TCS. The Bank established the Civil Society Team in 2002 and in 2005 the Bank's board endorsed a paper titled 'Issues and Options for Improving Engagement Between the World Bank and Civil Society Organizations' which included specific action items. In 2006, the team expanded and was re-titled the Global Civil Society Team.[1] The team helps connect organizations looking to engage with the Bank with the specific Bank staff whose work is most relevant to the organizations' interests and it keeps the Bank aware of new civil society trends and agendas.

Despite these evolutions, the general patterns of TCSO behavior observed in the IDA-10 continue to hold true, along with their implications for TCS and democratization. To test the durability of the IDA-10 conclusions, the research examined two case studies. The first, the

Bank's cancellation of the Arun III dam project in Nepal, was selected because it is one of the few clearly effective TCS campaigns to have occurred since the IDA-10. Because it began soon after the height of the 10th IDA lobbying and featured the first use of the World Bank's Inspection Panel, it represents a natural follow-on to the earlier case. Moreover, because the campaign focused on a popular project in a democratic country, it represents an unusually strong opportunity to assess the conclusions reached in the previous chapter about TCS's impacts on national government.

The second case examined was the World Bank's adoption of a policy allowing for the use of borrower country systems for procurement. Between 2007 and 2008, the World Bank changed its standards for project financial management and purchasing to begin allowing borrowers to use their own national systems in lieu of the World Bank's system. TCSOs, along with industry lobbyists and the International Labor Organization, opposed the change. The case has the virtue of being one of the Bank's most recent places of policy engagement with TCS. It provides an opportunity to examine outside engagement with the Bank post-9/11 and in the context of growing global acceptance of a TCS role in governance; the case also involved the Bank's Global Civil Society Team.

Data from these two case studies support the book's conclusions about TCS. In particular, both cases show the self-interested behavior of TCSOs and highlight their use of national governments for influence. Particularly clear in both instances are the ways in which TCS can enhance the control of some stakeholders (by enhancing transparency, accountability, or dialogue) while undermining equality of input. The Arun III case also demonstrates the potential conflicts between international campaigns and democratic governments discussed in the previous chapter, and the country systems case shows that the general patterns identified in the research hold true more than a decade after the IDA-10. In short, the outward appearance of TCS engagement with the Bank may have changed, but the underlying dynamics affecting TCSOs' behavior and the collective impacts of their advocacy have not.

The Arun III project: 1994–96

The World Bank's Arun III dam project in Nepal was the first project ever appealed to the World Bank's Inspection Panel. As such it was the subject of international attention, much of it fomented by the TCSOs which had lobbied for the creation of the panel. The resulting campaign ignored much of the public sentiment on the ground, including the positions of two different democratically elected governments and the pro-dam sentiments of the communities living in the project-affected area. In spite of an Inspection Panel finding supporting the continuation of the project, pressure from TCSOs led the Bank to cancel the loan. The evidence highlights the capacity of TCS to impact international institutions and promote accountability and transparency, but it also showcases TCSOs use of nation-state influence and the tendency of TCSOs coming from outside a given state or area to manipulate or ignore local concerns.

Background

In the early 1990s, Nepal was a functioning democracy, albeit a young one. The Arun III dam, planned by the Nepalese government and the World Bank, was a hydroelectric project designed to exploit the energy of the Arun river. The proposed dam was unusual in that it was a run-of-the-river facility: the strength and consistency of the river's flow was such that the dam could function without the massive reservoirs typical of hydroelectric dams (Bissell 2003). Given that such reservoirs were the main cause of the problems often associated with big dams, such as forced resettlement and increased water borne disease, the dam itself had relatively few negative human and environmental impacts. However, it did require building an access road to the dam site that would cut through an otherwise rural region.

The dam soon became a football for Nepalese political parties opposing the government, which was pro-dam. The government promoted the dam as a solution to Nepal's energy needs, while opposition politicians worried that government plans to sell surplus power to India would make the dam's profitability dependent on India's willingness to buy the electricity at a fair price. There was also some concern that the high cost of the dam would increase the price of power nationally, and that many of the benefits of the dam building would redound to India, which was supplying most of the subcontractors for the project (Udall 1998, pp. 409–410).[2]

When the Inspection Panel opened its doors in 1994, Nepalese activists were its first claimants. In October 1994, a Nepalese NGO based in the capital city of Kathmandu requested a panel investigation of the project on behalf of just four people living in the Arun Valley (Shihata 2000, pp. 102–104). Their claims, in contrast to cases like Polonoroeste or Sardar Sarovar, showed no consistent evidence of government malfeasance. Two claims letters were attached to the Inspection Panel report. In one, the author complains that his claims for compensation for communal land taken to build the access road have been denied, adversely affecting his economic condition. In the second, the author complains that his economic condition was negatively impacted because the government compensated him in cash. 'Since I was not used to the cash economy', he writes, 'I already spent the money I received'. Both authors note that they do not understand how the project will benefit them personally and that 'I have been hearing that there have been many debate [sic] and controversies at local, national and international levels' (the letters use identical language). Thus, the writers each state, they are authorizing a representative of the Nepalese NGO INHURED to act on their behalf.[3]

Although claiming to act on behalf of the residents of the Arun Valley, INHURED expanded on their concerns, challenging the government's macroeconomic policies and energy development plans (Bissell 2003). INHURED and its allies formed an umbrella organization called the Arun Concerned Group. The group's primary objection to the project was that too much of its economic viability depended on the willingness of the Nepal's neighbor, India, to purchase excess power generated by the dam. They also felt that the project was too big and would require too much debt. A lawyer for the group explained that, 'It's no exaggeration to say that Nepal's economic future is at stake. Nepal is a poor country and this megaproject is completely inappropriate for it'.[4]

The Bank denied consideration to the economic elements of INHURED's claim. INHURED then moved to withdraw the entire appeal, casting doubt on its earlier claim to represent the valley residents. Due to the rules of the Inspection Panel, however, the claim, once initiated, could not be withdrawn.

TCS involvement

Even prior to the Inspection Panel claim, some local and foreign NGOs were working to halt the project. The Nepalese NGO Alliance for Energy and the UK-based Intermediate Technology Development Group conducted independent evaluations of the project's impacts, publicized their findings, and proposed alternative solutions to Nepal's energy needs. Washington-based NGOs pressured the Bank to operationalize its newly liberalized information disclosure policies, with the result that the Bank released some of its own evaluations of the project (Udall 1998, pp. 408–413). Nepalese NGOs opposing the dam engaged pro-dam factions in the press (Bissell 2003).

In June of 1994, the Bank invited organizations critical of the project to a Washington, DC consultation. Organizations attending included Alliance for Energy, Intermediate Technology, and the Arun Concerned Group, all of which were actively campaigning against the project. Some of these groups had 'extensive meetings' with members of the World Bank's board of directors and US government officials following the consultation, and later used such informal connections to influence the board's consideration of the project (Udall 1998, pp. 411–412; see also pp. 417–418). Protests against the dam during the Bank's annual meeting in September of 1994 helped attract the attention of the Bank's future president, James Wolfensohn, to the issue (Mallaby 2004, pp. 113–114; cf. Rich 2002).

The Inspection Panel appeal further catalyzed international attention. Anti-dam activists, who were gaining momentum following the Bank's 1993 cancellation of the Narmada Dam project in India, seized on the issue, as did the anti-Bank TCSOs involved in the Mott-supported 50 Years is Enough campaign.[5] The media outreach for the 50 Years is Enough campaign was led by IRN, an anti-dam advocacy group that shared staff with the EDF. IRN received money from the Charles Stewart Mott foundation specifically to coordinate the public messages of the twenty-three organizations involved in the 50 Years campaign.[6] EDF, which had been at the forefront of the creation of the Inspection Panel and was a founding member of 50 Years is Enough (50 Years, undated), also played a key role (Udall 1998; cf. Rich 2002). 50 Years members that were interested in the Arun III project joined with opposition political forces based in Kathmandu, Nepal's capital. All of this attention had the effect of sidelining the local debate. Richard Bissell, an Inspection Panel member who has written in support of the cancellation, has nonetheless noted that 'the least support came at the local level' (1998, p. 32).

Stakeholder representation

International campaigners fighting the dam quickly relabeled the Kathmandu-based national groups opposing the dam as 'local NGOs' (Mallaby 2004; cf. Udall 1998). However, the project enjoyed substantial support among those citizens to be most directly affected by its implementation.[7] Residents of the Arun Valley lived primarily in mountainous villages in which all goods were moved by porters traveling on foot. They viewed the construction of the dam's access road as a significant economic boon and local leaders lobbied heavily to have the road pass through their villages. Significant grievances with the project developed only when the Bank pushed to lay the access road along a cheaper, shorter path that would affect fewer villages. Aside from the debate over the course of the road, valley residents had few concerns about the project (Bissell 2003, pp. 29–33).

The project's stakeholders also included the rest of the national population, who would be obliged to buy the power generated by the dam and, through their taxes, repay the debt the government would undertake in building it. Nepal was a democratic country and the building of the dam was a subject of vigorous public debate; one contemporary commentator described the Arun III as 'being discussed threadbare' for 'nine long years' (Upadhyay 1995; cf. Mahat undated). Only 12 per cent of Nepal's population had access to electricity, and press accounts indicate that there was widespread support for the project (Chatterjee 1995; Nepal Digest 1995b).[8] US-based TCSOs claimed that the World Bank had pressured the Nepalese government to support the project despite government misgivings.[9] Such claims, however, were contradicted by reports that 'all Nepal's political parties', including the opposition, supported the dam (Nepal Digest 1995a).[10] Any claim that the ruling government had acted against the wishes of the people was challenged by a national election in November of 1994, in the midst of the dam controversy. Members of an opposition party, the Communist Party of Nepal, displaced the Congress Party as the dominant political faction. The new government also chose to support the dam project their predecessors had initiated and even pushed for the project to be reopened after its cancellation (Chatterjee 1995; Nepal Digest 1995b).

In short, there was no evidence that the project was opposed by a majority of the Nepalese people or by a majority of people living in the Arun Valley. To the contrary, the project seemed to have significant support except among a minority of political elites based in the nation's capital.

Outcomes

As the Inspection Panel moved to review the Arun III claim, the Bank's management submitted new plans to bring the project into full compliance with the Bank's social and environmental safeguards. The final Inspection Panel report concluded that, with these modifications, the Arun III project was in compliance with the Bank's own policies. Although the panel expressed some reservations regarding the Nepalese government's capacity to implement the project as planned, it affirmed that the project was 'moving towards and intends to comply in substance with the requirements of [the Bank's] operational directives'.[11]

Nonetheless, Wolfensohn, who became Bank President in 1995, was extremely sensitive to the international civil society campaign. TCSOs, including some Nepalese anti-dam campaigners who had traveled to the US, had met with US legislators sitting on the Congressional sub-committees overseeing Bank funding (Udall 1998, p. 441). The new Republican-led Congress had cut the second year IDA-10 disbursement by 50 per cent, and was refusing to enter into negotiations for the IDA-11 replenishment. While there is no record of an explicit congress-ional threat linking Arun III with further cuts to Bank funding, Wolfensohn was already in a precarious position and publicly begging Congress to continue IDA funding (Lobe 1995).

Wolfensohn was also just beginning his tenure at the World Bank. He was determined to put his own stamp on the institution and move beyond its recent negative publicity (Mallaby 2004; Rich 2002). The Bank's public image had been badly scarred by the fallout over the Sardar Sarovar project and Wolfensohn 'was not interested in inherit-ing the problematic projects of earlier presidents'.[12]

When the Inspection Panel gave tentative approval to the Arun III project, Wolfensohn commissioned his own review. Like the Panel's investigation, Wolfensohn's review 'confirmed that the environmental and social mitigation actions that were currently stipulated in the pro-posed project were satisfactory'.[13] However, Wolfensohn indicated that he was concerned that the Nepalese government would be unable to meet implementation standards established by the Bank, that building the dam and continuing to provide social services would require tax increases in Nepal which the government might struggle to imple-ment, and that 'some cofinancing partners did not feel that they were in a position to commit the necessary funds within the next 12–18 months'.[14] On the basis of these concerns, Wolfensohn made a uni-lateral decision to cancel the project in 1996.

The cancellation caused significant outrage in Nepal.[15] Even one of the members of the Arun Concerned Group later admitted that, 'after the cancellation, there was widespread panic that Nepal would perhaps end up in darkness since the one project that had been in preparation for eight years was suddenly no more'.[16] The TCSOs involved, however, hailed the outcome as a major success. They saw the cancellation as legitimating the authority of the Inspection Panel (BIC 2003; CIEL, undated). The success of the claim encouraged other groups to submit claims to the Inspection Panel (Bissell 2003, p. 40; cf. BIC 2003; cf. Hunter 1996).

Civil society trends

The Arun III case study shows how several key patterns observed in the 10th IDA continued beyond the IDA advocacy.

TCSO position-taking

Major environmental organizations from the global North perceived the campaign against the Arun III to be a continuation of a larger, global anti-dam campaign. It was also part of a continued attack on the World Bank and its support for infrastructure development. Perhaps most importantly, it was seen as a crucial opportunity to vindicate the Inspection Panel mechanism by proving that the Inspection Panel could genuinely overturn Bank policy. In short, the Northern TCSOs working against the dam were doing so in service to pre-existing goals.

The behavior of Nepalese TCSOs was similar. The main Nepalese opponents acknowledged that the project had widespread support and that their economic concerns were not shared by the majority of Nepal's population. INHURED added their economic complaints to the four appeal requests they received from project-affected villagers, using the locals' appeal as a vehicle for a pre-existing agenda. The lack of interest in local needs was highlighted by the fact that when the panel refused to evaluate the economic complaints they had added, INHURED sought to withdraw the entire claim. This behavior, in particular, illustrates the potential gaps between TCSOs' nominal stakeholders, in this case the valley residents, and their authoritative stakeholders, in this case the elites running INHURED and its allies.

Choosing to participate

The idea that organizations participate in advocacy when their participation is funded or when they anticipate a high return on investment also matches the patterns of participation observed in the case. Several of the major US-based NGOs working on the campaign, including International Rivers, Environmental Defense Fund, and Friends of the Earth, were receiving funds from the Charles Stewart Mott Foundation. IRN, in particular, was receiving foundation funding designed to facilitate coordination. In addition, organizations like IRN or EDF were advancing an anti-dam agenda for which they already had donor or member support. Many of the organizations involved were apparently also following up on their investment in the 10th IDA protests by making sure that the World Bank Inspection Panel became an effective tool for advocacy in its debut appeal.

The Nepalese TCSOs were based in Kathmandu and represented a Kathmandu-based population. INHURED's attempt to withdraw the Inspection Panel claim when it no longer suited its agenda supports the observation made earlier that organizations prefer to engage in those activities likely to yield a good return for the organization (in terms of publicity, member or donor support, or policy success related to the organization's mission) on its investment of time and resources.

Mechanisms and distribution of influence

TCS activism surrounding the Arun III did enhance some means of citizen access at the World Bank, but influence was dominated by TCSOs based in donor countries. TCSOs used many of the same mechanisms of influence observed in the IDA-10, including generating and disseminating information, fomenting public accountability, and opening dialogues with key policymakers. Most importantly, TCSOs reinforced a key means of structural accountability by supporting the Nepalese Inspection Panel appeal.

The decision to cancel the project, however, ultimately rested not on the universally accessible Inspection Panel, but on a private decision by James Wolfensohn. Wolfensohn was seeking to restore the Bank's public image by placating and engaging with its most critical TCS opponents. He was also fighting for the full release of the remaining US funds promised for the IDA-10, while US environmental organizations sought to obstruct their release. Wolfensohn seemed to focus on the demands of a very small group of TCSOs and his reasons for canceling the project, including concerns regarding implementation and Nepal's tax regime, closely paralleled the economic concerns put forward by the campaigners rather than popular sentiment in Nepal or the will of the Nepalese government. This pattern supports the idea that state influence, exercised through financial leverage or other means, plays a key role in TCSO impacts, as well as the idea that the most powerful channels for influence may only be available to a small group of TCSOs.

Local representation

As noted, there is no evidence that the TCSOs of the anti-dam campaign represented a majority of local stakeholders, that is, Nepalese citizens. Instead, media accounts, local politics, and the Bank's own assessments suggest that the project had significant local support.

Moreover, there is little indication that TCSOs acted to protect the recognized rights of a disadvantaged minority. To the contrary, the Arun Concerned Group sought to drop the appeal to the Inspection Panel once it was clear that the panel would consider only alleged violations of the rights of project-affected people. In short, the case again indicates that claims by TCSOs to represent populations beyond their authoritative stakeholders should be treated skeptically and that partnerships between Northern TCSOs and Southern TCSOs may do little to make a campaign more representative. To the contrary, the case demonstrates the propensity of well-resourced TCSOs to choose local partners on the basis of whether the local agenda aligns with the international one, rather than on the basis of credible claims of local input by the local organizations.

Interestingly, a number of the TCSOs involved in the Arun III campaign have justified their actions by claiming that they were nonetheless acting in the best interests of the Nepalese people. Such assertions are common in civil society activism and it is important to note that they are irrelevant to the question of democracy. The unique feature of democracy is that the people themselves, however misguided or benighted, are entitled to determine their own collective best interest, albeit indirectly via their chosen representatives. Once an unelected minority is empowered to determine the collective good, governance has ceased to function democratically.

In spite of a lack of grassroots support, the anti-dam campaign used international influence and the Inspection Panel mechanism to challenge the policies of two different democratically elected governments. While permitting the Inspection Panel investigation might have been justified as a necessary adherence to Bank policies, the Panel investigation did not conclude that the project needed to be canceled. Wolfensohn's decision to cancel the project despite the findings of the Inspection Panel disregarded local democratic processes in favor of capitulation to NGO pressure. INHURED and other Nepalese actors clearly had a democratic right to contest the decisions of their government. However, the involvement of international allies and the use of the Inspection Panel moved the locus of decision-making from the local to the international realm, where most Nepalese citizens lacked power or voice. Powerful transnational activism undermined the ability of the Nepalese government to carry out development in the manner it saw fit. In short, not only did the TCSOs involved fail to improve the representation of the majority of stakeholders, they undermined the national government's role as a representative of its citizens' interests internationally and even its ability to make democratically informed decisions domestically.

The bottom line is that TCS's role in the Arun III project produced mixed results. By supporting the first Inspection Panel appeal, TCS helped foster transparency, accountability, and dialogue, as well as stakeholder control over the World Bank. However TCS failed to foster equal authority among stakeholders or to improve stakeholder representation. To the contrary, TCS represented only a small Nepalese minority, along with many environmentally interested citizens from donor countries. Within Nepal, it reinforced the power of a small group of local elites and used international mechanisms to overturn the will of a democratic government.

Country systems for procurement: 2007–08

In 2008 the World Bank's board of directors approved a plan, generated by Bank staff, to allow borrowers to use their own national systems to conduct procurement and manage finances for Bank-funded projects. In principle, the new policy would incentivize institutional reform, increase local ownership of projects, and facilitate donor harmonization. However, the policy raised substantial concerns from TCSOs about ways in which the use of national processes might facilitate corruption and undercut aid effectiveness. The lobbying against the policy in 2007–08, while ultimately unsuccessful, demonstrated a number of the dynamics seen in the IDA-10, especially the reliance of activists on donor government influence. The case also involved the Global Civil Society Team and demonstrated interesting parallels between the behavior of TCSOs and commercial actors, some of whom were also involved in the lobbying.

Business and the World Bank

The information liberalization measures forced on the Bank by TCS in 1993 had the unintended effect of making the Bank significantly more business-friendly. In 1990, the Bank's phone directory was considered a confidential document. Within the decade, interested parties could use the Bank's own website to identify the task team leader or project manager responsible for any given Bank project. The Bank's switchboard answered calls to the Bank's main line and freely gave out the extensions of the requested staff before connecting the call. Project information appeared online, including preliminary Project Information Documents (PIDs) and more detailed Project Appraisal

Documents (PADs). Such documents allowed companies to spot opportunities to sell goods and services to the World Bank. Bank-funded projects became a potential beachhead for an increasing number of corporations looking to expand operations into the developing world.

During the same period, internal Bank assessments of its procurement and financial management procedures identified significant shortcomings (Pallas and Wood 2009, p. 216). The resulting policy changes increased transparency and accountability in the purchase of goods and services for Bank projects, and raised Bank procurement procedures to the level of an international 'gold standard'. They were widely acknowledged to be the best in the world, even when compared with national governments. The result was that industry access to commercial opportunities through the Bank substantially widened, resulting in significantly increased business interest in Bank policy. When businesses began to recognize ways in which the Bank's country systems proposal might limit the transparency and accountability that facilitated competition among potential suppliers, businesses began lobbying the Bank and allied themselves with some of the TCSOs pursuing the same agenda.[17]

Background of the country systems policy

The use of country systems policy (UCS) had its genesis in 2002 at the UN International Conference on Financing for Development. The conference resulted in the Monterrey Consensus, which committed donors to increase the quantity of aid, streamline funding processes, and address borrower governance problems.[18] The OECD Development Assistance Committee (OECD-DAC) responded by setting up a working group on these issues. The Bank joined with the working group to develop a set of standards for evaluating borrower procurement procedures, since procurement (the purchasing of goods and services) was one of major governance issues affecting aid disbursement. In 2004 the Joint Venture for Procurement developed a benchmarking tool to assess borrower procurement procedures. After several revisions, this tool became known as the 'OECD-DAC 3'.

The working group also convened a meeting of multilateral development banks, governments, and non-profit donors, predominantly from the global North. Held in 2005, the meeting produced the Paris Declaration on Aid Effectiveness, which called for increased aid harmonization, local ownership of development decisions, and the wider use of country systems. Donor harmonization refers to cooperation among donors, especially the use of common standards among donors for grant applications, reporting, and other aspects of aid bureaucracy. Aid recipients frequently face unique standards from each donor, resulting in a drain on staff time and finances which can undercut their ability to manage projects well. By linking harmonization, ownership, and country systems, the Paris Declaration proposed a magic bullet of sorts: countries would use their own systems for procurement in all aid projects, resulting in greater local control and a common standard for use in all aid-financed spending.

The use of country systems for procurement was developed as a proposal for a change in Bank policy and submitted to the Bank's board. The proposal, however, met with strenuous opposition from TCS and industry. Opponents in the US and Europe questioned whether replacing the Bank's existing guidelines was even necessary (see, for example, Bretton Woods Project 2004). They also expressed concern that the OECD-DAC 3 tool was too weak to identify crucial flaws in borrowing country procedures and that the use of country systems would facilitate corruption and mismanagement. Bank management reluctantly withdrew the proposal from board consideration. It revised the benchmarking tool and resubmitted the proposal in 2007.

Renewed protest

The Bank's stated rationale for reintroducing the proposal was its belief that the use of local procurement procedures would develop local ownership and simplify lending. At the same time, it argued that the need to assess existing national systems would give the Bank grounds for evaluating a borrower's governance practices and making recommendations for their improvement. Thus harmonization and good governance would develop simultaneously.[19]

Nonetheless, critics of the proposal, including large manufacturers, anti-corruption watchdogs, and labor advocates, suspected that the Bank's management was motivated by a desire to maintain market share. For much of the 20th century, the Bank had been one of the only sources of development financing available for poor nations. By 2000, however, a large number of private financial institutions had become involved in sovereign lending. New bilateral donors, like India and China, were also becoming more active. These newer lenders required fewer conditions than did the Bank, giving them an advantage in making deals with developing country governments. The Bank was also facing significant pressure from some of its more powerful borrowers, countries like Brazil and Russia, to allow them to use their own procurement and financial management systems. At one of the later public meetings on country systems, even a senior Bank staff member opined that the new proposal was necessary for the Bank to 'stay relevant'.

As a result of competition with other lenders, opponents feared, the Bank was engaging in a race to the bottom. Rather than focusing on improving borrower governance, the Bank was developing ways of sidestepping its own guidelines. Such fears were reinforced by two additional facts. The new benchmarking tool introduced in 2007 seemed weaker than the rejected OECD-DAC 3, a problem the Bank even admitted in one early meeting (although it later retracted the statement). The Bank also planned to keep the results of the borrowers' systems evaluations confidential and to make confidential any agreed upon plan of remediation. Thus there would be no means of observing how the Bank applied the new standards, nor any means of verifying that the Bank was actually enforcing any borrower promises to upgrade their procedures. This latter point was particularly important, since the Bank proposed giving some of those borrowers who failed to pass the benchmarking test conditional approval to use their own systems (Pallas and Wood 2009, pp. 221–222).

Opponents of the proposal made their displeasure known through the Bank's donor governments. In response to potential opposition from the board, especially the US Executive director, the Bank's management announced that it would open the proposal for public consultation before submitting it to the board for final approval (Pallas and Wood 2009, p. 224).

The consultation process

The Bank department responsible for the country systems proposal was Operations Policy and Country Services (OPCS). In response to the board's demands, OPCS staff set up dozens of meetings with governments, industry, and civil society in Africa, Europe, Southeast Asia, Latin America, and the United States between September and December 2007. Many of these meetings were billed as public consultations.

The consultations helped establish a dialogue between the Bank and the industry and civil society members interested in the proposal. Transnational civil society efforts were led by Transparency International and the International Labor Organization (ILO).[20] The Bretton Woods Project, a watchdog group based in London, also played a role, as did Christian Aid (Bretton Woods Project 2008). Industry-based civil society organizations like the American Society of Civil Engineers also acted as advocates for their members. Commercial bodies such as the Federation of German Industries (BDI) and US-based

National Association of Manufacturers (NAM) helped coordinate meetings between their members and the Bank. Many individual commercial concerns, including firms like General Electric and Philips, also advocated for their own interests, although some of these withdrew from the process later as it lost momentum.[21]

The Bank expressed a strong interest in the public feedback it received. Staff stated that they welcomed the criticism they were receiving about the substance of the proposal and implied that public comments would be taken into account in the final draft of the policy.[22] Nonetheless, the consultations appeared to have little immediate impact. Although the Bank claimed to welcome public input, the staff posture at public consultations was often defensive.[23] The Bank's responses to its critics changed regularly. Initially the Bank defended the latest version of the OECD-DAC benchmarking tool. When industry developed a detailed critique of the tool,[24] highlighting the numerous ways in which it was weaker than current Bank policy, Bank staff switched tacks. They began to emphasize that the evaluation of borrowers' governance systems would be a three-stage process, of which the OECD-DAC benchmarking would only be the first phase. Problems with the Phase 1 review would be dealt with in the Phase 2 and Phase 3 evaluations. However, the plans for these stages existed only as summary proposals. As opponents began to critique them, the Bank argued that critics did not understand what the final product would look like.

Bank staff also mishandled the consultations. Although most consultations were public, the Bank failed to release records of most of its meetings. Even though OPCS made audio recordings of many of the meetings, it refused to release recordings or transcripts of even the public consultations. Instead, it insisted on writing summary reports of each gathering. On several occasions these summaries were contested by the meetings' participants. The BDI, for instance, complained that the Bank had downplayed the concerns of German businesses in one BDI-facilitated discussion. The report on a meeting with civil society in Washington, DC entirely omitted concerns raised by the ILO about labor standards. Many meetings never received a public report at all. Likewise, electronic comments sent to a website set up for the purpose were not published or publicly responded to (Pallas and Wood 2009, pp. 226–227).

The Bank's Global Civil Society Team was conscious of the problems in the consultation. Team members helped coordinate the DC meeting with CSOs and attended the consultation. They were aware of the issues with the website feedback and more general problems with the consultations. In general, they seemed to feel that the OPCS team had not adhered to the Bank's best practice on civil society consultations. According to a source familiar with these issues, the Global Civil Society Team's role was to assist Bank operational units in how to design and carry out consultations with CSOs. They also worked to guide Bank staff on their interaction with civil society. However, while they could identify and suggest best practices, they did not have the mandate to enforce them, as the Bank's participation policies were not mandatory.

The country systems staff had designated a four-month period for public consultation. By holding dozens of consultations all over the world, they established a strong record of dialogue with key stakeholders. Yet because the minutes of the meetings were withheld or redacted, and the final text of the proposal was not yet written, the consultations created little record of public objections. When challenged about the missing meeting reports and the incomplete proposal, Bank staff replied that their commitment to extensive public commentary had used up the staff time that otherwise could have been used on reporting or policy writing.

This tactic overwhelmed opposition from many TCSOs and the ILO. These organizations had never coordinated a joint policy position; instead, each pursued its usual agenda. The ILO pushed for labor standards to be included in the new system. Transparency International worked for greater transparency. Christian Aid emphasized local control over key decisions. Lobbying tactics were the subject of even less intra-civil society consultation than the policy agenda.

Industry and industry-based CSOs, however, pushed back hard against the Bank. These organizations worked to canvas the consultations and establish an independent record of the public meetings.[25] Transparency International also allied itself with this effort.

This group of opponents developed detailed criticisms of the proposal, which they shared with key staff in the US government.[26] This prompted a reaction from OPCS staff, who requested meetings with the chief critics in January, after the consultation period had ended. The proposal that resulted called for a very limited implementation of the new system on a pilot basis and the creation of a Technical Working Group involving civil society, industry, and government representatives which would monitor and evaluate the implementation.

Opponents were still dissatisfied, however, and made their case directly to the US Treasury. Treasury staff had been monitoring the proposal and attending some of the consultations,[27] but the Treasury had yet to take a public stand. Treasury Deputy Undersecretary Clay

Lowery agreed to a meeting with the policy's opponents to allow them to make their case. The morning of the meeting, however, coincided with the bankruptcy announcement of the Lehman Brothers investment bank. According to one of the participants in the meeting, the Deputy Undersecretary paid scant attention to the industry and civil society presentation while he sent and received messages on his Blackberry. Several days later, he told Bank staff that he thought that American industry was basically in agreement with the proposal and that the US would support it.

Once Bank staff realized that the proposal's opponents lacked US support, they rapidly revised the country systems proposal. Two days before the Bank's board voted on the proposal, they attached a confidential addendum to the policy undercutting previous concessions, reducing the authority and scope of the Technical Working Group. The oversight role of civil society in particular was weakened. The board approved the policy in April 2008, and by 2009 Bank staff were planning to implement the 'pilot' as widely as possible.

Transnational civil society behavior

In spite of the weak impact of civil society on the World Bank's final country systems policy, TCSO and industry allies still had a profound effect upon the process. Like the Arun III dam, this case study confirms several of this book's core findings.

Civil society agendas and participation

As in the IDA-10, the TCSOs that met with Bank staff each pressed their own agenda. This led to largely atomized behavior. The ILO focused almost exclusively on labor standards. Transparency International focused on means of limiting corruption. Christian Aid seemed ambivalent about the proposal and openly supported some elements of local control. Professional organizations like the ASCE focused on rules governing consulting contracts of the sort often sought by their members. It is also interesting to note that environmental organizations were involved in protesting the use of country systems for social and environmental safeguards in 2004 (Bretton Woods Project 2004; BIC 2004). However, they refrained from involvement in the debate over the use of country systems for procurement. This pattern of TCSO advocacy is in keeping with the IDA-10 finding that organizations' policy positions reflect their core mission or values.

The TCSOs involved in the issue also lacked coordination, despite their small numbers. During the meetings I attended, the organizations present appeared to have no prior knowledge of one another's interests or goals in the consultation, nor did the representatives attending appear to use the consultations to establish relations with one another. At a tactical level, only Transparency International and some of the professional organizations allied themselves with business groups and participated in some of the additional meetings arranged between opponents of the policy and Bank and government officials.

The contrast between industry and industry-allied CSOs and the rest of the TCSOs involved is informative. Industry-linked lobbying of the Bank was initially highly coordinated, because participants shared a set of financial incentives. As certain actors began to sense that the Bank was unwilling to yield on the policy (and thus that the efforts spent on lobbying would yield a poor return on investment), they backed out of the process individually. In this regard, industry-related lobbying illustrated the importance of material incentives, both in motivating action and driving coordination.

Mechanisms of influence

As in the 10th IDA and Arun III cases, the country system activists reinforced a number of channels for citizen influence at the World Bank. The most profound of these was dialogue. In part because of civil society pressure, dozens of dialogues were held in Bank donor and borrower nations, and included government, industry, and civil society.

Opponents of the policy change also helped enhance the Bank's transparency. They canvassed meetings, exchanged information, and sought to establish a clear record of the Bank staff's actions and statements about the new policy. Their efforts to gather and disseminate information both aided transparency and made the Bank accountable for distortions in the record.

That being said, the activists continued to rely on donor power. It was pressure from the US executive director, prompted by businesses and TCSOs, that was the primary impetus for the massive dialogue effort. Likewise, when the Bank realized that activists had lost US government support for changes in the new policy, the OPCS staff felt free to renege on many of the promises that they had made. In this regard, the country systems debate presents an interesting null-case confirmation of one of this book's core contentions. Not only can it be shown that TCS lobbying succeeds primarily via the influence of the Bank's donor states; when TCS activism lacks donor state influence, it fails.

The role of the Global Civil Society Team also highlights the importance of donor power. The GCS Team is tasked specifically with developing dialogue between Bank staff and outside parties. To a certain extent, the team also develops transparency by recommending best practices for dialogues or exposing the Bank's internal workings to outsiders looking for access. However, the mere development of norms was not enough to give the team authority. During the donor-mandated country systems negotiations, the GCS Team succeeded in facilitating or enhancing dialogue. However, the dialogues had relatively little effect on the final policy or on the long-term behavior of the OPCS team. Even in the area of transparency, the GCS Team's knowledge of best practices and its job as designated intermediary between civil society and the Bank gave it limited authority. Instead, OPCS staff consistently misstated or withheld comments generated in the dialogues and acted in pursuit of their own agenda.

Borrower governments and local representation

Sources indicate that pressure from emerging-market borrowers was one of the major drivers of the Bank's policy change, a fact Christian Aid and the Bretton Woods Project acknowledged. Most TCSOs involved in the policy negotiations made few explicit claims to represent developing country citizens. This may reflect the fact that two of the major organizations involved, Transparency International and the ILO, are organizations whose authority is established by either their technocratic expertise or UN mandate, rather than claims to developing world representation. On the whole, however, organizations seemed to privilege their own views of best practice with little regard for developing country input or, in the case of industry-related CSOs, straightforwardly lobbied on behalf of their members' interests.

Transnational civil society, governments, and the Bank

The critical approach this book takes towards civil society organizations' democratic credentials can easily eclipse the fact that the Bank itself is in need of democratic reform. The UCS case, however, supports some of the perennial accusations made against the institution: namely, that Bank staff are focused on their own agendas, uninterested in outside input, and may deal with the public in dubious or duplicitous ways.

The fact that the Bank suffered such a stunning loss in its battle with TCS during the 10th IDA can easily eclipse the fact that the Bank was still able to struggle against the changes. It used its connections with IDA deputies and member governments to seek to preserve its existing policies and independence, even though it was largely unsuccessful in stopping the specific policy changes proposed at that time. In the case of country systems, Bank staff worked hard to escape TCS and industry influence in order to implement the policy they thought would best serve the institution and its clients. Once donors, particularly the US, had withdrawn support for the UCS opponents, Bank autonomy became even more pronounced. This agency is important to note. Too much research on the World Bank treats the institution as though it is only passive or reactive. Accurate modeling of global governance must encompass the complex three-way interactions between governments, TCS, and the Bank.

With regards to TCS, the case study reinforces observations made throughout this book about the tendency of TCSOs to advance established agendas and to react strongly to financial incentives. The individualistic agendas of TCSOs and the lack of coordination among organizations without a shared financial incentive closely parallel the IDA-10. While less dramatic than the IDA-10 or the Arun cases, the ways TCSOs involved in the UCS pursued their agendas reflect a continued weakness in many TCSOs' value for developing country governments and local stakeholder input. Ultimately TCS, as in the IDA-10 and Arun III cases, helped enhance democratic preconditions at the Bank by developing dialogue and transparency. However, failure of TCS advocacy in the absence of strong donor support confirms that much of TCS's influence at the Bank passes via the governments of donor states, and that influence will continue to accrue disproportionately to those TCSOs that can motivate donor action on behalf of their agendas.

Conclusions

The outward appearance of Bank-TCS relations has evolved over the past twenty years. The Bank has become more transparent and more amenable to input from TCSOs. Interactions between the Bank and TCS have become more regularized, with the creation of the Inspection Panel, the development of the Global Civil Society Team, and the proliferation of ad hoc policy dialogues. Nonetheless, the cases in the chapter indicate that the patterns identified in the 10th IDA continue to hold true in subsequent interactions between TCS and the World

Bank. The fundamental dynamics governing TCSO influence and behavior remain unchanged.

The case studies of the Arun III dam and UCS policy reinforce this book's analysis of the motivation and participation of TCSOs, their mechanisms of influence, and their mixed impact on stakeholder representation. The two cases also support the idea that TCS is an authority in the international system, acting as a means of stakeholder influence that exists alongside states and international institutions.

The cases studies reinforce this book's contentions regarding the democratic legitimacy of TCS in the context of the World Bank. The data continue to indicate that TCS has democratic outputs in the form of improved citizen control over the Bank. However, the data also indicate that TCS lacks democratic inputs. Stakeholders do not have equal authority in determining its policy positions, nor do they enjoy equal control over its means of influence, either directly or via representatives. Moreover, TCS does not appear to improve the representation of many of those stakeholders currently marginalized in international policymaking; instead, it often appears to reinforce the power of stakeholders in already powerful nations.

Yet the country systems case study reminds us of the starting point for this research. Scholars look to TCS to reform the World Bank, and global governance more generally, because it is genuinely in need of reform. The Bank tends to be technocratic, insular, and disproportionately beholden to powerful donors. Although its policies affect the lives of billions of people, it is accountable to only a small fraction of them. Although TCS does not currently act to democratize the World Bank, a subsequent question emerges: Under what conditions or constraints can TCS become an effective force for the democratization of the World Bank? That question is explored in this book's final chapter.

8

Transnational Civil Society and the Democratization of Global Governance

The introduction of this book outlined two schools of thought regarding TCS. One suggested that TCS would remedy the democratic deficits present in global governance institutions like the World Bank. The other challenged the capacity of TCS to democratize global governance and even suggested that TCS might worsen existing imbalances in power between the citizens of poor and rich nations. Data on TCS engagement with the World Bank support and challenge some of the contentions of each school. The data present a new picture of TCS and its role in global governance and suggest new directions for further research. This chapter begins with a discussion of this book's findings and directions for future research, analyzes the consequences of these findings for our understanding of TCS's potential to democratize global governance, and then explores ways in which TCS's influence can be shaped and channeled to enhance its democratizing effects.

Transnational civil society and the World Bank

Research on the World Bank confirms the globality of TCS. Participants in the IDA-10 came from both the global North (including North America, Europe, Japan, and Australia) and the global South (including Malaysia, India, Latin America, and Africa). They included advocacy organizations, development actors, and faith groups. In the IDA-10, Southern CSOs were sometimes recruited as partners by Northern-based CSOs, but participants also included networks of developing world organizations. The other case studies confirm the diversity of TCS. Northern CSOs from multiple countries participated in the campaign against the Arun III dam project alongside local, Nepalese CSOs. A wide variety of organizations from North America and Europe participated in the use of country systems discussions. The data make clear that TCS has global reach and membership, and actors from the global South can and do participate independently in some transnational policy advocacy. This globality lends credence to the vision of TCS as a transnational force with the potential to diversify and democratize stakeholder input in global policymaking.

Yet the data from the World Bank emphatically contradict claims that this potential is being fully realized. The data indicate that TCSOs tend to pursue their goals or interests individualistically. Alliances may form where interests or goals overlap, as in the case of anti-dam environmentalists during the Arun III campaign or industry-related advocacy groups involved in UCS. Outside donors can prompt collective action by conditionalizing their funding, as in the case of the Mott foundation and its grant recipients. Similar objectives may give the superficial appearance of unity even where organizations have had no official dialogue or coordination, as in the common opposition of Transparency International and the ILO to aspects of the country systems policy. Nonetheless, coordination or its appearance often results from factors external to TCSOs themselves – overlapping funding streams, pressure from donors or members, or the need for access to resources. There appears to be nothing intrinsic to TCS itself that makes it more likely to produce dialogue, consensus, or coordination.

Atomized actors

Individual organizations seem to choose their policy activities based on a combination of mission and material concerns. Mission, such as environmental conservation or labor rights, seems to be the primary determinant of most organizations' policy interests. However, mission alone does not predict advocacy. Rather, the decision to participate in activism and policymaking is heavily influenced by funding, which is a key component of organizational survival. Because resources are invariably limited, organizations will choose to participate in those activities for which they receive specific funding or for which there is a high return on investment in terms of publicity, power, sustained or increased membership, revenue, or the achievement of pre-existing mission-based objectives.

An environment of scarce funding creates competition that undermines incentives for collaboration and dialogue. Few of the TCSO staff involved in any of the cases discussed in this book recounted meaningful dialogue between their organizations and other organizations. Organizations receive funding from their members or foundations to support a particular agenda or lobby in order to protect or advance their financial interests. Staff in any given organization recognize the impact of such financial pressures on other organizations. During the IDA-10 in particular, many CSO leaders perceived compromise to be impossible and dialogue a waste of time because of such pressures. Even actors from organizations with similar views expressed some tension with one another. Organizations with overlapping agendas competed for funding, at times making them disinclined to collaborate or share credit.

Much of the existing research on TCS suggests that cooperation and collective action are the typical modes of operation for TCSOs and the natural outgrowth of aligned missions. Such research often stresses civil society networks as the locus of campaign formation. Yet recent research has suggested that the mere existence of a network does not guarantee the undertaking of advocacy, even if the issue under consideration is clearly aligned with the network's goals (Carpenter 2007). The data presented in this book help explain why: organizations are incentivized to pursue their goals individualistically, either working on their own or employing partners only in an instrumental fashion. The emergence of an international campaign therefore requires the alignment of not just mission but also a variety of other factors across multiple organizations. As a result massive, network-based campaigns represent a special case within the realm of advocacy, rather than a general case.

It appears to me that the focus on large, successful campaigns has created a selection bias in the larger body of research, allowing investigators to overlook the fact that large, successful transnational campaigns are relatively uncommon phenomena. The tendency to use the campaign or network as the unit of analysis in examinations of TCS exacerbates this problem. When dealing with campaigns as discrete units, it may be easy to assume that the common denominator among members, the shared interest in the issue addressed by the campaign, is also the campaign's causal factor. For example, if a campaign consists entirely of conservation-minded TCSOs, the TCSOs must have joined *because* they are conservation-minded. This research shows that such assumptions are likely erroneous or, at best, give an incomplete picture of TCSO motivations.

To better understand TCS, future research must investigate when and why campaigns occur but also when and why they do not. In examining any given campaign, it should test assumptions about TCSO motivations for joining by comparing TCSOs that join with TCSOs that do not. Investigators should be open to the possibility that campaigns result not from a common ideal, but rather from the temporary alignment of disparate interests.

Influence and architecture

Both activists and academics credit TCS for numerous changes in policy or behavior on the part of international institutions. Certainly the cases in this book support such claims. Yet those explanations of TCS influence that credit it with marshaling or representing overwhelming public opinion are at odds with the atomized nature of TCS and the competitive environment in which TCSOs function. Indeed, there is no strong evidence of massive moral suasion driving policy change in any of the cases studied here. In the case of the IDA-10, the most successful faction of activists was also the smallest, and in the case of the Arun III dam, civil society defied both the wishes of a democratic government and the well-documented desires of the project-affected population.

Given the data presented here, it seems that TCS's impact at the World Bank is linked less to its claims of popular representation or moral authority than to the architecture of global governance. The architecture of the World Bank affords power to those TCSOs able to influence key states. In the IDA-10, the Bank's concerns about US threats to its funding weighed heavily in its decision to accede to the demands of actors with strong connections to key US politicians. Such threats were also a factor in the Arun III. Similarly, the Bank rejected the demands of lobbyists in the country systems case when it became clear that they did not have strong US government backing. Certainly some TCSOs used tactics besides leveraging state influence, such as public accountability or the monitoring of institutional activities, but there is little evidence that these tactics played a role in successful policy change.

Recognizing the role of state power is not to say that TCSOs lack the power or autonomy frequently attributed to them. Although TCS influence at the Bank makes significant use of the leverage of powerful donor states, TCS retains some degree of independence. Even where TCSO influence relies on donor leverage, TCSOs can seek to manipulate key donors via their domestic political processes, including relationships with key decision-makers. Naturally such manipulation is most likely to be successfully achieved by TCSOs from those donor states, particularly those with large memberships or connections to key politicians. The result is an impactful but highly unequal TCS, in which some members have far more power than others.

These findings challenge more purely constructivist conceptions of TCS influence, particularly where such conceptions focus on TCS as mobilizing some form of mass public as opposed to elites. Further studies of TCS influence on global governance should examine equally both the behavior of TCSOs and the states and international institutions that act as their interlocutors. In particular, such examinations must identify those features of institutional and state architecture that effect institutional and state reactions to TCSOs and those elements that constitute points of leverage or access for TCSOs.

The stakeholder dilemma

TCSOs frequently claim to represent large groups of stakeholders and to use their influence on behalf of marginalized populations. The representational claims made by the organizations studied in this book, however, could not be proven and were often suspect. This finding was consistent regardless of whether Northern TCSOs were partnered with TCSOs from developing countries. Instead, there are significant indications that claims made by Northern organizations to represent the interests of the Bank's poorest members were overstated. Such claims may have been sincere, if perhaps uninformed or paternalistic, but they also represented good tactics. The data suggest that claims of broad presentation can enhance the credibility or influence of TCSO policy proposals, particularly if claims to representivity are accepted by allied policymakers.

Representational claims by Northern TCSOs are imbued with two dangers: moral hazard and systemic disempowerment. Moral hazard, a term borrowed from the finance industry and applied to TCS advocacy by Robert Wade (2009), describes the problem that occurs when a party making a decision is insulated from its consequences. Policy input by Northern TCSOs on development-related issues is liable to significant moral hazard since the TCSOs themselves will never be subject to the policies they endorse. Consider that 100 per cent of the US-based TCSOs opposing the Arun III hydroelectric project had continual access to electricity while 89 per cent of Nepalese citizens did not. This sort of disparity deprives many representational claims made by TCSOs of a basic accountability check. It also suggests that we should treat with extreme caution claims by TCSOs to represent the 'best interests' of a given group of stakeholders rather than those stakeholders' expressed will. Lastly, we must be wary of the feedback cycle that can occur when both TCSOs and international policymakers operate in an environment of moral hazard and plan policies for a group of stakeholders in the absence of any direct representation from that group.

Claims to representivity are central to the capacity of TCSOs to challenge the authority or legitimacy of governments, particularly those of poorer countries. Such challenges can have long-term, systemic consequences. On the positive side, TCS can force governments to become more transparent, accountable, or respectful of the rights of their citizens. However, TCSOs can exploit their connections with powerful states to force TCSO agendas on weaker states. When TCSOs attack governments and undercut their authority or credibility in an international policymaking process, TCSOs may weaken the capacity of these governments to represent their citizens internationally, closing off a potential means of representation for developing country stakeholders and possibly creating or exacerbating a more systemic disempowerment. Future research on TCS's impacts on stakeholder representation should therefore include a counterfactual analysis that considers the possible role of the stakeholder's state in the absence of TCS advocacy.

The inverse boomerang

The data discussed here suggest an addition to the dominant boomerang model of network advocacy (Keck and Sikkink 1998). The model is typically employed to describe transnational advocacy efforts that begin in the global South, acquire partners in the global North, and return to the global South with increased influence. Some of the data in this book, particularly regarding the Narmada Dam, support the idea of Southern initiation.

However, transnational campaigns do not occur only because Southerners reach out to interested Northerners. Sometimes Northerners do the reaching out. The data reveal the potential for an 'inverse boomerang', following a North-South-North pattern. A Northern TCSO may strategize an international campaign based on its own values, agenda, or funding incentives. It may then seek out local Southern partners, selecting those local organizations whose interests or issues reinforce the Northern agenda.[1] This local support, in turn, helps legitimate or globalize the campaign, giving it greater credibility with key decision-makers. Northern-based IDA-10 campaigners from both pro-Bank and anti-Bank factions demonstrated this pattern, as did Northern-based opponents of the Arun dam, facilitating the participation in the policy process of Southern counterparts whose positions aligned with those of the Northern TCSOs. Thus at least two boomerangs exist: a South-North-South model initiated by marginalized populations and a North-South-North model driven by a Northern agenda.

In examining transnational campaigns, one must ask when different organizations within the campaign first espoused the campaign's public agenda; exactly which organizations control the public face of a campaign; and how decisions are made internally (if there is some measure of internal deliberation within the campaign, which this research has shown should not be assumed). Recognizing the two possible boomerang patterns and posing some of the questions described here can lead to a more nuanced understanding of the mechanics of transnational advocacy and its implications for remedying the democratic deficit in global governance.

A global community or a class of actors?

Conventional wisdom on TCS depicts TCS as a global community, marked by widespread participation, equality of access, and consensual decision-making. It also views TCS as an autonomous power, able to directly impact international affairs via its influence on public opinion. The empirical reality is strikingly different. Individual TCSOs are highly atomized. Their decision-making processes with regards to advocacy are often self-focused and sharply constrained by their operational environment. Influence is dependent upon the architecture of the states and institutions with which they interact and, often, their relationships with key individuals within those bodies. Representational claims have little credibility and may reflect the pursuit of tactical advantage. The result is that TCS as a whole is marked by sharp disparities in power and that even when TCS influences international policymaking, there is no guarantee that such influence reflects the will of either the majority of stakeholders or the majority of TCSOs.

This research suggests that rather than seeing TCS as a global community, it should be regarded merely as an emerging class of actors, akin to multinational corporations, states, and international institutions. Although similarities exist between actors within this class, their behavior in any given situation is often best understood by examining the interests of individual organizations and the constraints of their operational environment. Just as the behavior and influence of other classes of international actors, such as states and institutions, must be understood within the context of the international system, so too must the behavior of TCSOs be understood with reference to their broader international economic and political situation.

Transnational civil society and democratic global governance

This book uses the ideas of Dahl, Moravcsik, Held, and others to develop a definition of democracy as a system or pattern of equal citizen authority or influence expressed via some representative mechanism and resulting in government or institutional responsiveness to the will of the majority, but under which the government or institution is also constrained to protect the liberal rights of its citizens or stakeholders. This definition is designed to escape state-centered understandings of democracy that are focused on voting or other structures, while still maintaining the core values and pragmatism inherent in state models (an effort in which I follow Moravcsik in particular).

This book mates this concept of democracy with the work of Uhlin, Dingwerth, and Scharpf. These authors disaggregate democratic legitimacy, dividing it into input, throughput, and output components. This book takes these components and links them to context, arguing that in order to be democratically legitimate, civil society actors must seek to complete those elements of democracy which are lacking in their own context. Because of the international context in which TCS operates, the input and output components are the most relevant for assessing its democratic legitimacy. However, for the purposes of engaging with the broader literature, I would like here to first discuss the contributions (or lack thereof) of TCS as a whole – i.e. the aggregate impact of all TCSOs involved – at the World Bank within each of the three aforementioned categories.

Democratic inputs refer to TCS's contribution to stakeholders' equal representation or inclusion in global governance. In the case of the World Bank, TCS generally fails to contribute to equal representation or to inclusivity. As noted, organizations' policy positions seem to be determined by pre-existing agendas rather than consultations with the stakeholders they claim to represent, and funding considerations may determine which organizations participate in a given policy campaign. Organizations with strong connections to the Bank's major donor governments wield disproportionate power and may actively use their influence to restrict the input of some weaker organizations and developing country governments. Dialogue among organizations is rare and the absence of compromise prevents the creation of consensus positions. As a result, the power dynamics among TCSOs may actively impede the capacity of TCS as a whole to improve the equality of stakeholder access to policymaking or the inclusivity of decision-making processes. Because these factors, TCS largely fails to contribute to democratic inputs in the governance of the World Bank.

Democratic throughputs include transparency, accountability, participation, and deliberation. TCS contributes heavily in most of these areas. TCSOs have significantly increased transparency at the World Bank by monitoring and researching the Bank's activities; promoting self-monitoring in the form of environmental and social impact assessments; and forcing changes in the Bank's information policy. TCSOs have held the Bank accountable through public awareness campaigns and attacks on Bank funding, and by promoting the creation of the Inspection Panel. New dialogues between the Bank and civil society have facilitated the participation of the TCSOs invited to attend and possessing the resources to sustain involvement. The net impact of TCSO activities has been a significant contribution to throughput.

Democratic outputs include increased stakeholder control over policy and the protection of liberal rights. In general, the Bank's scope of activity precludes its direct involvement in the formation of rights. However, there is some limited evidence that where the Bank's activities have led indirectly to the abrogation of stakeholders' rights (as in the case of the initially uncompensated forced resettlement of the Narmada oustees, for example), TCSOs have acted to protect liberal rights. At the same time, TCS has increased stakeholder control over the World Bank, making the Bank less independent and technocratic and more directly responsive to stakeholder input. In this regard, the data indicate that TCS has contributed to democratic outputs.

The authority role

This book suggests that within the anarchical transnational space, TCS acts as an authority: an independent and powerful means of citizen influence not subject to the regulation of any state or body. Because TCSOs, civil society networks, and advocacy campaigns are generally not answerable to any other actor or body for their impacts, those impacts must be judged by whether the processes that produced them reflect the core elements of democracy (as opposed to enhancing or fostering the democratic performance of some other actor). Because democracy requires equal citizen input and majoritarian control over government, the democratic legitimacy of authorities is judged by input and output. Regardless of whether TCS is acting as an alternative to the current system of global governance or seeking to participate in and reform the current system, it must recognize and understand the will of the stakeholders it represents, develop equal authority among stakeholders, and work towards outcomes that represent the will of the majority or which protect the core liberal rights of the minority. Only if TCS meets these standards can it be considered democratically legitimate.

The democratic legitimacy of transnational civil society

This book supports the popular contention that TCS increases transparency and accountability in global policymaking. However, improving throughput, as these activities do, is not sufficient to democratize global governance. Rather, democratic inputs and outputs are the key standards by which TCS's impacts must be assessed. TCS contributes to the latter but not the former. Therefore it cannot be said to be democratizing global governance.

It is important to note that this is not a normative judgment on TCS's overall impact on the Bank. The World Bank in the early 1990s was an institution much in need of reform and the undemocratic tactics pursued by many TCSOs were instrumental in achieving important changes. Many of the respondents I interviewed for this research noted that although they were critical of the more coercive tactics used by some TCSOs, in hindsight they were glad for the outcomes. Positive outcomes, however, while they may grant TCS some moral legitimacy, do not equate with democratic legitimacy. A benevolent aristocracy is still an aristocracy. While the structures and attitudes that facilitate and justify elite dominance of policymaking can, in the short term, produce some positive outcomes, they offer no protection against the self-seeking behavior or misguided paternalism that may occur over the long term.

The empirical data about the World Bank illustrates the importance of democratic inputs and outputs to true democratization at the global level. In the three case studies researched here, TCS failed to improve, and even actively obstructed, equality of access and influence in transnational decision-making. In the absence of such inputs, improved throughputs (accountability, transparency, and the like) only served to magnify the power of elite actors and led to outputs that seemed disconnected from the will of the majority of stakeholders.

This perspective lends support to those authors critical of TCS's capacity to democratize global governance. If the trends manifest in TCS engagement with the World Bank hold true elsewhere, TCSOs may increase the control of some stakeholders over international policymaking. However, their efforts will do little to increase the influence of marginalized stakeholders in international decision-making or otherwise improve representation or equality of authority. Far from correcting the current imbalances in the global governance system, TCS may actually make the problem worse.

Future research

Given the Bank's long history of engagement with TCS, it seems likely that the Bank constitutes a leading indicator and that the patterns described in the book will hold true elsewhere. However, the Bank is a unique institution and, in keeping with the arguments made above, TCS's behavior and impacts may vary with changes in the interests of the TCSOs involved and their operational context, particularly the architecture of the institutions with which they engage. TCSOs in different issue areas, such as human rights, engaging with other institutions, such as the UN, or subject to different organizational imperatives, may have different impacts than the TCSOs studied here.

Additional research is necessary regarding the impact of TCS on the democratization of global governance. Democracy should be used as an analytical yardstick and, within a given piece of research, clearly defined. Using democracy as a measure has a normative value. Responding to citizen interests has become a primary concern of decision-makers in certain international institutions, including the World Bank. Such decision-makers recognize the usefulness of democratic credentials in establishing their institution's legitimacy. The language of democracy is therefore persuasive to some policymakers and can broaden the audience for research. Even more importantly, democracy is essential for stakeholders. Democratic mechanisms ensure that stakeholder concerns are heard and, ideally, that their rights are protected and their interests valued fairly. Using the language of democratic legitimacy helps shine a spotlight on issues of stakeholder access and influence.

From an academic perspective, using explicit analytical standards facilitates comparison of different findings and pieces of research. Not every author will use the standard of democracy put forth in this book. However, if all authors were to define the standard of democracy they are using in clear and explicit terms, it would greatly facilitate the comparison of their findings with those in other works.

Improving stakeholder representation at the World Bank

The data in this book suggest that TCS is failing to deliver democratizing change at the World Bank. Yet the data also reinforce claims that such change is indeed necessary. How then can TCS's impacts be improved? The findings of this research speak to the importance of four policy initiatives: increasing formal dialogues between the Bank and civil society; limiting state power in Bank decisions; holding individual TCSOs accountable; and improving the composition of civil society campaigns engaging the World Bank to make such campaigns more representative.

Formal dialogues are important because they can, in theory, provide an equal playing field for the organizations involved. In the absence of formal dialogues, TCSOs are prone to using personal connections or other informal channels to access and influence policymakers at the Bank. These personal channels are often only accessible to elite organizations, particularly those that can afford to keep offices in Washington, DC where their staff hone their political skills and connections through regular interactions with staff at the Bank's headquarters. As seen in this book, this can contribute to a preponderance of Northern influence in general and strong advantages for US-based TCSOs in particular.

It is important to note, however, that dialogues must be more than just spaces for conversation. As the country systems case shows, the Bank's reputation for obfuscation and even deception is not undeserved. Bureaucrats within the Bank are likely to continue to seek to advance their own agendas regardless of civil society input, even if such input can be managed to better reflect stakeholder interests. Thus mechanisms must be developed to hold Bank staff accountable to agreements negotiated with civil society.

Currently TCS' contributions to policymaking mirror the imbalances inherent in the state-driven system. States continue to be key players in the international system and TCSOs from powerful nations show little hesitation in exploiting the power of their states to achieve their goals. At the World Bank in particular, the system of voting shares privileges powerful states. Rebalancing state power at the World Bank is a noble goal, but one that has made limited progress over the past two decades (Bretton Woods Project 2010). A more realistic solution might be to limit the power of all states by magnifying the Bank's technocratic nature. This could be done by imbuing policy dialogues with real decision-making power. This would have the dual effects of increasing TCS power vis-à-vis Bank staff while decreasing the role of state influence with its concomitant inequalities.

In order for formal dialogues to produce democratic decisions, policies must be developed that ensure a representative cross-section of civil society actors and enhance the accountability of TCSOs. Resources play a significant role in prompting or facilitating organizations' participation in policymaking. Wealthy populations tend to field more TCSOs, particularly professional advocacy NGOs, than poor ones, creating a real possibility that Southern voices would be drowned out in an open dialogue. Developing a means for selecting a representative group of participants is an obvious requirement if policy dialogues are to really enhance democracy.

Creating a representative group of participants requires determining for whom each TCSO actually speaks. Identifying representative TCSOs on the basis of their own claims is difficult; it seems unlikely that an organization can be trusted to consistently represent a population to which it is not accountable. Mere consultation between an organization and a local population does not ensure accountability, nor does partnership between a TCSO and grassroots organizations. Therefore alternative means must be developed of ensuring that TCSOs are accountable to specific populations in ways that allow their representative claims to be verified. Once policymakers can determine on whose behalf TCSOs actually speak, it should be possible to assemble dialogues in which various stakeholder groups are represented, via TCSOs, in an equitable fashion. Both the Bank and TCSOs can help facilitate such an outcome.

Initial steps for the World Bank

The Bank should focus on increasing the number of formal dialogues with TCS, imbuing such dialogues with greater power, and limiting the number of informal interactions with civil society. It should also manage TCS's participation in formal dialogues in such a way as to obtain a cross-section of representative participants and incentivize TCSOs to develop their own credentials as stakeholder representatives. These steps would have the effect of regularizing and expanding TCS's influence, while channeling that influence through representative and accessible mechanisms.

As noted, using TCS to democratize Bank decision-making should begin with the creation of more formal policy dialogues. In the same way that the Bank has developed a standard practice of engaging with national and local civil society in its project decisions, so too it could engage with civil society regarding changes in its international policies. These dialogues must also be given some measure of real authority in the decision-making process (cf. Ebrahim and Herz 2011; McKeon 2010). If this could be achieved, it would mitigate some of the problems of elite or state-based influence. It would also create positive incentives for constructive interactions among TCSOs. If major policies are more often shaped by formal dialogues, powerful CSOs may turn their attention towards gaining access to such dialogues or lobbying the other participants, rather than pursuing the support of policy elites. Due to their resources and expertise, currently powerful TCSOs would doubtless be influential even within formal dialogues or while acting as lobbyists, but they would have to contend with a more democratic setting.

In order to create equal access and representation, the Bank should stipulate that the organizations involved in formal dialogues each be accountable to a specific population. Access to the dialogue itself can then be structured to involve a cross-section of potential representatives of the impacted stakeholders. Given that other international institutions, such as the UN, have an accreditation process for CSOs, it does not seem unreasonable for the Bank to screen would-be participants and create criteria for participation.

As shown in this research, simple claims of representation, even when backed by on-the-ground consultations, are not reliable indicators of representivity. Funding, however, does create an accountability link between an organization and the stakeholders that fund it. Thus one possible screening mechanism would be to look at organizational funding. Such a move would likely privilege grassroots organizations over professionalized NGOs. The developing world is rife with civil society, in the form of village associations, church groups, farmers' collectives, and the like. All of these are funded by contributions from their members and many would be eager to engage on the international policies effecting them if provided with the opportunity (cf. McKeon 2010). The Bank has already demonstrated a facility for locating such organizations for project consultations. Therefore it should be capable of identifying them for invitations to participate in international dialogues.[2] Of course, for such organizations to participate, the Bank would need to fund the travel and expenses of their members and provide translation services. The Bank has already begun to do this by sponsoring limited CSO attendance at the Annual and Spring meetings of the World Bank and IMF (Scholte 2012, p. 199). Expanding this effort could be costly, but should be feasible within the overall expense structure of the Bank.

Initial steps for transnational civil society organizations

As shown in this book, TCS can act as an effective channel for citizen input into international relations. The problem is that such input is not evenly distributed or shared among all stakeholders. TCS must increase its input legitimacy so that it can more equitably represent the interests of the people affected by its influence in policymaking. Two steps may be helpful in this process. First, TCSOs should delimit their primary stakeholders and develop accountability to their stakeholder population. Second, organizations should engage in meaningful dialogue, incorporating disparate voices and developing commonly agreed proposals. Unlike changes at the World Bank, which involve the creation and implementation of new structures, change within TCS requires that certain organizations seek to pioneer and advance new norms. Insofar as these innovations must arise from within the practitioner community, there may be additional solutions that have not yet penetrated the academic literature and were not uncovered by this research. Nonetheless, the steps described here may provide a useful framework for discussion. The reader interested in practical solutions is also advised to consider Ebrahim (2007), McKeon (2010) and Scholte (2012), whose work both reinforces many of the points made here and offers some alternative suggestions.

To become more accountable to their stakeholders, TCSOs need to begin by defining clearly their stakeholder populations. A population might include all of the people affected by a certain development policy; the citizens of a certain country; or adherents to a certain faith. The key is to make clear on exactly whose behalf an organization is speaking. Organizations may lobby on behalf of certain ideas or principles or seek to build a new movement, but even issue- or idea-based organizations should be able to define their stakeholder population. Such populations, in turn, must be at least roughly enumerated. Insofar as democratic governance is a majoritarian affair, it is necessary to know approximately how large a given stakeholder population is.

To enhance claims of representivity, TCSOs should seek to be directly accountable to the populations they claim to represent. Accountability implies the potential for reward and punishment. Financial accountability has already been discussed. Other forms of accountability include an established creed or internal democratic structures. Faith-based groups may be considered representative in matters pertaining to the faith because both leaders and adherents are held to the same theological standard. Many grassroots organizations in the developing world allow members to elect their leader or chief officers. Certain US organizations, like Bread for the World, hold annual meetings at which members vote on organization priorities. Friends of the Earth International practices meaningful North-South dialogue, granting all of its national chapters equal voice in deciding the international organization's agenda (see Doherty 2006). Unions also tend to use internal votes on key decisions. Provided that such populist mechanisms are binding on the leadership, such voting could be considered proof of accountability.

TCSOs may also need to revise and narrow their representative claims to match their scope of accountability. Many TCSOs, particularly those based in the global North, already have de facto accountability to a set of Northern donors or members. The problem in such cases is not a general lack of accountability per se, but claims to represent stakeholders (often large groups of stakeholders) well outside the population to which the TCSO is accountable. An effort to limit the claims of one's group to the population to which it is accountable may help reveal the absence of Southern voices in international policymaking and create a space Southern voices can grow to fill.

Increasing transparency and accountability would require time and money from those organizations which do not currently release financial records or have internal democratic mechanisms. Organizations might also be reluctant to release funding information, particularly if their funding stream comes from a very limited set of donors. Indeed, both organizations and donors might be resistant to increased transparency. Organizations might also be inclined to defend existing claims to representivity, rather than delimiting a narrower stakeholder group, lest they undermine the credibility of previous or ongoing advocacy work. It is important to acknowledge that most powerful organizations are likely the ones with the most to lose. Major advocacy NGOs based in the global North have significant power and many have already established their credibility with key policymakers. For such actors, reforming representation may entail more risks than rewards.

Nonetheless, given that many CSOs already claim representation as a value, it is possible for a norm of enhancing representation through accountability to develop and spread over time. The fact that some civil society organizations, including some American NGOs, practice internal democracy indicates that such practices are possible. If the reforms are feasible, then the primary barriers to widespread reform are ones of opinion or interest, not logistics or practicality. If a few actors were to release financial donation records, improve stakeholder voice within the organizations, or engage more meaningfully with Southern partners, the reform process could snowball.

Enhancing dialogue is perhaps a more complicated task. It is easy to say that dialogues among TCSOs should feature diverse partners, focus on developing consensus or majoritarian policy positions and proposals, and prioritize stakeholder interests over organizational interests. However, many TCSOs already claim to uphold these norms, even if the data contradicts such claims. One partial solution is better facilitating the participation of Southern civil society. As noted earlier, actors from the developing world may lack the resources necessary to participate in international dialogues and developing country actors receiving funding from an outside organization may be inclined to adjust their positions to favor their patrons. Similarly, would-be patrons may be inclined to select partners based on the degree to which those partners support the patron's view.

A possible solution involves developing a practice of collective funding. Wealthy CSOs involved in a particular issue or policy process could pool a portion of their resources in order to fund the involvement of developing country actors. To avoid the temptation to manipulate the process, would-be funders could assemble around a broad issue (such as the environment, trade, or labor standards) without defining specific policy objectives. The resulting funding coalitions would then seek to choose their partners on their merits as representatives, as judged by their accountability to a group of claimed stakeholders, rather than their adherence to a particular policy position. Sponsoring Southern civil society organizations' involvement in TCS dialogues will not, by itself, make TCS dialogues democratic. However, the presence of independent Southern voices might help catalyze more inclusive, meaningful debate.

Transnational intervention in domestic processes

It is important to note that increasing the representivity of TCS does little to deal with the problems associated with TCS intervention in the affairs of democratic states. The passion most TCSOs have for their issues (and the unfortunate contempt in which many Northern TCSOs seem to hold Southern governments) makes them unlikely to withdraw from policy advocacy in favor of the government. However, as much as possible, TCSOs should seek to distinguish between democratic and undemocratic governments. Tests of democracy could go beyond mere elections to encompass the protection of rights or a lack of corruption; however, the standards should be transparent and should not be more stringent than those applied to recognized Northern democracies. When engaging with issues in democratic countries, TCSO should to seek to localize the discussion by supporting local partners as they foment debate, rather than internationalizing local decisions through transnational campaigns that risk undermining local democratic processes.

Final considerations

The vast majority of the world's citizens live in poverty in underdeveloped nations. Some of these nations are undemocratic, and many of them lack strong influence in the global arena. If the growing importance of global governance is to impact these persons in a positive way, by protecting rights, alleviating poverty, or facilitating development, such populations must have an equitable say in the decisions affecting them. For transnational actors, whether international institutions or TCSOs, claiming to develop policy on behalf of such populations is no substitute for creating democratic institutions and mechanisms that allow them to speak for themselves. As this book has shown, TCS has the power to both enhance stakeholder authority and to inhibit equality and representivity. Enabling TCS to fulfill its potential as a democratizing force will require continued research on the motivations and constraints that determine TCSO behavior and the creation of new, data-driven policies and norms that reshape TCSOs' behavior and impacts.

Notes

Chapter 1   Waiting on Democracy

1   To take just one recent example, the UN Convention on Genocide did not, despite much anticipation, lead to UN intervention in Darfur once genocide was publicly declared (see Bellamy and Williams 2006).

Chapter 2   Context, Role, and Legitimacy

1   Portions of this chapter were first published in Pallas, Christopher L. 2010. Revolutionary, Advocate, Agent, or Authority: Context-based Assessment of Democratic Legitimacy in Transnational Civil Society. *Ethics and Global Politics*, 3(3): 217–238.
2   Because not all of the contexts discussed in this chapter are transnational, this chapter uses the more general terms 'civil society' and 'civil society organization (CSO)'.
3   Granted, Habermasian depictions of deliberative democracy are non-majoritarian. However, deliberative democracy requires open access in order to function. Only when all ideas can be brought to the debate is it guaranteed that discussion will reveal the ultimate good. There is abundant evidence that international policy discussions are not universally accessible, and that TCS itself may be dominated by elites. Were this standard applied to TCS, it seems unlikely that any international network or campaign would pass muster.
4   See, for example, the cases in Fox and Brown (1998b) and Clark et al (2003).
5   Each of these three contexts includes substantial internal variation. For example, the context of democratic states includes states with varying forms (and, some would say, 'quality') of democracy. For the sake of parsimony, this book does not model the variation within these three contexts or detail methods for evaluating the contexts themselves (e.g. by specifying the threshold at which a state becomes democratic). I would argue that these are second order concerns compared to the question of how different contexts create different standards for CSOs' democratic legitimacy, which much of the civil society literature to date has ignored.
6   To put the issue metaphorically, a midfielder does not become a goalkeeper simply because he grabs the ball with his hands. Were he or she to do such a thing, we would not refer to him as tending goal but rather as committing a handball.
7   Many CSOs combine the agent role with other activities. For instance, religious organizations in the US may receive government funds to run homeless shelters and yet also act as advocates on behalf of the homeless. It is likely that taking on the role of agent either diminishes or magnifies an organization's capacity for advocacy or revolution, but in the interest of parsimony, the various roles are treated here discretely.

8   Tvedt (2002) makes a detailed discussion of these issues.
9   In those instances in which CSOs operate in multiple contexts without any pretense toward establishing a global norm, institution, or regulation, or toward benefiting a transnational population, their legitimacy must be judged by the political context of the intended beneficiaries of their actions. Reasons for this are discussed later in this chapter, under 'Intervention in Local Settings'.

Chapter 3   Beating the Bank: Transnational Civil Society and the 10th IDA

1   Popular participation was initially intertwined with engagement with formal NGOs. The United Nations Development Programme, for instance, defined participation as dialogue with NGOs for much of the 1980s (Howell and Pearce 2002, pp. 97–98). However, the concept as used by the World Bank and the NGO Working Group referred to engagement with grassroots stakeholders, especially project-affected people, which could occur through civil society organizations (church groups, agricultural collectives, etc.) or ad hoc meetings. For the sake of clarity, I am here referring only to the evolution of this latter, more populist conception of participation. This is the usage most germane to the actors discussed in this chapter, and it has also been the more widely accepted definition since the mid-1990s (cf. Howell and Pearce 2002, p. 98).
2   Wade's account was also verified for this book by two environmental staffers active during this period.
3   Friends of the Earth has seventy-six member groups internationally. However, all references to Friends of the Earth or FoE in this book refer to Friends of the Earth US.
4   According to a source at NWF, the organization helped fund the involvement of Japanese environmental organizations.
5   One source for this data was from a major environmental group which eschewed the committee; another was from a development and justice NGO which joined the committee.
6   101st US Congress, PL 101-240, December 1989.
7   World Bank, 1991, OD 4.00: Environmental Assessment.
8   See, for example: Invitation issued by the Bank Information Center (BIC), CIEL, EDF, and others for a cocktail party launching 'The New International Alliance of the Indigenous-Tribal Peoples of the Tropical Forests', 19 March 1992; and fax from Jonathan Miller of BIC to Andy Storey of Trocaire, 25 June 1992. Documents provided to the author as scanned copies of the originals by the Bank Information Center (BIC), December 2007. See also Crossette (1992b).
9   Fax from Jonathan Miller of BIC to Andy Storey of Trocaire, 25 June 1992.
10 See, for example, 'Position Paper from Irish Non-Governmental Organizations (NGOs) Regarding the Tenth Capital Replenishment of the International Development Association', dated June–September, 1992.
11 US Treasury, 'Tenth Replenishment of the International Development Association (IDA 10)', 24 January 1992.

12 US Treasury, 'IDA X: Quality of Project Lending', 21 April 1992.

13 See statements by MPs Michael Meacher and John Denham, during UK Parliamentary debate on a motion by the Under-Secretary of State for Foreign and Commonwealth Affairs that funding for IDA-10 be approved. UK Parliamentary record, 12 July 1993, 11:10pm. Meacher criticizes the 'anti-social and anti-development policies of the World Bank' while Denham notes that he was forced to obtain Bank documents via US NGOs.

14 Author's interview with Maureen Smyth, Senior Vice President for Programs and Communications, Charles Stewart Mott Foundation, interview by phone, 21 March 2008. Hereafter: 'Interview: Smyth'.

15 A letter from John Kerin, Australia Minister for Trade and Overseas Development to Gregg Barrett, Third World Forum, 7 September 1992 addresses the NGO's concerns regarding Narmada and welcomes the 'vital role which NGOs and their widespread networks play' in monitoring the Bank. The letter notes that Kerrin has asked Robin Casson, Australian's lead IDA deputy, to 'arrange a meeting with interested NGOs' prior to the September IDA meeting and 'where appropriate, incorporate [their concerns] into the Australian position'.

16 Fax from Andy Storey of Trocaire to Jonathan Miller of BIC, 1 July 1992.

17 'Position Paper from Irish Non-Governmental Organizations (NGOs) Regarding the Tenth Capital Replenishment of the International Development Association', dated 'June–September, 1992 [sic]'.

18 US Treasury, 'IDA Deputies Meeting, Dublin, July 1–2, 1992, "The Environment"', 30 July 1992.

19 World Bank, 'Meeting Between IDA Deputies, Executive Directors, and NGOs', 16 September 1992.

20 Document is unattributed; obtained from BIC. See also Bruce Rich, Lori Udall, and Deborah Moore, all of EDF, 'Letter to the Editor: Before We Let the World Bank Squander More', *The New York Times*, 6 January 1993.

21 Advertisement, 'Your Tax Money – Funding Yet Another World Bank Disaster: Why thousands of people will drown before accepting the Sardar Sarovar Dam', *The New York Times*, 21 September 1992.

22 Fax from David Reed, Director, International Institutions Policy Program, WWF to George A. Folsom, Deputy Assistant Secretary, International Development, Debt and Environment Policy, US Treasury, 3 September 1992.

23 Letter from Mazide N'diaye, Co-Chair, NGO/World Bank Working Group, to Lewis Preston, President, World Bank, 30 October 1992.

24 Ibid.

25 Fax from Lori Udall to US NGOs, 23 November 1992.

26 Ibid.; fax from Randy Hayes of Rainforest Action Network to Lori Udall of EDF 24 November 1992; and fax from BIC to US Representative Barney Frank, 2 March 1993.

27 Bruce Rich, Lori Udall, and Deborah Moore, Director, staff lawyer, and staff scientist of EDF's international program (respectively), 6 January 1993.

28 Willi Wapenhans, 'Letter to the Editor: World Bank Keeps Improving Its Approach', *The New York Times*, 23 January 1993.

29 World Bank, 'Additions to IDA Resources: 10th Replenishment', December 1992, pp. 4–5.

30 Kapur notes that the US was 'almost unique' among Bank donors in having 'two genuinely independent decision-making branches that always [were] at least in semi-conflict and both of which [needed] wooing' (Kapur et al 1997, p. 1145).

31 Hearings before the US House of Representatives Subcommittee on Foreign Operations, Export Financing, and Related Programs on the Foreign Operations, Export Financing, and Related Programs Appropriations for 1994, 1 March 1993 (Hereafter: Hearings, US House, 1 March 1993); hearings before the US House of Representatives Subcommittee on International Development, Finance, Trade, and Monetary Policy on Authorizing contributions to IDA, GEF, and ADF, 5 May 1993 (Hereafter: Hearings, US House, 5 May 1993); hearings before a US Senate subcommittee of the Committee on Appropriations, on Foreign Operations, Export Financing, and Related Programs Appropriations for Fiscal Year 1994, 15 June 1993 (Hereafter: Hearings, US Senate, 15 June 1993).

32 Hearings, US House, 1 March 1993 and Hearings, US House, 5 May 1993.

33 Hearings, US House, 1 March 1993.

34 Hearings, US House, 5 May 1993.

35 This account comes from a former Oxfam staff member, present at the time.

36 Congressional Record, 103rd Congress, 1st session, June 17, 1993.

37 Ibid.

38 US Congress, PL 103-87, 30 September 1993.

39 US Congress, PL 103-306, 23 August 1994.

Chapter 4   Principles and Paychecks: Positions and Participation in the IDA-10

1 See testimony by Glenn Prickett, Senior Associate, International Programs, Natural Resources Defense Council, during Hearings, US House, 5 May 1993.

2 Fax from David Reed, Director, International Institutions Policy Program, WWF to George A. Folsom, Deputy Assistant Secretary, International Development, Debt and Environment Policy, US Treasury, 3 September 1992.

3 Hearings, US House, 5 May 1993.

4 Letter from Mazide N'diaye, Co-Chair, NGO/World Bank Working Group, to Lewis Preston, President, World Bank, 30 October 1992.

5 Hearings, US House, 5 May 1993.

6 Hearings, US House, 1 March 1993.

7 Hearings, US House, 5 May 1993.

8 World Bank, 'Meeting Between IDA Deputies, Executive Directors, and NGOs', 16 September 1992.

9 Hearings, US House, 1 March 1993; and Hearings, US House, 5 May 1993.

10 Scholars frequently fold funding needs into the broader category of 'organizational imperatives'. However, respondents for this research used the much balder language of money and financing. To reflect faithfully the data provided, this section therefore focuses narrowly on the issue of funding.

11 Ashish Mandloi, Sanjay Sangvai, Devrambhai Kanera, Manglya Vasave, Kamala Yadav, and Medha Patkar, 'NBA Responds to Inquiries on Foreign Funding', *The South Asian* (thesouthasian.org), 9 July 2006.
12 Interview: Smyth.
13 Charles Stewart Mott Foundation, 'Mott Grants, Program Area: Reform of International Finance and Trade, 1990–1994'. Database print out, prepared 22 May 2008. Provided to the author by the foundation. (Hereafter: Mott Grants 1990–1994)
14 Ibid.
15 Hearings, US Senate, 15 June 1993.
16 Hearings, US House, 1 March 1993.
17 Mott Grants 1990–1994.

Chapter 5   Mechanisms of Influence and the Distribution of Authority

1 See statement by John Denham, during UK Parliamentary debate on a motion by the Under-Secretary of State for Foreign and Commonwealth Affairs that funding for IDA-10 be approved. UK Parliamentary record, 12 July 1993, 11:10pm.
2 Human Rights Watch and the National Resources Defense Council, *Defending the Earth: Abuses of Human Rights and the Environment* (New York: Human Rights Watch and NRDC, 1992), pp. 49–70.
3 In 1990 the Bank formed the Learning Group on Participatory Development, which involved NGO input. The Learning Group issued its report in 1994. Manuals on participatory consultations were produced in 1995 and updated in later years.
4 US Treasury, 'IDA 10 Deputies' Report, Revised Draft', 1993. See also Kapur et al 1997, pp. 1149–1150.
5 Republicans controlled the executive under George H.W. Bush from 1989–1992, including the period when the replenishment agreement was negotiated. Democrats controlled Congress through 1994, when most of the funding for the agreement was to be authorized.
6 The sole exception being Bread for the World, represented by Nancy Alexander. According to a source at Bread, Alexander had close relationships with the environmental community.
7 Fax from Chad Dobson, Secretary of the Bank Information Center, to Congressman Barney Frank, 11 December 1992.
8 Fax from Chad Dobson to meeting invitees, 14 January 1993. Affiliations of the invitees were listed as EDF, NRDC, FoE, Global Legislators for a Balanced Environment, Environment and Energy Study Institute, World Resources Institute, Audubon, CIEL, Bread, Sierra Club, Committee on Agricultural Sustainability in Developing Countries, Conservation International, International Union for the Conservation of Nature, WWF, Interaction, Church World Service, Greenpeace, and the Nature Conservancy.
9 These were Bread for the World and Church World Service.
10 Fax from Chad Dobson to Congressman Barney Frank, 27 January 1993.

11 Fax from Chad Dobson to invited NGOs, 29 January 1993. See also fax from Glenn Prickett, NRDC to Congressman Barney Frank, 2 April 1993.
12 Fax from the Bank Information Center to Representative Barney Frank, 3 February 1993.
13 Fax from Chad Dobson to Sydney Key, staff for the House Subcommittee on International Development, Finance, Trade, and Monetary Policy, 14 April 1993.
14 Fax from Chad Dobson to Sydney Key, staff for the House Subcommittee on International Development, Finance, Trade, and Monetary Policy, 15 March 1993; Fax from Chad Dobson to Sydney Key, and Tim Reiser, Senate Committee on Appropriations, 4 April 1993.
15 Letter from Kathryn S. Fuller, President WWF, to Congressman David Obey, Chair US House Subcommittee on Foreign Operations, Export Financing, and Related Operations, 25 March 1993.
16 Both pro- and anti-IDA TCSOs submitted additional written testimony.
17 Hearings, US House, 1 March 1993.
18 Hearings, US House, 5 May 1993.
19 Hearings, US House, 1 March 1993.
20 US Congress, 5 May 1993.
21 US House of Representatives Record Ref. Vol. 139, No. 86, 17 June 1993.
22 States also, of course, retain control over bilateral and multilateral policy-making, which may not involve any international institutions. However, such state-to-state negotiations have different dynamics than institutional policymaking and are thus beyond the scope of this book.
23 To be clear, the creation of a mechanism of input is itself an output, just as the creation of a constitution specifying regular elections would be considered a democratic output. It is the elections themselves, if implemented in a free and fair way, that would constitute a democratic input.

Chapter 6 Transnational Civil Society and Local Representation

1 In addition to share votes, each country also receives a number of basic votes. The system of share and vote allocation in place in the era of the IDA-10 is detailed in William Gianaris, 'Weighted Voting in the International Monetary Fund and the World Bank', *Fordham International Law Journal* 14(1990): 927–928. The current process for vote allocation is described at World Bank, 'Voting Powers', http://go.worldbank.org/ VKVDQDUC10, accessed 19 April 2013.
2 World Bank Annual Report 1996.
3 The EDs for FY1996 came from the US, Japan, Germany, France, UK, Austria, Canada, Netherlands, Mexico, India, Italy, Pakistan, Sweden, Brazil, Switzerland, New Zealand, China, Saudi Arabia, Russia, Kuwait, Malawi, Thailand, Argentina, and Comoros. Of these, India, Pakistan, China, Malawi, and Comoros were eligible for IDA funds.
4 Borrowers were granted observer status in the mid-1990s.
5 World Bank, 'International Development Association', http://go. worldbank.org/83SUQPXD20, accessed 14 July 2009.

6 Hearings, US House, 5 May 1993.
7 During the 1980s, Bank funding was used for security-oriented resettlement by the governments of both Brazil and Indonesia, and had come under heavy attack by transnational activists.
8 Hearings, US House, 5 May 1993. See also Nelson (1997a, p. 427).
9 Hearings, US House, 5 May 1993.
10 Hearings, US House, 1 March 1993.
11 Ibid.
12 Hearings, US House, 5 May 1993.
13 Ibid.
14 Ibid. See testimony of David Reed of WWF for a similar statement.
15 Hearings, US House, 1 March 1993; emphasis added.
16 Ibid.
17 See also Mbogori and Chigudu (1999), and Wiesen et al (1999).
18 US Treasury, 'IDA Deputies Meeting, Dublin, July 1–2, 1992, "The Environment"', 30 July 1992. Deputy interest in meeting with CSOs from borrower countries culminated in the meeting held 16 September 1992 between deputies and six NGOs, hosted by the World Bank.
19 Author's interview with Bruce Rich, 19 February 2008, Washington, DC.
20 See, for instance, advertisement, 'Your Tax Money – Funding Yet Another World Bank Disaster: Why thousands of people will drown before accepting the Sardar Sarovar Dam', *The New York Times*, 21 September 1992; Udall (1995) also exemplifies this.
21 Hearings, US House, 5 May 1993.
22 Author's interview with John Clark, formerly of Oxfam-UK, 7 December 2007, Washington, DC.
23 Ibid; Patel and Mehta (1995).

Chapter 7   Beyond the 10th IDA

1 Information on the GCS Team comes from the author's interviews with Bank staff with direct knowledge of the team's activities, including a former team member. See also the team's website, http://go.worldbank.org/8DJ82AMKB0, viewed 16 February 2008.
2 Also, World Bank, *Accountability at the World Bank: The Inspection Panel Ten Years On*, pp. 51–57.
3 The World Bank Inspection Panel Report, 'The Inspection Panel Report on Request for Inspection Nepal: Proposed Arun III Hydroelectric Project and Restructuring of the Arun III Access Road Project (Credit 2029-NEP)', 16 December 1994.
4 Gopal Siwakoti, quoted by Lori Udall, Washington Director, International Rivers Network, in 'Arun III Hydroelectric Project in Nepal: Another World Bank Debacle?' 1 March 1995. See also Statement by Bikash Pandey (Alliance for Energy, Nepal) to the World Bank Board of Executive Directors, 'Experience with the Arun (Nepal) Claim', 3 February 1998.
5 Cf. Report by Environmental Defense Fund, Friends of the Earth, International Rivers Network. 'Gambling with People's Lives: What the

World Bank's New 'High-Risk/High-Reward' Strategy Means for the Poor and the Environment', September 2003.

6 Mott Grants 1990–1994.

7 World Bank press release, 'World Bank and Nepal to Develop Alternatives to Arun Project', 3 August 1995. Release notes that the Bank has cancelled the project in spite of 'support for the Arun III, both among all of Nepal's political parties and from most of the residents in the valley.' Bissell (2003) confirms general support in the valley.

8 See also World Bank, 'Memorandum of the President of the International Development Association to the Executive Directors on a Country Assistance Strategy Progress Report of the World Bank Group for the Kingdom of Nepal', 18 November 2002. The report indicates that cancellation of the project 'generated wide negative publicity for the Bank' in Nepal and that 'even in 2002 there is frequent mention of the Bank and this particular project in the Nepali press'.

9 See press release by Lori Udall, Washington Director, International Rivers Network, 'Arun III Hydroelectric Project In Nepal: Another World Bank Debacle?', 1 March 1995.

10 See also World Bank press release, 'World Bank and Nepal to Develop Alternatives to Arun Project', 3 August 1995.

11 World Bank, *Accountability at the World Bank: The Inspection Panel Ten Years On*, pp. 56–57. See also World Bank press release, 'World Bank and Nepal to Develop Alternatives to Arun Project', 3 August 1995.

12 Report by Environmental Defense Fund, Friends of the Earth, and International Rivers Network, 'Gambling with People's Lives: What the World Bank's New 'High-Risk/High-Reward' Strategy Means for the Poor and the Environment', September 2003.

13 World Bank press release, 'World Bank and Nepal to Develop Alternatives to Arun Project', 3 August 1995.

14 Ibid.

15 World Bank, 'Memorandum of the President of the International Development Association to the Executive Directors on a Country Assistance Strategy Progress Report of the World Bank Group for the Kingdom of Nepal', 18 November 2002.

16 Statement by Bikash Pandey (Alliance for Energy, Nepal) to the World Bank Board of Executive Directors, 'Experience with the Arun (Nepal) Claim', 3 February 1998.

17 Business interests were represented primarily by associations, such as the Federation of German Industries (BDI) and the US Council for International Business. Development Finance International (DFI), a DC-based consultancy serving corporations seeking to engage with the Bank, also played a prominent role. Some individual corporations participated directly; for instance, General Electric sent a representative to 10 December 2007 consultation in Washington, DC. Sources indicate alliances between TCS and business occurred through industry proxies, rather than with the representatives of individual corporations.

18 United Nations Department of Economic and Social Affairs, 'Monterrey Consensus of the International Conference on Financing for Development', 2004.

19 Operations Policy and Country Services, 'Use of Country Systems in Bank-Supported Operations – Status Report (Incorporating R2007-0079 and R2007-0079/3)', 9 October 2007, pp. 1–3.
20 The ILO is a tripartite organization representing the interests of labor, business, and government. Representatives, however, attended the Washington consultation with civil society, where they focused particularly on the potential impact of UCS on labor standards.
21 For more detailed notes on business participation, see meeting reports available at http://go.worldbank.org/B9QAG7P2X0. Viewed 19 July 2010.
22 Author's coverage of the public consultation, New York, NY, 14 December 2007.
23 Author's coverage of the public consultations in Washington, DC, 10 December and 13 December 2007, and the public consultation in New York, NY, 14 December 2007, plus conversations with others present at additional consultations.
24 DFI played a particularly prominent role in this process. See DFI PowerPoint attached to Bank report of 10 December 2010 consultation at http://go.worldbank.org/B9QAG7P2X0. Viewed 19 July 2010.
25 Key participants shared with the author internal correspondence demonstrating this effort. See also World Bank: Country Systems Consultations: Summary of Feedback. Available at http://go.worldbank.org/B9QAG7P2X0. Viewed 19 July 2010.
26 One such criticism, authored by DFI, can be seen online at: http://siteresources.worldbank.org/INTPROCUREMENT/Resources/ConsultationTranscript-Presentation-HQ.pps. Viewed 19 July 2010. Evidence of discussions with government staff comes from author's correspondence with key participants.
27 These included the 10 December 2007 meeting in Washington, DC at which DFI presented its detailed critique of the proposal.

Chapter 8 Transnational Civil Society and the Democratization of Global Governance

1 Clifford Bob (2005) has also elaborated on these dynamics in the selection of local partners by Northern NGOs.
2 Scholte (2012), writing regarding the IMF, notes that such engagement may also need to reflect diversity in other ways, e.g. by deliberately including rural or female-led CSOs. See also McKeon (2010).

References

50 Years is Enough Network. Undated. History, http://www.50years.org/pdf/ 10thAnniversary/history.pdf, accessed 8 July 2009.

Anderson, Kenneth. 2000. 'The Ottawa Convention Banning Landmines, the Role of International Non-governmental Organizations and the Idea of International Civil Society.' *European Journal of International Law* 11(1): 91–120.

Archibugi, Daniele. 2004. 'Cosmopolitan Democracy and Its Critics: A Review.' *European Journal of International Relations* 10(3): 437–473.

Atkinson, Jeff. 2007. 'International NGOs in Southern Advocacy: Case Studies of Two Oxfam Campaigns in Southern Asia.' London: ESRC Non-Governmental Public Action Programme Working Paper. Available online at http://webfirstlive.lse.ac.uk/internationalDevelopment/research/NGPA/fel-lowships/practitionerfellowships/pdfs/Oxfam_Atkinson_Report.pdf, accessed 14 June 2013.

Barnett, Michael and Martha Finnemore. 1999. 'The Politics, Power, and Pathologies of International Organizations.' *International Organization* 53(4): 699–732.

Barrett, Marlene (ed.) 2000. *The World Will Never Be the Same Again.* London: Jubilee 2000 Coalition and World Vision.

Bellamy, Alex and Paul Williams. 2006. 'The UN Security Council and the Question of Humanitarian Intervention in Darfur.' *Journal of Military Ethics* 5(2): 144–160.

Bernhard, Michael. 1993. 'Civil Society and Democratic Transition in East Central Europe.' *Political Science Quarterly* 108(2): 307–326.

Berry, Jeffrey M. 1999. 'The Rise of Citizen Groups.' In *Civic Engagement in American Democracy*, edited by T. Skocpol and M. Fiorina. Washington, DC: Brookings Institution Press.

Bexell, Magdalena, Jonas Tallberg and Anders Uhlin. 2010. 'Democracy in Global Governance: The Promises and Pitfalls of Transnational Actors.' *Global Governance* 16: 81–101.

BIC. 2003. Bank Information Center, 'BIC Toolkit for Activists: Issue 3. The World Bank's Policy Framework: The "Safeguard" Policies, Compliance and the Independent Inspection Panel', http://www.bicusa.org/en/Article.295.aspx, accessed 14 July 2009. See also the Center for International Environmental Law, 'Brief Summaries of Inspection Panel Claims', http://www.ciel.org/Ifi/ ifibs.html#Arun, accessed 14 July 2009.

BIC. 2004. Bank Information Center, Country Systems Approach to World Bank Social and Environmental Safeguards: Concerns and Challenges, http://www. bicusa.org/en/Article.1775.aspx, accessed 14 July 2009.

Bissell, Richard. 2003. 'The Arun III Hydroelectric Project, Nepal.' In *Demanding Accountability: Civil-Society Claims and the World Bank Inspection Panel*, edited by D. Clark, J. Fox and K. Treakle. Oxford: Rowman and Littlefield Publishers, Inc.

Bob, Clifford. 2005. *The Marketing of Rebellion: Insurgents, Media and International Activism*. Cambridge: Cambridge University Press.

Bowden, Brett. 2006. 'Civil Society, the State, and the Limits to Global Civil Society.' *Global Society* 20(2): 155–178.

Bradlow, Daniel. 1993a. The Case for a World Bank Ombudsman. Policy paper submitted to the US House of Representatives Subcommittee on International Development, Finance, Trade and Monetary Policy of the Banking, Finance and Urban Affairs Committee, May 1993.

Bradlow, Daniel. 1993b. 'International Organizations and Private Complaints: The Case of the World Bank Inspection Panel.' *Virginia Journal of International Law* 34: 553–613.

Bretton Woods Project. 2004. UK NGO Meeting with Executive Director Tom Scholar, 14 December 2004, http://www.brettonwoodsproject.org/art-90445, accessed 19 February 2009.

Bretton Woods Project. 2008. World Bank and Procurement: Development Tool or TNC Sop? http://www.brettonwoodsproject.org/art-561019, accessed 10 March 2009.

Bretton Woods Project. 2010. Analysis of World Bank Voting Reforms: Governance Remains Illegitimate and Outdated, http://www.brettonwoodsproject.org/art-566281, accessed 10 January 2013.

Brown, L. David, Alnoor Ebrahim and Srilatha Batliwala. 2012. 'Governing International Advocacy NGOs.' *World Development* 40(6): 1098–1108.

Busby, Joshua. 2007. 'Bono Made Jesse Helms Cry: Jubilee 2000, Debt Relief, and Moral Action in International Politics.' *International Studies Quarterly* 51: 247–275.

Carpenter, R. Charli. 2007. 'Setting the Advocacy Agenda: Theorizing Issue Emergence and Nonemergence in Transnational Advocacy Networks.' *International Studies Quarterly* 51: 99–120.

Chatterjee, Pratap. 1995. 'No Reconsideration of Arun III: Wolfensohn.' *Inter-Press Service*, published in *The Nepal Digest*, 23 October.

CIEL. Undated. Center for International Environmental Law, Brief Summaries of Inspection Panel Claims, http://www.ciel.org/Ifi/ifibs.html#Arun, accessed 14 July 2009.

Clark, Ann Marie. 2001. *Diplomacy of Conscience: Amnesty International and Changing Human Rights Norms*. Princeton: Princeton University Press.

Clark, Dana. 2003. 'Understanding the World Bank Inspection Panel.' In *Demanding Accountability: Civil Society Claims and the World Bank Inspection Panel*, edited by D. Clark, J. Fox and K. Treakle. Oxford: Rowman and Littlefield Publishers, Inc.

Clark, Dana, Jonathan Fox and Kay Treakle (eds) 2003. *Demanding Accountability: Civil Society Claims and the World Bank Inspection Panel*. Oxford: Rowman and Littlefield Publishers, Inc.

Clark, John. 1991. *Democratizing Development: The Role of Voluntary Organizations*. London: Earthscan Publications Ltd.

Colas, Alejandro. 2002. *International Civil Society: Social Movements in World Politics*. Oxford: Wiley-Blackwell.

Cooley, Alexander and James Ron. 2002. 'The NGO Scramble: Organizational Insecurity and the Political Economy of Transnational Action.' *International Security* 27(1): 5–39.

Cornia, Giovanni, Richard Jolly and Frances Stewart. 1987. *Adjustment with a Human Face: Protecting the Vulnerable and Promoting Growth*. Gloucestershire, UK: Clarendon Press.

Covey, Jane G. 1998. 'Is Critical Cooperation Possible? Influencing the World Bank through Operational Collaboration and Policy Dialogue.' In *The Struggle for Accountability*, edited by J. Fox and L.D. Brown. Cambridge: MIT Press.

Crossette, Barbara. 1992a. 'The Earth Summit: What Some Preach in Rio is Not What They Practice at Home.' *The New York Times*, 15 June.

Crossette, Barbara. 1992b. 'Movement Builds to Fight Harmful Projects in Poor Nations.' *The New York Times*, 23 June.

Dahl, Robert. 1999. 'Can International Institutions Be Democratic?' In *Democracy's Edges*, edited by I. Shapiro and C. Hacker-Cordon. Cambridge: Cambridge University Press.

Daley-Harris, Sam. 2007. Imagine: A Nation that Cares for Itself, and for All Humanity, http://www.results.org/website/article.asp?id=31, accessed 30 September 2008.

Dingwerth, Klaus. 2007. *The New Transnationalism: Transnational Governance and Democratic Legitimacy*. New York: Palgrave Macmillan.

Doherty, Brian. 2006. 'Friends of the Earth International: Negotiating an International Identity.' *Environmental Politics* 15(5): 860–880.

Ebrahim, Alnoor. 2007. 'Toward a Reflective Accountability in NGOs.' In *Global Accountabilities: Participation, Pluralism, and Public Ethics*, edited by A. Ebrahim and E. Weisband. Cambridge: Cambridge University Press.

Ebrahim, Alnoor and Steven Herz. 2011. 'The World Bank and Democratic Accountability: The Role of Civil Society.' In *Building Global Democracy? Civil Society and Accountable Global Governance*, edited by J.A. Scholte. Cambridge: Cambridge University Press.

Edwards, Michael and John Gaventa. 2001. *Global Citizen Action*. Boulder, CO: Lynne Rienner.

Evangelista, Matthew. 1999. *Unarmed Forces: The Transnational Movement to End the Cold War*. London: Cornell University Press.

Fatton Jr., Robert. 1995. 'Africa in the Age of Democratization: The Civic Limitations of Civil Society.' *African Studies Review* 38(2): 67–99.

Fioramonti, Lorenzo. 2005. 'Civil Societies and Democratization: Assumptions, Dilemmas and the South African Experience.' *Theoria* 52(107): 65–88.

Fisher, William. 1995. 'Development and Resistance in the Narmada Valley.' In *Toward Sustainable Development? Struggling over India's Narmada River*, edited by W. Fisher. New York: M.E. Sharpe.

Florini, Ann (ed.) 2000. *The Third Force: The Rise of Transnational Civil Society*. Washington, DC: Carnegie Endowment for International Peace.

Florini, Ann and P.J. Simmons. 2000. 'What the World Needs Now?' In *The Third Force: The Rise of Transnational Civil Society*, edited by A. Florini. Washington, DC: Carnegie Endowment for International Peace.

Foley, M.W. and B. Edwards. 1996. 'The Paradox of Civil Society.' *Journal of Democracy* 7(3): 38–52.

Fox, Jonathan. 2003. 'Introduction: Framing the Inspection Panel.' In *Demanding Accountability: Civil Society Claims and the World Bank Inspection Panel*, edited by D. Clark, J. Fox and K. Treakle. Oxford: Rowman and Littlefield Publishers, Inc.

Fox, Jonathan and L. David Brown. 1998a. 'Assessing the Impact of NGO Advocacy Campaigns on World Bank Projects and Policies.' In *The Struggle for Accountability: The World Bank, NGOs, and Grassroots Movements*, edited by J. Fox and L.D. Brown. Cambridge: The MIT Press.

Fox, Jonathan and L. David Brown (eds) 1998b. *The Struggle for Accountability: The World Bank, NGOs, and Grassroots Movements*. Cambridge: The MIT Press.

Gill, M.S. 1995. 'Resettlement and Rehabilitation in Maharashtra for the Sardar Sarovar Narmada Project.' In *Toward Sustainable Development? Struggling over India's Narmada River*, edited by W. Fisher. New York: M.E. Sharpe.

Goodhart, Michael. 2005. 'Civil Society and the Problem of Global Democracy.' *Democratization* 12(1): 1–21.

Grzybowski, Candido. 2000. 'We NGOs: A Controversial Way of Being and Acting.' *Development in Practice* 10(34): 436–444.

Gulbrandsen, Lars and Steiner Andresen. 2004. 'NGO Influence in the Implementation of the Kyoto Protocol: Compliance, Flexibility Mechanisms, and Sinks.' *Global Environmental Politics* 4(4): 54–75.

Gwin, Catherine. 1994. *US Relations with the World Bank 1945–92*. Washington, DC: The Brookings Institution.

Hammond, Ross and Lisa McGowan. 1993. *The Other Side of the Story: The Real Impact of World Bank and IMF Structural Adjustment Programs*. Washington, DC: Development Group for Alternative Policies.

Held, David. 1995. *Democracy and the Global Order: From the Modern State to Cosmopolitan Governance*. Cambridge: Polity Press.

Held, David. 2004. 'Democratic Accountability and Political Effectiveness from a Cosmopolitan Perspective.' *Government and Opposition* 39(2): 364–391.

Held, David. 2006. *Models of Democracy, 3rd ed.* Cambridge: Polity.

Holmes, Steven. 1992. 'India Cancels Dam Loan from World Bank.' *The New York Times*, 31 March.

Howell, Jude. 2000. 'Making Civil Society from the Outside – Challenges for Donors.' *European Journal of Development Research* 12(1): 3–22.

Howell, Jude and Jenny Pearce. 2002. *Civil Society and Development: A Critical Exploration*. Boulder, CO: Lynne Rienner Publishers, Inc.

Hunter, David. 1996. The Planafloro Claim, http://www.ciel.org/Ifi/planafl.html, accessed 14 July 2009.

Ibrahim, Saad E. 1998. *Nurturing Civil Society at the World Bank: An Assessment of Staff Attitudes Towards Civil Society*. Washington, DC: World Bank.

Jolly, Richard. 1991. 'Adjustment with a Human Face: A UNICEF Perspective on the 1980s.' *World Development* 19(12): 1807–1821.

Kapur, Devesh, John Prior Lewis and Richard Charles Webb. 1997. *The World Bank: Its First Half Century, Vol. 1*. Washington, DC: Brookings Institution Press.

Keck, Margaret E. 2004. 'Governance Regimes and the Politics of Discursive Representation.' In *Transnational Activism in Asia: Problems of Power and Democracy*, edited by N. Piper and A. Uhlin. London: Routledge.

Keck, Margaret E. and Kathryn Sikkink. 1998. *Activists Beyond Borders: Advocacy Networks in International Politics*. Ithaca, NY: Cornell University Press.

Kopecky, Petr and Cas Mudde. 2003. 'Rethinking Civil Society.' *Democratization* 10(3): 1–14.

Korten, David C. 1998. *Globalizing Civil Society: Reclaiming Our Right to Power*, *1st ed.* New York: Seven Stories Press.

Lipschutz, Ronald. 1992. 'Reconstructing World Politics: The Emergence of Global Civil Society.' *Millennium: Journal of International Studies* 21(3): 389–420.

Lobe, Jim. 1995. 'Finance: IDA on the Edge.' Washington, *Inter Press Service*, 9 October.

Long, Carolyn. 2001. *Participation of the Poor in Development Initiatives: Taking Their Rightful Places.* Sterling, VA: Earthscan Publications.

Mahat, Ram. Undated. The Loss of Arun III, Nepal Study Center, University of New Mexico, http://nepalstudycenter.unm.edu/MissPdfFiles/The%20Loss%20of%20 Arun%20IIIRevised.pdf, accessed 13 July 2009.

Mallaby, Sebastian. 2004. *The World's Banker: A Story of Failed States, Financial Crises, and the Wealth and Poverty of Nations.* New York: The Penguin Press.

Manji, Firoze and Carl O'Coill. 2002. 'The Missionary Position: NGOs and Development in Africa.' *International Affairs* 78(3): 567–583.

Mansbach, Richard W., Yale H. Ferguson and Donald E. Lampert. 1976. *The Web of World Politics: Nonstate Actors in the Global System.* Englewood Cliffs, NJ: Prentice-Hall.

Marschall, Miklos. 1999. 'From States to People: Civil Society and Its Role in Governance.' In *Civil Society at the Millennium*, edited by K. Naidoo. Hartford: Kumarian.

Matthews, Jessica. 1997. 'Power Shift.' *Foreign Affairs* 76(1): 50–66.

Mbogori, Ezra and Hope Chigudu. 1999. 'Civil Society and Government: A Continuum of Possibilities.' In *Civil Society at the Millennium*, edited by K. Naidoo. Hartford: Kumarian Press.

McKeon, Nora. 2010. 'Who Speaks for the Poor and Why Does It Matter?' *UN Chronicle* 3: 39–42.

Mehta, Pradeep. 1994. 'Fury Over a River.' In *Fifty Years is Enough: The Case Against the World Bank and the International Monetary Fund*, edited by K. Danaher. Boston: South End Press.

Meyer, Carrie 1997. 'The Political Economy of NGOs and Information Sharing.' *World Development* 25(7): 1127–1140.

Mitchell, John. 1991. 'Public Campaigning on Overseas Aid in the 1980s.' In *Britain's Overseas Aid Since 1979*, edited by A. Bose and P. Burnell. Manchester: Manchester University Press.

Moravcsik, Andrew. 2004. 'Is there a "Democratic Deficit" in World Politics? A Framework for Analysis.' *Government and Opposition* 39(2): 336–363.

Murphy, Jonathan. 2005. 'The World Bank, INGOs, and Civil Society: Converging Agendas? The Case of Universal Basic Education in the Niger.' *Voluntas: International Journal of Voluntary and Nonprofit Organizations* 16(4): 353–374.

Naidoo, Kumi and Rajesh Tandon. 1999. 'The Promise of Civil Society.' In *Civil Society at the Millennium*, edited by K. Naidoo. Hartford: Kumarian Press.

Nanz, Patrizia and Jens Steffek. 2004. 'Global Governance, Participation and the Public Sphere.' *Government and Opposition* 39(2): 314–335.

Näsström, Sofia. 2010. 'Democracy Counts: Problems of Equality in Transnational Democracy.' In *Transnational Actors in Global Governance*, edited by C. Jönsson and J. Tallberg.

Nelson, Paul. 1997a. 'Conflict, Legitimacy, and Effectiveness: Who Speaks for Whom in Transnational Networks Lobbying the World Bank.' *Nonprofit and Voluntary Sector Quarterly* 26(4): 421–441.

Nelson, Paul. 1997b. 'Deliberation, Leverage, or Coercion? The World Bank, NGOs, and Global Environmental Politics.' *Journal of Peace Research* 34(4): 467–470.

Nelson, Paul. 2000. 'Heroism and Ambiguity: NGO Advocacy in International Policy.' *Voluntas: International Journal of Voluntary and Nonprofit Organizations* 13(4): 478–490.

Nepal Digest. 1995a. 'Meeting on Hydro Project Held in Nepal.' *The Nepal Digest*, 10 August.

Nepal Digest. 1995b. 'Premier Unhappy with World Bank Cancellation of Hydropower Project.' Text of a report by Radio Nepal, 9 August 1995, published in *The Nepal Digest*, 13 August.

Pallas, Christopher L. 2005. 'Canterbury to Cameroon: A New Partnership Between Faiths and the World Bank.' *Development in Practice* 15(5): 677–684.

Pallas, Christopher L. and Johannes Urpelainen. 2012. 'NGO Monitoring and the Legitimacy of International Cooperation: A Strategic Analysis.' *Review of International Organizations* 7(1): 1–32.

Pallas, Christopher L. and Johannes Urpelainen. 2013. 'Mission and Interests: The Strategic Formation and Function of North-South NGO Campaigns.' *Global Governance* 19: 401–423.

Pallas, Christopher L. and Jonathan Wood. 2009. 'The World Bank's Use of Country Systems for Procurement: A Good Idea Gone Bad?' *Development Policy Review* 27(2): 215–230.

Patel, Anil. 1995. 'What Do the Narmada Valley Tribals Really Want?' In *Toward Sustainable Development? Struggling over India's Narmada River*, edited by W. Fisher. New York: M.E. Sharpe.

Patel, Anil and Ambrish Mehta. 1995. 'The Independent Review: Was It a Search for Truth?' In *Toward Sustainable Development? Struggling over India's Narmada River*, edited by W. Fisher. New York: M.E. Sharpe.

Patkar, Medha. 1995. 'The Struggle for Participation and Justice: A Historical Narrative.' In *Toward Sustainable Development? Struggling over India's Narmada River*, edited by W. Fisher. New York: M.E. Sharpe.

Payne, Rodger. 1996. 'Deliberating Global Environmental Politics.' *Journal of Peace Research* 33(2): 129–136.

Pincus, Jonathan and Jeffrey Winters (eds) 2002. *Reinventing the World Bank*. Ithaca: Cornell University Press.

Price, Richard. 2003. 'Transnational Civil Society and Advocacy in World Politics.' *World Politics* 55(4): 579–606.

Putnam, Robert. 1988. 'Diplomacy and Domestic Politics: The Logic of Two-Level Games.' *International Organization* 42(3): 427–460.

Putnam, Robert. 2000. *Bowling Alone: The Collapse and Revival of American Community*. New York: Simon and Schuster.

Raustiala, K. 1997. 'States, NGOs, and International Environmental Institutions.' *International Studies Quarterly* 41(4): 719–740.

Reuters. 1992. 'Save Summit Call by Greenpeace.' *Herald Sun*, 28 April.

Rich, Bruce. 1994. *Mortgaging the Earth: The World Bank, Environmental Impoverishment, and the Crisis of Development*. Boston: Beacon Press.

Rich, Bruce. 2002. 'The World Bank under James Wolfensohn.' In *Reinventing the World Bank*, edited by J. Pincus and J. Winters. Ithaca: Cornell University Press.

Risse, Thomas. 2000. 'The Power of Norms versus the Norms of Power: Transnational Civil Society and Human Rights.' In *The Third Force: The Rise of Transnational Civil Society*, edited by A. Florini. Washington, DC: Carnegie Endowment for International Peace.

Robinson, Eugene. 1992. 'At Earth Summit, South Aims to Send Bill North; Developing Nations, Putting Priority on Growth, Say Cleanup is Possible – for a Price.' *The Washington Post*, 1 June.

Sabatier, Paul and Hank C. Jenkins-Smith (eds) 1993. *Policy Change and Learning: An Advocacy Coalition Approach*. Oxford: Westview Press.

Scharpf, Frizt. 1999. *Governing Europe: Effective and Democratic?* Oxford: Oxford University Press.

Schedler, Andreas. 1998. 'What is Democratic Consolidation?' *Journal of Democracy* 9(2): 91–107.

Scholte, Jan Aart. 2004. 'Civil Society and Democratically Accountable Global Governance.' *Government and Opposition* 39(2): 211–233.

Scholte, Jan Aart. 2011. 'Introduction.' In *Building Global Democracy? Civil Society and Accountable Global Governance*, edited by J.A. Scholte. Cambridge: Cambridge University Press.

Scholte, Jan Aart. 2012. 'A More Inclusive Global Governance? The IMF and Civil Society in Africa.' *Global Governance* 18(2): 185–206.

Scholte, J.A., Renate Bloem, Richard Samans, Kumi Naidoo, Chantana Banpasirichote Wungaeo, Virginia Vargas and Barry Aminata Touré. 2009. 'Global Civil Society Forum and Poverty.' In *Global Civil Society 2009: Global Civil Society and Poverty Alleviation*, edited by M. Glasius, M. Kaldor and H. Anheier. London: SAGE Publications.

Shaw, Martin. 1992. 'Global Society and Global Responsibility: The Theoretical, Historical, and Political Limits of International Society.' *Millennium: Journal of International Studies* 21(3): 421–434.

Shihata, Ibrahim F.I. 1991. *The World Bank in a Changing World, Vol. 2*. Boston: M. Nijhoff Publishers.

Shihata, Ibrahim F.I. 2000. *The World Bank Inspection Panel: In Practice, 2nd ed.* Oxford: Oxford University Press.

Simbi, Margaret and Graham Thom. 2000. 'Implementation by Proxy: The Next Step in Power Relationships between Northern and Southern NGOs?' In *New Roles and Relevance: Development NGOs and the Challenge of Change*, edited by D. Lewis and T. Wallace. Hartford: Kumarian.

Spiro, Peter J. 1995. 'New Global Communities: Nongovernmental Organizations in International Decision-Making Institutions.' *The Washington Quarterly* 18(1): 45–56.

Stiglitz, Joseph. 1999. 'The World Bank at the Millennium.' *The Economic Journal* 109(459): 577–597.

Stone, Diane. 2005. 'Knowledge Networks and Global Policy.' In *Global Knowledge Networks and International Development*, edited by D. Stone and S. Maxwell. New York: Routledge.

Turner, Rik and Colin Harding. 1992. 'Minister's Dismissal Raises Green Doubts about Collor.' *The Independent*, 24 March.

Turner, Scott. 1998. 'Global Civil Society, Anarchy, and Governance: Assessing an Emerging Paradigm.' *Journal of Peace Research* 35(1): 25–42.

Tvedt, Terje. 2002. 'Development NGOs: Actors in a Global Civil Society or in a New International Social System.' *Voluntas: International Journal of Voluntary and Nonprofit Organizations* 13(4): 363–375.

Udall, Lori. 1995. 'The International Narmada Campaign: A Case of Sustained Advocacy.' In *Toward Sustainable Development? Struggling over India's Narmada River*, edited by W. Fisher. New York: M.E. Sharpe.

Udall, Lori. 1998. 'The World Bank and Public Accountability: Has Anything Changed?' In *The Struggle for Accountability: The World Bank, NGOs, and Grassroots Movements*, edited by J. Fox and L.D. Brown. Cambridge: MIT Press.

Uhlin, Anders. 2010. 'The Democratic Legitimacy of Transnational Actors: A Framework for Analysis.' In *Legitimacy Beyond the State? Re-examining the Democratic Credentials of Transnational Actors*, edited by A. Uhlin and E. Erman. New York: Palgrave.

UNICEF. 2012. Jim P. Grant Biography, http://www.unicef.org/about/who/index_bio_grant.html, accessed 10 January 2013.

Upadhyay, Akhilesh. 1995. 'Nepal-Development: New Rulers Seek Revival of Arun III.' *Inter Press Service*, 9 October.

Vidal, John. 1992. 'Earth Summit: Money the Root of All Change.' *The Guardian*, 4 June.

Wade, Robert. 1997. 'Greening the Bank: The Struggle Over the Environment, 1970–1995.' In *The World Bank: Its First Half Century Volume 2: Perspectives*, edited by D. Kapur, J. Lewis and R. Webb. Washington, DC: The Brookings Institution.

Wade, Robert. 2009. 'Accountability Gone Wrong: The World Bank, Non-governmental Organizations and the US Government in a Fight over China.' *New Political Economy* 14(1): 25–48.

Walker, James and Andrew Thompson (eds) 2008. *Critical Mass: The Emergence of Global Civil Society*. Waterloo: Wilfred Laurier University Press.

Walzer, Michael. 1995. 'The Concept of Civil Society.' In *Toward a Global Civil Society*, edited by M. Walzer. Providence, RI: Berghahn Books.

Washington Office on Africa. 1996. Africa: US & Internet. Programs, 04/26/96, http://www.africa.upenn.edu/Urgent_Action/dc_42696.html, accessed 4 July 2009.

Wendt, Alexander. 1995. *Social Theory of International Politics*. Cambridge: Cambridge University Press.

Wiesen, Caitlin, Geoffrey Prewitt and Barbar Sobhan. 1999. 'Civil Society and Poverty: Whose Rights Count?' In *Civil Society at the Millennium*, edited by K. Naidoo. Hartford: Kumarian Press.

Willetts, Peter (ed.) 1996. *The Conscience of the World: The Influence of Nongovernmental Organisations in the UN System*. London: Hurst and Company.

Woods, Ngaire. 2000. 'The Challenge of Good Governance for the IMF and World Bank Themselves.' *World Development* 28(5): 823–841.

Woods, Ngaire. 2005. 'Making the IMF and the World Bank More Accountable.' In *Reforming the Governance of the IMF and the World Bank*, edited by A. Buira. London: Anthem.

Woods, Ngaire. 2007. 'Multilateralism and Building Stronger International Institutions.' In *Global Accountabilities: Participation, Pluralism, and Public Ethics*, edited by A. Ebrahim and E. Weisband. Cambridge: Cambridge University Press.

Zürn, Michael. 2004. 'Global Governance and Legitimacy Problems.' *Government and Opposition* 9(2): 260–287.

Index

Printed and bound in the United States of America